Composing Gender

A BEDFORD SPOTLIGHT READER

Composing Gender

A BEDFORD SPOTLIGHT READER

Rachael Groner
Temple University

John F. O'Hara
The Richard Stockton College of New Jersey

Bedford/St. Martin's
Boston | New York

For Bedford/St. Martin's
Publisher for Composition: Leasa Burton
Executive Editor: John E. Sullivan III
Publishing Services Manager: Andrea Cava
Production Supervisor: Victoria Anzalone
Marketing Manager: Emily Rowin
Editorial Assistant: Rachel Greenhaus
Project Management: Westchester Publishing Services
Photo Researcher: Laura Ulring Moore
Senior Art Director: Anna Palchik
Text Design: Castle Design
Cover Design: Billy Boardman
Cover Photo: © John Lund/Paula Zacharias/Getty Images
Composition: Westchester Publishing Services
Printing and Binding: RR Donnelley and Sons

President, Bedford/St. Martin's: Denise B. Wydra
Editorial Director, English and Music: Karen S. Henry
Director of Marketing: Karen R. Soeltz
Production Director: Susan W. Brown
Director of Rights and Permissions: Hilary Newman

Manufactured in the United States of America.
8   7   6   5
f   e   d   c   b

For information, write: Bedford/St. Martin's, 75 Arlington Street, Boston, MA 02116 (617-399-4000)

ISBN 978-1-4576-2854-2

Acknowledgments

Composing Gender

A BEDFORD SPOTLIGHT READER

Rachael Groner
Temple University

John F. O'Hara
The Richard Stockton College of New Jersey

Bedford/St. Martin's

Boston | New York

For Bedford/St. Martin's

Publisher for Composition: Leasa Burton
Executive Editor: John E. Sullivan III
Publishing Services Manager: Andrea Cava
Production Supervisor: Victoria Anzalone
Marketing Manager: Emily Rowin
Editorial Assistant: Rachel Greenhaus
Project Management: Westchester Publishing Services
Photo Researcher: Laura Ulring Moore
Senior Art Director: Anna Palchik
Text Design: Castle Design
Cover Design: Billy Boardman
Cover Photo: © John Lund/Paula Zacharias/Getty Images
Composition: Westchester Publishing Services
Printing and Binding: RR Donnelley and Sons

President, Bedford/St. Martin's: Denise B. Wydra
Editorial Director, English and Music: Karen S. Henry
Director of Marketing: Karen R. Soeltz
Production Director: Susan W. Brown
Director of Rights and Permissions: Hilary Newman

Manufactured in the United States of America.
8   7   6   5
f   e   d   c   b

For information, write: Bedford/St. Martin's, 75 Arlington Street, Boston, MA 02116 (617-399-4000)

ISBN 978-1-4576-2854-2

Acknowledgments

About the Bedford Spotlight Reader Series

The Bedford Spotlight Reader Series is a new line of single-theme readers, each featuring Bedford's trademark care and quality. The readers in the series collect thoughtfully chosen readings sufficient for an entire writing course — about thirty selections — to allow instructors to provide carefully developed, high-quality instruction at an affordable price. Bedford Spotlight Readers are designed to help students make inquiries from multiple perspectives, opening up topics such as money, food, sustainability, and gender to critical analysis. An Editorial Board, made up of a dozen compositionists at schools focusing on specific themes, has assisted in the development of the series.

Spotlight Readers offer plenty of material for a composition course while keeping the price low. Combine a Spotlight Reader with a handbook or rhetoric and save 20 percent off the combined price. Or package your Spotlight Reader with *Critical Reading and Writing: A Bedford Spotlight Rhetoric*, a brief rhetoric covering the essentials of critical reading, the writing process, and research, for free (a $10 value).

Each volume in the series offers multiple perspectives on the topic and its effects on individuals and society. Chapters are built around central questions such as "What Determines What We Eat?" and "What Rituals Shape Our Gender?" and so offer numerous entry points for inquiry and discussion. High-interest readings, chosen for their suitability in the classroom, provide a mix of genres and disciplines, as well as accessible and challenging selections to allow instructors to tailor their approach to each classroom. Each chapter thus brings to light related — even surprising — questions and ideas.

A rich editorial apparatus provides a sound pedagogical foundation. A general introduction, chapter introductions, and headnotes provide context. Following each selection, writing prompts provide avenues of inquiry tuned to different levels of engagement, from reading comprehension ("Understanding the Text"), to critical analysis ("Reflection and Response"), to the kind of integrative analysis appropriate to the research paper ("Making Connections"). A Web site for the series offers support for teaching: **bedfordstmartins.com/spotlight**.

One of the convenient things about using gender as the basis for a writing course is the fact that we all already have a lifetime of direct experience with it. Everyone is, in some sense, an "expert" on gender, even if that expertise is like fluency in one's native language: One can speak it without necessarily being aware of the grammar and syntax that make it work. Children, for example, do a fine job communicating, but only gradually — through education — do they become aware of the structures of their language, its development, the changing meanings of words, and so on. Similarly, for most people, gender is so fundamental that it remains paradoxically invisible. Like a language, it is so deeply interwoven with the experience of life and the whole organization of society that most people, most of the time, do not pay attention to it — until they begin to analyze it.

The analogy between performing gender and speaking a language is appropriate to this book. As with speaking, performing gender for most people just seems to "happen." It feels "natural." Yet performing gender, like communicating, means adhering to a complex set of social codes that people must *learn to speak*, learn to live within and in relation to. Whether we are conscious of it or not, almost every facet of our lives — our bodies, behaviors, interests, activities — is constituted through gender codes and categories. Like with language, gender does not just reflect reality but shapes it. Even our most routine acts (such as waking up and choosing to wear or not to wear certain clothing or hair styles) represent subtle choices having to do with performing gender. More significantly, the shapes our bodies take, the spaces we occupy, our social interactions, our values, aspirations and goals, our professional limits and potential, are all intertwined with gender.

We have extensively taught the approach and material that makes up *Composing Gender*. For over a decade, we and others in the First-Year Writing Program at Temple University have used gender as a basis for introducing critical thinking, analytical writing, and academic discourse — in part because of how well we all speak the language of gender without perhaps having thought too much about its "rules" and "grammar," much less its role in helping constitute individuals and society. The subject of gender thus presents students with a familiar subject, yet de-familiarizes their experience of it by asking them to analyze how gender is constructed, articulated, and institutionalized in our culture — and what the implications might be to their personal, social, and political lives. As a way to begin to understand the complex intersections of individuality and society — and to practice the intellectual work that opens doors to academic participation — gender offers a relatable, flexible, and salient subject.

Features of *Composing Gender*

We created this book with the hope that it could offer for a wider audience what we have found in our own experience to be the benefits of a single-themed writing course in gender studies. In many ways, we created the book we would have liked to have had available to us over the years. As most writing teachers know, "content" or subject matter is often a pretense in a writing course, a means to an end. Our goal is not to teach gender studies per se (though we introduce the subject to students); instead, we prioritize intellectual preparation for college-level critical thinking and writing. The goal is to equip students with a *critical apparatus* — the ability to read, think, explore, and respond to intellectual issues articulated within a recognizable (and ultimately researchable) domain of discourse.

The readings in this book offer many inroads for academic inquiry related to the sources and consequences of gender construction in America. They ask us to think about gender within overarching intellectual frameworks relevant to many academic fields: social construction, identity, ideology, language, representation, embodiment, diversity. They ask us to examine the roles played by commercial media and consumer culture as they become habituated into everyday life in the United States. They elicit conversations and reflections about current events and contemporary social issues (social norms and values, stereotypes, inequality, civil rights), and inspire critical thinking about the causes and effects of contemporary social values about men and women. Questions about gender relate to all of us personally, traverse fields of study and academic interests, and remain important to many kinds of public debate. On their own or clustered in different ways, the readings can be used to generate critical responses, experiential essays, integrative analyses, and research-based papers on a wide variety of subjects. We hope you will find fruitful pathways into diverse forms of analysis through the selections. Teachers and students are encouraged to limit, expand, and alter the discussion and writing prompts to suit their classroom needs.

The expanding body of research in gender studies, and the continuously unfolding current events relevant to the gender issues raised in this book make these readings constantly renewable and open to new kinds of analysis.

Acknowledgments

The authors would like to thank the many people who helped bring *Composing Gender* into being, most of all our students who have over the years helped us clarify for ourselves the most useful constellations of readings and questions for a writing class. We would like to thank our colleagues at Temple University who have tried out many of our selections and prompts and provided invaluable feedback. We would like to thank especially Eli Goldblatt, Director of the First-Year Writing Program at Temple, for his support. We were fortunate to have reviewers provide insightful advice as we worked on this project; we are grateful for their help: Holly Bauer, University of California, San Diego; Steve Kaczmarek, Columbus State Community College; Erica Rand, Bates College; and Anita Turlington, Gainesville State College, as well as the members of the Bedford Spotlight Reader Series Editorial Board. Many thanks also to the editors and staff at Bedford/St. Martin's, especially John Sullivan, Leasa Burton, and Jane Smith.

Rachael Groner
John F. O'Hara

Bedford/St. Martin's offers resources and format choices that help you and your students get even more out of the book and your course. To learn more about or order any of the following products, contact your Bedford/St. Martin's sales representative, e-mail sales support (sales_support@bfwpub.com), or visit the Web site at **bedfordstmartins .com/spotlight/catalog**.

Choose the Flexible *Bedford e-Portfolio*

Students can collect, select, and reflect on their coursework and personalize and share their *e-Portfolio* for any audience. Instructors can provide as much or as little structure as they see fit. Rubrics and learning outcomes can be aligned to student work, so instructors and programs can gather reliable and useful assessment data. Every *Bedford e-Portfolio* comes pre-loaded with *Portfolio Keeping* and *Portfolio Teaching*, by Nedra Reynolds and Elizabeth Davis. *Bedford e-Portfolio* can be purchased separately or packaged with the book at a significant discount. An activation code is required. To order *e-Portfolio* with the print book, use ISBN 978-1-4576-7927-8. Visit **bedfordstmartins.com/eportfolio**.

Watch Peer Review Work

Eli Review lets instructors scaffold their assignments in a clearer, more effective way for students — making peer review more visible and teachable. *Eli* can be purchased separately or packaged with the book at a significant discount. An activation code is required. To order *Eli Review* with the print book, use ISBN 978-1-4576-7929-2. Visit **bedfordstmartins .com/eli**.

Select Value Packages

Add value to your course by packaging one of the following resources with *Composing Gender* at a significant discount. To learn more about package options, contact your Bedford/St. Martin's sales representative or visit **bedfordstmartins.com/spotlight/catalog**.

- ***Critical Reading and Writing: A Bedford Spotlight Rhetoric, by Jeff Ousborne***, provides a brief overview of the critical reading, writing, and research process — for free when packaged (a $10 value). To order *Critical Reading and Writing* packaged with *Composing Gender,* use ISBN 978-1-4576-7546-1.

- ***EasyWriter*, Fifth Edition, by Andrea Lunsford**, distills Andrea Lunsford's teaching and research into the essentials that today's writers need to make good choices in any rhetorical situation. To order *EasyWriter* packaged with *Composing Gender*, use ISBN 978-1-4576-8323-7.

- *A Pocket Style Manual*, **Sixth Edition, by Diana Hacker and Nancy Sommers**, is a straightforward, inexpensive quick reference, with content flexible enough to suit the needs of writers in the humanities, social sciences, sciences, health professions, business, fine arts, education, and beyond. To order *A Pocket Style Manual* with *Composing Gender*, use ISBN 978-1-4576-8324-4.

- *LearningCurve for Readers and Writers*, Bedford/St. Martin's adaptive quizzing program, quickly learns what students already know and helps them practice what they don't yet understand. Game-like quizzing motivates students to engage with their course, and reporting tools help teachers discern their students' needs. An activation code is required. To order LearningCurve packaged with *Composing Gender*, use ISBN 978-1-4576-7922-3. For details, visit **bedfordstmartins.com /englishlearningcurve**.

- *Portfolio Keeping*, **Third Edition, by Nedra Reynolds and Elizabeth Davis**, provides all the information students need to use the portfolio method successfully in a writing course. *Portfolio Teaching*, a companion guide for instructors, provides the practical information instructors and writing program administrators need to use the portfolio method successfully in a writing course. To order *Portfolio Keeping* packaged with *Composing Gender*, use ISBN 978-1-4576-7926-1.

Try *Re:Writing 2* for Fun

What's the fun of teaching writing if you can't try something new? The best collection of free writing resources on the Web, *Re:Writing 2* gives you and your students even more ways to think, watch, practice, and learn about writing concepts. Listen to Nancy Sommers on using a teacher's comments to revise. Try a logic puzzle. Consult our resources for writing centers. All free for the fun of trying it. Visit **bedfordstmartins .com/rewriting**.

Instructor Resources

You have a lot to do in your course. Bedford/St. Martin's wants to make it easy for you to find the support you need — and to get it quickly.

- **Teaching Central** (bedfordstmartins.com/teachingcentral) offers the entire list of Bedford/St. Martin's print and online professional resources in one place. You'll find landmark reference works, sourcebooks on pedagogical issues, award-winning collections, and practical advice for the classroom — all free for instructors.

- *Bits* (bedfordbits.com) collects creative ideas for teaching a range of composition topics in an easily searchable blog format. A community of teachers — leading scholars, authors, and editors — discuss revision, research, grammar and style, technology, peer review, and much more.

- **Bedford Coursepacks** (bedfordstmartins.com/coursepacks) allow you to easily download digital materials from Bedford/St. Martin's for your course for the most common course management systems — Blackboard, Angel, Desire2Learn, Web CT, Moodle, or Sakai.

Contents

Chapter 4   How Do We Define Sexuality?   183

Chapter 5   How Do the Media Shape Gender?   241

Composing Gender

A BEDFORD SPOTLIGHT READER

Introduction for Students

What Is College Writing?

Composing Gender is a textbook for college writers. As you can see by surveying the table of contents, all of the articles and essays included in the book are focused on one particular theme — gender — and all are relatively bound in place and time: American contemporary culture. You may be wondering why a college writing textbook would seem to be "about" something so specific, but there is a good explanation for this having to do with what college writing — and thinking — is.

College writing represents a conjunction of skills that includes not just *writing* but also *critical reading* and *critical thinking*. *Critical reading* means being able to comprehend complex texts by reading closely, working to understand terms and theories, applying your own knowledge to them, cross-referencing other sources, asking questions of the text, and using strategies like note-taking and journal-keeping that result in enhanced understanding of a piece of writing. *Critical thinking* means being able to evaluate the merit of what you are studying by reflecting upon and critically judging the information and arguments you are engaged with by thinking about them from multiple perspectives, probing their claims, recognizing biases, and interrogating assumptions made by the authors. This conjunction of critical reading, critical thinking, and writing amounts to the development of an intellectual apparatus you will need in the future as growing intellectuals and professionals — in whatever field you study.

Many students might say to themselves, "I am going to college to become a dentist, so when am I ever going to need to write a paper about gender?" Or, "I am majoring in chemistry, so why do I need to learn about gender?" These are understandable questions, but there are answers to them we think most educated people would agree with. First, the intellectual processes involved in apprehending complex ideas, applying those ideas to your own observations and experiences, formulating rational questions (and provisional answers to the dilemmas posed by your questions), and producing negotiated responses all constitute a basic structure inherent in every academic field and professional environment. Second, it is vital to your college studies to cultivate curiosity about subjects that may seem initially obvious or uninteresting. Developing skills as a critical thinker, reader, and writer will allow you to engage with new discourses in potentially exciting and challenging ways. This is one of the fundamental lessons of college studies: not all themes will engage you, so you'll need to engage with them in active and curious ways.

As you advance in college, and eventually graduate — and perhaps move on to graduate or professional school or your first "real job" — you will transform in many ways. One of the major aspects of this transformation involves moving from student to professional, a turn from being a receiver of knowledge to being a producer of knowledge. To be a producer of knowledge means simply that you will be shaping the world by contributing your ideas and practices to it, and overwhelmingly you will do this through language: listening, reading, speaking, thinking, and writing. To be able to contribute to professional organizations and social institutions capably, responsibly, intelligently, and sensitively is a long-term goal college writing can help you begin to achieve.

Why Gender?

In short, "gender" is a topic that will allow you to practice and hone your critical reading, thinking, and writing skills. You might ask, then, "Why gender? Why not something else?" This is a fair question. We feel gender is among the best single themes for a college writing course for several reasons:

Gender is familiar. Everybody is, in a sense, already an "expert" on gender. From the earliest stages of your life, you have been developing this "expertise" constituted by your ability to live within and interact through the codes of gender. To be able to perform complex thinking and response, it is arguably necessary to have a great deal of knowledge about the subject matter. Students in many writing classes are often asked to read about unfamiliar subjects, and then asked to think and write about them in high-level ways. Reading and writing about gender alleviate some of the pressure of this "learning curve," and provide you with subject matter you are already well prepared to engage more deeply.

Gender is relevant. Gender is a crucial dimension of every social, academic, and professional arena. If you can think of a single place where gender is not a factor, then you are imagining a place where there are no people. When you consider gender in relation to science, business, economics, political science, art, music, literature, history — or indeed any field of study — you will no doubt see that ideas and assumptions about gender are important both to the shape of those fields and to the work done within them. Further, the readings we have chosen are particularly relevant to American readers and writers because debates and conversations about gender can be found all around us in the news, on television and in film, and perhaps even among those in your own family or social circles. Therefore, understanding gender will help you understand an important facet of your future life and work. This relevancy will hopefully allow you to respond to these readings in a way that wouldn't be possible with a less accessible or timely theme. Because gender discourses span many fields of study, gender offers a relatively convenient research topic that accommodates diverse interests and many different kinds of writing (personal, analytical, argumentative, etc.).

Gender is a "discourse." All academic endeavors involve participation in an ongoing conversation called a "discourse." This is not the same type of conversation you might have with a roommate, or with a group of friends, but the type of conversation that takes place among many people over many years in various types of expression: books, essays, articles, speeches, and many other kinds of articulations. All university students are expected to develop skills to absorb, assimilate, and synthesize information gathered from various sources within various discourses, and to find their own voice within them. This is a basic pattern in the production of knowledge. This book offers a sample of interrelated readings that represent part of a larger unique discourse, and it provides a place where you can position your own voice.

Gender is a foundation of identity. For most people, college is not just a place where they learn "material," but a place where they learn more about themselves and others. It can be a fascinating experience to begin to see what you take for granted about yourself and others in light of the social processes that construct identity and identity categories. It can be enlighten-ing to see, for example, how stereotypes and prejudices are developed and perpetuated, how social conventions may limit or expand individuals' potential life courses, and how commonly shared assumptions structure our worldviews. In fact, it is essential in a democratic, multicultural society to learn about and engage with identity, identity categories, and their formulations. Like studying race, class, ethnicity, or nationality, studying gender can help you understand yourself better, as well as help you tolerate and value other people and other people's perspectives.

Gender is political. Because gender is tied so tightly to sex categories, sexualities, and questions of law, it provides fertile ground for debate on all sorts of current events having to do with equality for all citizens. From wage and income disparities, to other occupational and social inequalities, to matters involving family law, civil rights, violence, public health, public service, equal access, and so on, gender is a key dimension in many political contestations and negotiations. Gender discourses invoke issues of conformity and resistance, social change, and social justice that all citizens are responsible for knowing about and participating in.

Gender is personal. We believe that a valuable by-product of writing about gender is learning about yourself. As you will see while reading this book, gender codes can be both productive and constraining. Almost everyone has been subject to a gender stereotype in their lives, judged for an inadequate performance of gender, or pressured to do something in order to satisfy an expectation of his or her gender. Understanding gender as a social process provides a bulwark against these things by giving you a vocabulary for contesting them and asserting yourself as an individual.

Gender Regulations: The Units in This Book

The field of gender studies is vast. Gender studies as a field of knowledge began to gain coherence and direction as an academic discipline with the rise of the women's rights movements of the 1960s. Early work in gender studies attempted to "demystify," or make less powerful, many of the myths that existed about women. Among many others, the study of gender took on the myths that women were naturally weaker, less intelligent, and more emotional, dependent, and domestic than men. Such commonly held assumptions about women had long contributed to their educational, professional, and personal oppression. The result was a denial of opportunities and rights for women that helped make real some of the very stereotypes that were assumed — a self-fulfilling prophecy. Gender studies helped change all that, and since then women have undoubtedly made progress in terms of social and political equality, though many issues remain and many battles are still being fought. Women continue to earn, on average, about 70 percent of men's income for the same jobs — an issue of inequality serious enough to be a major policy focus for President Barack Obama leading up to his 2012 election. In 2012, "secretary" remained the number one occupation for women in America (as it was in 1950), and issues of reproductive rights, violence against women, and workplace harassment and discrimination remain central issues in gender studies.

Over five decades of concerted work in gender studies, many thousands of books and many more thousands of articles and reports have studied gender from just about every conceivable angle. Men have come to be as important to gender studies as women, for men too are equally subject to gender expectations, gender codes, and gender stereotypes that affect their lives in consequential ways. For example, men tend to lose out in custody battles and child support arrangements. They are not given child-care leave from work as frequently as women. And, on average, men are tasked with more dangerous and unhealthy forms of work, are more at risk to engage in unhealthy behaviors such as drinking and smoking, and tend not to live as long as women. Other forms of gender identity also came into prominence as gender studies developed. Gay, lesbian, bisexual, transsexual, and transgender persons have become more visible in the field of gender and in culture at large — and consequently ideas about gender itself have become more and more complicated.

For your editors to create a book of readings in gender studies without being so broad as to eviscerate the goal of the single-themed writing course, we decided the best way to proceed would be to create a constellation of interrelated readings within the larger subject of gender studies. Anticipating an audience of beginning undergraduates, we focused primarily on *the social construction of gender* throughout the most formative years of life, from childhood to the early years of adulthood. We wanted the material to be as familiar as possible, so we concentrated on the ways gender codes begin to shape the experience of life and map its future course: how children are raised in the United States within gender boundaries, how gender is taught, learned, and performed among many people and institutions throughout adolescence and young adulthood, how gender codes facilitate and limit life opportunities, and how media messages about gender contribute to individuals' self-perception and social values.

By concentrating on these specific aspects of gender studies, we crafted five units that share ideas among them even while each is distinct in its own way. Each unit is designed to add a new dimension to understanding gender *formation* and *regulation* — how gender is built and reinforced, and what the effects may be on individuals and society. Each reading in the units is intended to be able to be put into conversation with the others, so as you read, note where intersections and discrepancies appear. Part of critical thinking and reading involves integrating sources, allowing them to "speak to" one another by noting where they agree and disagree, where they help clarify and expand one another, and where one sheds new light upon another.

The Structure of *Composing Gender*

Chapter 1, *Is Gender Either/Or (or Something Else)?*, is intended to lay out major theories concerning the social construction of gender. Traditional notions of gender held to its "two-ness": men and women were born male or female, and were assumed to fulfill a sort of "biological destiny." Men and women behaved the ways they did because — well, they were born that way. Any outliers were assumed to be curiosities at best, pathologies at worst. This assumption of biological destiny (which incidentally was a key to other forms of oppression such as slavery) was based on a powerful intellectual supposition of older times known in philosophy as *dualism*, which saw *opposition* as a fundamental principle of the ordering of nature. Self and other, civilization and savagery, rational and irrational, moral and immoral, good and evil — and many more such pairs — were widely seen as stable categories assured by nature itself. Theories of social construction upset this traditional viewpoint, and held not only that individuals were "products of their environment" but also that ideas of right and wrong, good and evil, rational and irrational, and so on, were dependent upon the values and outlooks of those defining them. Right and wrong, and good and evil, for example, came to be seen by most intellectuals as social phenomena, not facts of nature. *People* perpetuated these dualisms, not nature. The first unit includes readings that define the social construction of gender and interrogate dualism in relation to gender. They examine the conventions, habits, beliefs, and attitudes about men and women that structure our notions of masculinity and femininity, and affect the ways we socialize individuals differently based on sex categories.

Chapter 2, *How Do We Become Boys and Girls?*, addresses gender construction in perhaps the most formative time in a person's life: childhood. Each article delves into a different facet of children's experience of gender, from the toys children are given at the earliest ages, to the ways parents and caregivers respond to children's performances of gender, to how role models are developed, to how gender is regulated in schools, in popular media, in youth sports, and in other locations of childhood culture. As you read, try to think about how these dynamics work — how children come to learn the "truth" about gender — and how they have changed over time.

Chapter 3, *What Rituals Shape Our Gender?*, contains a number of pieces related to ritual reaffirmations of gender roles and categories. When many people think of "rituals," their almost automatic response is to associate them with ancient or tribal cultures, a kind of "primitive" social phenomenon. However, as this chapter's readings show, rituals are present in our everyday lives even in modern, twenty-first-century first-world culture, and like all rituals they serve to support and maintain social values, including beliefs about gender roles and categories. From dating and mating practices between women and men to "rites of passage" that help demarcate the transition from girl to woman, and boy to man, our culture is rife with rituals that help enact accepted gender practices through pre-scripted life events and ceremonies. In the same way "primitive" rituals are anthropologically significant to understanding ancient and tribal cultures, our rituals — weddings, holidays, and other such kinds of ceremonies, even the controversial issue of routine male infant circumcision — are significant to understanding our lives and, obviously, our performances of gender.

Chapter 4, *How Do We Define Sexuality?*, examines the relationship of sexuality to gender, taking as its premise that sexuality is another instance of gender performance many people take to be a natural product of one's gender status. Women and men are often thought to be unproblematically ("naturally") attracted to the opposite sex, yet the articles in this chapter complicate this assumption by addressing the ways sexuality itself is socially constructed through many of the same processes outlined in the previous chapters. What is a "normal" expression of sexuality, and what is not, are notions that have changed over time and place. All people are born with sexual impulses, but how and where those impulses are directed is a socio-logical matter at least as much as it a biological one. What people find sexually attractive or erotic varies from person to person, culture to culture, era to era. The "beauty standard" itself for men and women in contemporary America can look quite different from decade to decade. Having sex — what Walt Whitman characterized as the thing on which "all beauty, all purity, all sweetness, all friendship, all strength, all life, all immortality depend" — may be something that is itself learned through a variety of what sociologists call "sexual scripts," literally the behaviors, positions, and expectations of the sex act. If this seems untoward to talk about, or uncomfortable, we must remem-ber that college writing, in addition to challenging your intellect, may also challenge you in other ways. In college writing, like in college generally, no subject is "off the table," nor in our opinion should it be. College is for adults thinking in adult ways.

In addition to questioning the nature of sexuality in relation to sex category and gender, this chapter also takes up the issue of homosexuality, bisexuality and omni-sexuality, especially the ways such categories are conceived in a social world that has traditionally sanctioned only one possible, moral, correct direction for sexual expression. As you know, attitudes about such things are rapidly changing, and we hope this chapter provides for you a way to under-stand these changes in context with gender and social construction.

Chapter 5, *How Do the Media Shape Gender?*, adds the "media" as a dimension in understanding contemporary trends in representations of gender and sexuality. The impacts of visual media in structuring attitudes about gender, beauty, race, and sexuality, including the very controversial though important question of children's sexuality, are some of the subjects addressed in this unit. This last question about children's sexuality we find particularly important as today we have a paradoxical phenomenon occurring: at the very moment when children's sexuality is so taboo — and the most grotesque of all social images is that of the pedophile — we have a media environment that presents children in unprecedented sexual ways, as objects of sexual fascination and sexual allure. It takes little more than a glance at an average clothing catalogue, a set of music videos, or even children's television shows to see that children are invested by image producers with a precocious sexuality. As one selection from this unit, *The American Psychological Association Task Force Report on the Sexualization of Young Girls*, shows, the impact of this popular cultural trend may be dire for young girls and women.

Across all the chapters, you will see many opportunities to share your experiences of gender socialization and gender construction, to add your observations about the current cultural machinery that produces contemporary gender categories, to place the readings in relation to one another, to engage with gender issues, and in general to work within this discourse on the social construction of gender to challenge the readings as much as they will challenge you. You will see that what seems familiar, routine, or even natural about gender is actually very complicated, and that to understand gender means understanding complex theories of social science and cultural studies. Most of all, we hope you will see that the intellectual processes you will engage in by reading, thinking, and writing within this discourse will translate to the kind of applications of critical reading, thinking, and writing you will be performing throughout college and into your personal and professional life.

The title of this book, *Composing Gender*, is a play on words. On one hand, to "compose gender" alludes to the many social processes that construct the elements we associate with masculinity, femininity, and other gender types. Yet, on the other hand, "composing" refers to the goal, ultimately, of developing your ability to "compose" academic papers, essays, and other forms of written expression — to write. The word "composition" comes from the Latin word *composito*, or "putting together, connecting, or arranging." As college writers, *putting together, connecting*, and *arranging* translate to reading and writing meaningfully: understanding ideas, extracting claims and examples, placing ideas in dialogue with one another, and adding your own outlooks and ideas (and perhaps even those from outside resources), in order to better understand the relationship between the individual and society, and in order to become better equipped to express yourself intelligently in this context.

A Note on the Questions

At the end of each reading, we have included three sets of questions we hope will help you think about the readings. The first set, "Understanding the Text," is aimed at helping you comprehend the reading on its own terms. In these questions, we ask for clarifications of the dominant arguments in the articles, interpretations of the meaning of unique claims, and extrapolations of the examples and illustrations the author uses to support his or her overall positions. These are "reading comprehension" questions we hope will help you read the pieces closely and understand the author. They amount to what we are calling "author-centered" questions.

The second set of questions, "Reflection and Response," asks more for your contributions of examples, gathered through your experiences and observations, and your opinions or ideas about the articles as a whole or about their discrete claims. These questions are intended to bring you into the conversation, and we consider them "reader-centered questions."

The third set of questions, "Making Connections," is intended to offer more complex writing prompts that ask you to consider reading in clusters, in light of one another, or to consider sources outside of *Composing Gender*, and in light of what positions or arguments you can articulate in relation to the ideas communicated by the readings. In these we ask you to think further, to include your own claims and examples, or counterclaims and counterexamples. Because each question calls for understanding the texts, positioning yourself within the discourse, and combining and cross-referencing other texts, we think of these as "discourse-centered questions."

We do not presume to tell, nor can we predict, how your instructors will utilize this text. One teacher may prefer focusing on "Reflection and Response," for instance, in a writing class that favors expressive, essay writing, or writing from experience. Another may value research-based writing and stay in the "Making Connections" section more often than not. Still another may prefer to modify these questions, combine them, or even reject them and invent his or her own writing assignments. No matter how these readings are used, however, there are two things we feel very confident about as editors: one, that this subject matter opens up multiple ways to learn college writing; and two, that they elicit what we think is the most important common thread to all good writing: *relevancy.* The relevancy of gender construction provides an undeniable immediacy and importance to whatever kind of work you produce about it. After all, these readings address the very basis of our identities, the fundamental categories we use to understand one another, how these categories change (and resist change), and how they shape the potential experiences and opportunities we ourselves and the next generation will have in life.

Best of luck, and happy writing!

Rachael Groner
John F. O'Hara

1

Is Gender Either/Or (or Something Else)?

Ask a child what the opposite of *dog* is, and you are likely to get the response *cat*. Ask what the opposite of *sun* is, and you will probably hear the reply *moon*. As with many things typically taken as *binary pairs* in our lexicon — coffee and tea, fork and spoon, land and sea — a little consideration reveals them to be *false dichotomies*: they oppose two things that are not mutually exhaustive (there are other possibilities for an opposite of *dog*), or mutually exclusive (dogs and cats are both animals). Of course, it is not only children who speak (and think) in dichotomies. Many adults are prone to similar reductionism, and arguably with higher consequences, when they speak too easily of black people and white people, the rich and the poor, socialism and capitalism, Democrats and Republicans, and so on. The problem with false dichotomies is they tend to lead to dualistic thinking, which makes it difficult to account for the real complexity of a given problem or issue or to offer compromise solutions and negotiated perspectives about them.

The readings in this chapter, "Is Gender Either/Or (or Something Else)?," all seek in some way to break down persistent false dichotomies used to mark the differences between men and women, masculinity and femininity, sex and gender. They address popular, ubiquitous notions of the "two" sexes, the "two" genders, and the "two sides" of biology and culture — dichotomies that deeply affect our sense of ourselves and our expectations of others in society — and they challenge the uncritical acceptance of dualistic thinking about men and women that at once constructs and regulates gender boundaries.

One of the primary challenges to dualistic thinking that these readings share is a critique of a long-standing, almost intuitive sense that men's and women's biological differences produce two (and only two) genders. It is commonly thought that a person's sex category (male or female) forms the basis of that person's gender displays. The categories of "male" and "female," which are used to differentiate people biologically based on reproductive organs and hormonal processes, are seen from a sociobiological perspective to mark the beginning of the many different characteristics men and women exhibit in the social world. In this deterministic formulation, the social behaviors associated

Consider how the male and female bodies in this image are portrayed in this photo. Are they opposites? Do you see similarities in their poses or expressions?

with masculinity and femininity, and the roles men and women are expected to play in society, are understood as natural, determined at birth. As they develop, then, men's and women's biological predispositions are seen to extrapolate into different capabilities, capacities, and behaviors.

This sociobiological perspective has been a subject of great debate in gender studies in part because, like many dichotomies, even biological sex categories like male and female do not offer clear-cut distinctions. Many people are born with ambiguous sex traits, with perhaps as many as 1 in 100 births featuring atypical characteristics. Furthermore, human beings are among the least dimorphous species on the planet, with men and women marked more by biological similarity than by difference. And yet, perhaps because of a sense of inherent biological opposition to one another, males

Masculine	Feminine
Thinking	Feeling
Dominant	Subordinate
Aggressive	Compliant
Rational	Emotional
Stronger	Weaker
Competitive	Cooperative
Active/proactive	Passive/patient
Stoic	Expressive
Mathematical	Linguistic
Scientific	Artistic
Purposeful	Meandering
Domineering	Receptive
Leading	Following
Worldly	Domestic
Distant	Close
Serious	Playful
Authoritative	Negotiative
Visual	Tactile
Focused	Dreamy

and females are expected to play different social roles, to occupy different statuses, and to think and act in distinct ways. This false dichotomy between male and female, masculinity and femininity, takes for granted essential differences between the sexes, then socializes men and women differently from the earliest ages on, holding them to looser and stricter expectations throughout the life course. The conventions of gender are upheld and supported by individuals, families, communities, social organizations, and institutions. One way of perceiving the cultural distinctions between men and women is to make a list of characteristics seen as "masculine" and "feminine" in American society.

By questioning the strict biological "division" between male and female and by emphasizing the gulf between biological sex category and gender conventions, the articles that follow propose a "social constructionist" model of understanding gender. From a social constructionist perspective, individuals are born with very limited predispositions based on sex categories, and the qualities we consider "masculine" and "feminine" are not seen as biological in origin, but as products of the social environment rooted in cultural practices, traditions, and values about men and women. That is to say, gender is seen in the social constructionist perspective to be fully dependent upon contingencies of the social world. Notions of masculinity and femininity change from year to year and decade to decade, and can look quite different in different places at different times. The only problem is that because of widespread notions about the inherent linkages between biological sex and gender display, many people consider the current social arrangements of gender as inherent to the species, when in fact gender codes and gender roles are dependent and transformable.

Judith Lorber, in "'Night to His Day': The Social Construction of Gender," looks at how individuals acquire and perform gender, not as a function of biological determinism, but according to social parameters for defining appropriate gender display. By questioning the power of false dichotomies (male and female, masculine and feminine), Lorber examines the pressures people experience to adhere to gender codes and to perform them adequately. She further argues that the dichotomy between masculinity and femininity helps constitute a value system that privileges masculine over feminine characteristics, and solidifies ongoing patriarchal privilege in western societies.

Aaron Devor, in "Becoming Members of Society: The Social Meanings of Gender," also examines the role gender plays in constructing a recognizable social order based on the assumption of gender polarity. In assessing the many cultural "proscriptions and prescriptions" that produce gender behaviors, attitudes, and identities, he points out that membership itself in society in some ways depends upon conformity to these social standards.

Ruth Hubbard, in "Rethinking Women's Biology," concentrates on the dichotomies established between sex and gender. In her analysis, the presumptive separation between "nature" and "nurture" to define differences between the "biological" and the "social" aspects of gender is itself a false dichotomy that ignores the interdependencies of the biological and the social. Social practices can shape and alter biological realities and construct male and female bodies differently. As individuals transform and train their bodies differently according to (and sometimes against) gender codes, they highlight how significantly embodiment itself is affected by cultural behaviors and patterns. If biology is thought to contribute to gender, Hubbard's work suggests, it is at least as true that gender practices can produce certain types of biological bodies — in short, that gender practices can impact male and female physiology.

In an excerpt by Petra Doan, from "The Tyranny of Gendered Spaces: Reflections from Beyond the Gender Dichotomy," a transgendered woman and gender scholar addresses the sometimes harrowing experiences of gender-variant individuals in a society where sex and gender dichotomies are prevalent. And the final selection by Barbara Kantrowitz and Pat Wingert, "Are We Facing a Genderless Future?," provides a profile of legal conflicts arising between the growing number of gender-variant people and the institutional settings where there are only two choices, man or woman.

Each article in this chapter offers a broad definition of gender alongside an analysis of how gender structures are produced and maintained through commonly accepted dualisms, how these dualisms affect identity and relations with others, and how they open and close opportunities for certain kinds of experiences of the world.

"Night to His Day": The Social Construction of Gender

Judith Lorber

Judith Lorber is a professor emerita of sociology and women's studies at the Graduate Center and Brooklyn College of the City University of New York. She was the founding editor of *Gender and Society* and has authored many books, including *Breaking the Bowls: Degendering and Feminist Change* (2005), *Paradoxes of Gender* (1994), and *Women Physicians: Careers, Status and Power* (1984). She has also coedited a number of books, such as *The Social Construction of Illness* (2002) and *Gender Inequality: Feminist Theories and Politics* (2009). She received the American Sociological Association's Jessie Bernard Career Award in 1996 for "scholarly work that has enlarged the horizons of sociology to encompass fully the role of women in society." This selection has been widely anthologized and originally appeared in *Paradoxes of Gender.*

Talking about gender for most people is the equivalent of fish talking about water. Gender is so much the routine ground of everyday activities that questioning its taken-for-granted assumptions and presuppositions is like wondering about whether the sun will come up.[1] Gender is so pervasive that in our society we assume it is bred into our genes. Most people find it hard to believe that gender is constantly created and re-created out of human interaction, out of social life, and is the texture and order of that social life. Yet gender, like culture, is a human production that depends on everyone constantly "doing gender" (West and Zimmerman 1987).

And everyone "does gender" without thinking about it. Today, on the subway, I saw a well-dressed man with a year-old child in a stroller. Yesterday, on a bus, I saw a man with a tiny baby in a carrier on his chest. Seeing men taking care of small children in public is increasingly common — at least in New York City. But both men were quite obviously stared at — and smiled at, approvingly. Everyone was doing gender — the men who were changing the role of fathers and the other passengers, who were applauding them silently. But there was more gendering going on that probably fewer people noticed. The

---

[1] Gender is, in Erving Goffman's words, an aspect of *Felicity's Condition*, "any arrangement which leads us to judge an individual's . . . acts not to be a manifestation of strangeness. Behind Felicity's Condition is our sense of what it is to be sane" (1983, 27). Also see Bem 1993; Frye 1983, 17–40; Goffman 1977.

baby was wearing a white crocheted cap and white clothes. You couldn't tell if it was a boy or a girl. The child in the stroller was wearing a dark blue T-shirt and dark print pants. As they started to leave the train, the father put a Yankee baseball cap on the child's head. Ah, a boy, I thought. Then I noticed the gleam of tiny earrings in the child's ears, and as they got off, I saw the little flowered sneakers and lace-trimmed socks. Not a boy after all. Gender done.

Gender is such a familiar part of daily life that it usually takes a deliberate disruption of our expectations of how women and men are supposed to act to pay attention to how it is produced. Gender signs and signals are so ubiquitous that we usually fail to note them — unless they are missing or ambiguous. Then we are uncomfortable until we have successfully placed the other person in a gender status; otherwise, we feel socially dislocated. In our society, in addition to man and woman, the status can be *transvestite* (a person who dresses in opposite-gender clothes) and *transsexual* (a person who has had sex-change surgery). Transvestites and transsexuals carefully construct their gender status by dressing, speaking, walking, gesturing in the ways prescribed for women or men whichever they want to be taken for — and so does any "normal" person.

For the individual, gender construction starts with assignment to a sex category on the basis of what the genitalia look like at birth.[2] Then babies are dressed or adorned in a way that displays the category because parents don't want to be constantly asked whether their baby is a girl or a boy. A sex category becomes a gender status through naming, dress, and the use of other gender markers. Once a child's gender is evident, others treat those in one gender differently from those in the other, and the children respond to the different treatment by feeling different and behaving differently. As soon as they can talk, they start to refer to themselves as members of their gender. Sex doesn't come into play again until puberty, but by that time, sexual feelings and desires and practices have been shaped by gendered norms and expectations. Adolescent boys and girls approach and avoid each other in an elaborately scripted and gendered mating dance. Parenting is gendered, with different expectations for mothers and for fathers, and people of different genders work at different kinds of jobs. The work adults do as mothers and fathers and as low-level workers and high-level bosses shapes women's and men's life experiences, and these experiences produce different feelings, consciousness, relation-

---

[2] In cases of ambiguity in countries with modern medicine, surgery is usually performed to make the genitalia more clearly male or female.

ships, skills — ways of being that we call feminine or masculine.[3] All of these processes constitute the social construction of gender.

Gendered roles change — today fathers are taking care of little 5 children, girls and boys are wearing unisex clothing and getting the same education, women and men are working at the same jobs. Although many traditional social groups are quite strict about maintaining gender differences, in other social groups they seem to be blurring. Then why the one-year-old's earrings? Why is it still so important to mark a child as a girl or a boy, to make sure she is not taken for a boy or he for a girl? What would happen if they were? They would, quite literally, have changed places in their social world.

To explain why gendering is done from birth, constantly and by everyone, we have to look not only at the way individuals experience gender but at gender as a social institution. As a social institution, gender is one of the major ways that human beings organize their lives. Human society depends on a predictable division of labor, a designated allocation of scarce goods, assigned responsibility for children and others who cannot care for themselves, common values and their systematic transmission to new members, legitimate leadership, music, art, stories, games, and other symbolic productions. One way of choosing people for the different tasks of society is on the basis of their talents, motivations, and competence — their demonstrated achievements. The other way is on the basis of gender, race, ethnicity — ascribed membership in a category of people. Although societies vary in the extent to which they use one or the other of these ways of allocating people to work and to carry out other responsibilities, every society uses gender and age grades. Every society classifies people as "girl and boy children," "girls and boys ready to be married," and "fully adult women and men," constructs similarities among them and differences between them, and assigns them to different roles and responsibilities. Personality characteristics, feelings, motivations, and ambitions flow from these different life experiences so that the members of these different groups become different kinds of people. The process of gendering and its outcome are legitimated by religion, law, science, and the society's entire set of values.

Western society's values legitimate gendering by claiming that it all comes from physiology — female and male procreative differences. But gender and sex are not equivalent, and gender as a social construction does not flow automatically from genitalia and reproductive organs, the main physiological differences of females and males. In the

---

[3] See Butler 1990 for an analysis of how doing gender is gender identity.

construction of ascribed social statuses, physiological differences such as sex, stage of development, color of skin, and size are crude markers. They are not the source of the social statuses of gender, age grade, and race. Social statuses are carefully constructed through prescribed processes of teaching, learning, emulation, and enforcement. Whatever genes, hormones, and biological evolution contribute to human social institutions is materially as well as qualitatively transformed by social practices. Every social institution has a material base, but culture and social practices transform that base into something with qualitatively different patterns and constraints. The economy is much more than producing food and goods and distributing them to eaters and users; family and kinship are not the equivalent of having sex and procreating; morals and religions cannot be equated with the fears and ecstasies of the brain; language goes far beyond the sounds produced by tongue and larynx. No one eats "money" or "credit"; the concepts of "god" and "angels" are the subjects of theological disquisitions; not only words but objects, such as their flag, "speak" to the citizens of a country.

Similarly, gender cannot be equated with biological and physiological differences between human females and males. The building blocks of gender are socially *constructed* statuses. Western societies have only two genders, "man" and "woman." Some societies have three genders — men, women, and *berdaches or hijras* or *xaniths*. Berdaches, hijras, and xaniths are biological males who behave, dress, work, and are treated in most respects as social women; they are therefore not men, nor are they female women; they are, in our language, "male women."[4] There are African and American Indian societies that have a gender status called *manly hearted women* — biological females who work, marry, and parent as men; their social status is "female men" (Amadiume 1987; Blackwood 1984). They do not have to behave or dress as men to have the social responsibilities and prerogatives of husbands and fathers; what makes them men is enough wealth to buy a wife.

Modern Western societies' *transsexuals* and *transvestites* are the nearest equivalent of these crossover genders, but they are not institutionalized as third genders (Bolin 1987). Transsexuals are biological males and females who have sex-change operations to alter their genitalia. They do so in order to bring their physical anatomy in congruence with the way they want to live and with their own sense of gen-

---

[4] On the *hijras* of India, see Nanda 1990; on the *xaniths* of Oman, see Wikan 1982, 168–86; on the American Indian *berdaches*, see Williams 1986. Other societies that have similar institutionalized third-gender men are the Koniag of Alaska, the Tanala of Madagascar, the Mesakin of Nuba, and the Chukchee of Siberia (Wikan 1982, 170).

der identity. They do not become a third gender; they change genders. Transvestites are males who live as women and females who live as men but do not intend to have sex-change surgery. Their dress, appearance, and mannerisms fall within the range of what is expected from members of the opposite gender, so that they "pass." They also change genders, sometimes temporarily, some for most of their lives. Transvestite women have fought in wars as men soldiers as recently as the nineteenth century; some married women and others went back to being women and married men once the war was over.[5] Some were discovered when their wounds were treated; others not until they died. In order to work as a jazz musician, a man's occupation, Billy Tipton, a woman, lived most of her life as a man. She died recently at seventy-four, leaving a wife and three adopted sons for whom she was husband and father, and musicians with whom she had played and traveled, for whom she was "one of the boys" (*New York Times* 1989).[6] There have been many other such occurrences of women passing as men to do more prestigious or lucrative men's work (Matthaei 1982, 192–93).[7]

Genders, therefore, are not attached to a biological substratum. Gender boundaries are breachable, and individual and socially organized shifts from one gender to another call attention to "cultural, social, or aesthetic dissonances" (Garber 1992, 16). These odd or deviant or third genders show us what we ordinarily take for granted — that people have to learn to be women and men. Men who cross-dress for performances or for pleasure often learn from women's magazines how to "do" femininity convincingly (Garber 1992, 41–51). Because transvestism is direct evidence of how gender is constructed, Marjorie Garber claims it has "extraordinary power . . . to disrupt, expose, and challenge, putting in question the very notion of the 'original' and of stable identity" (1992, 16). . . .

For Individuals, Gender Means Sameness

Although the possible combinations of genitalia, body shapes, clothing, mannerisms, sexuality, and roles could produce infinite varieties in human beings, the social institution of gender depends on the

---

[5] Durova 1989; Freeman and Bond 1992; Wheelwright 1989.

[6] Gender segregation of work in popular music still has not changed very much, according to Groce and Cooper 1990, despite considerable androgyny in some very popular figures. See Garber 1992 on the androgyny. She discusses Tipton on pp. 67–70.

[7] In the nineteenth century, not only did these women get men's wages, but they also "had male privileges and could do all manner of things other women could not: open a bank account, write checks, own property, go anywhere unaccompanied, vote in elections" (Faderman 1991, 44).

production and maintenance of a limited number of gender statuses and of making the members of these statuses similar to each other. Individuals are born sexed but not gendered, and they have to be taught to be masculine or feminine.[8] As Simone de Beauvoir said: "One is not born, but rather becomes, a woman . . . ; it is civilization as a whole that produces this creature . . . which is described as feminine" (1953, 267). . . .

Many cultures go beyond clothing, gestures, and demeanor in gendering children. They inscribe gender directly into bodies. In traditional Chinese society, mothers once bound their daughters' feet into three-inch stumps to enhance their sexual attractiveness. Jewish fathers circumcise their infant sons to show their covenant with God. Women in African societies remove the clitoris of prepubescent girls, scrape their labia, and make the lips grow together to preserve their chastity and ensure their marriageability. In Western societies, women augment their breast size with silicone and reconstruct their faces with cosmetic surgery to conform to cultural ideals of feminine beauty. Hanna Papanek (1990) notes that these practices reinforce the sense of superiority or inferiority in the adults who carry them out as well as in the children on whom they are done: The genitals of Jewish fathers and sons are physical and psychological evidence of their common dominant religious and familial status; the genitals of African mothers and daughters are physical and psychological evidence of their joint subordination.[9]

Sandra Bem (1981, 1983) argues that because gender is a powerful "schema" that orders the cognitive world, one must wage a constant, active battle for a child not to fall into typical gendered attitudes and behavior. In 1972, *Ms. Magazine* published Lois Gould's fantasy of how to raise a child free of gender-typing. The experiment calls for hiding the child's anatomy from all eyes except the parents' and treating the child as neither a girl nor a boy. The child, called X, gets to do all the things boys *and* girls do. The experiment is so successful that all

---

[8] For an account of how a potential man-to-woman transsexual learned to be feminine, see Garfinkel 1967, 116–85, 285–88.

[9] Paige and Paige (1981, 147–49) argue that circumcision ceremonies indicate a father's loyalty to his lineage elders — "visible public evidence that the head of a family unit of their lineage is willing to trust others with his and his family's most valuable political asset, his son's penis" (147). On female circumcision, see El Dareer 1982; Lightfoot-Klein 1989; van der Kwaak 1992; Walker 1992. There is a form of female circumcision that removes only the prepuce of the clitoris and is similar to male circumcision, but most forms of female circumcision are far more extensive, mutilating, and spiritually and psychologically shocking than the usual form of male circumcision. However, among the Australian aborigines, boys' penises are slit and kept open, so that they urinate and bleed the way women do (Bettelheim 1962, 165–206).

the children in X's class at school want to look and behave like X. At the end of the story, the creators of the experiment are asked what will happen when X grows up. The scientists' answer is that by then it will be quite clear what X is, implying that its hormones will kick in and it will be revealed as a female or male. That ambiguous, and somewhat contradictory, ending lets Gould off the hook; neither she nor we have any idea what someone brought up in a totally androgynous manner would be like sexually or socially as an adult. The hormonal input will not create gender or sexuality but will only establish secondary sex characteristics; breasts, beards, and menstruation alone do not produce social manhood or womanhood. Indeed, it is at puberty, when sex characteristics become evident, that most societies put pubescent children through their most important rites of passage, the rituals that officially mark them as fully gendered — that is, ready to marry and become adults.

Most parents create a gendered world for their newborn by naming, birth announcements, and dress. Children's relationships with same-gendered and different-gendered caretakers structure their self-identifications and personalities. Through cognitive development, children extract and apply to their own actions the appropriate behavior for those who belong in their own gender, as well as race, religion, ethnic group, and social class, rejecting what is not appropriate. If their social categories are highly valued, they value themselves highly; if their social categories are of low status, they lose self-esteem (Chodorow 1974). Many feminist parents who want to raise androgynous children soon lose their children to the pull of gendered norms (Gordon 1990, 87–90). My son attended a carefully nonsexist elementary school, which didn't even have girls' and boys' bathrooms. When he was seven or eight years old, I attended a class play about "squares" and "circles" and their need for each other and noticed that all the girl squares and circles wore makeup, but none of the boy squares and circles did. I asked the teacher about it after the play, and she said, "Bobby said he was not going to wear makeup, and he is a powerful child, so none of the boys would either." In a long discussion about conformity, my son confronted me with the question of who the conformists were, the boys who followed their leader or the girls who listened to the woman teacher. In actuality, they both were, because they both followed same-gender leaders and acted in gender-appropriate ways. (Actors may wear makeup, but real boys don't.)

For human beings there is no essential femaleness or maleness, 15 femininity or masculinity, womanhood or manhood, but once gender is ascribed, the social order constructs and holds individuals to strongly gendered norms and expectations. Individuals may vary on

For human beings there is no essential femaleness or maleness, femininity or masculinity, womanhood or manhood, but once gender is ascribed, the social order constructs and holds individuals to strongly gendered norms and expectations.

many of the components of gender and may shift genders temporarily or permanently, but they must fit into the limited number of gender statuses their society recognizes. In the process, they re-create their society's version of women and men: "If we do gender appropriately, we simultaneously sustain, reproduce, and render legitimate the institutional arrangements. . . . If we fail to do gender appropriately, we as individuals — not the institutional arrangements — may be called to account (for our character, motives, and predispositions)" (West and Zimmerman 1987, 146).

The gendered practices of everyday life reproduce a society's view of how women and men should act. Gendered social arrangements are justified by religion and cultural productions and backed by law, but the most powerful means of sustaining the moral hegemony of the dominant gender ideology is that the process is made invisible; any possible alternatives are virtually unthinkable (Foucault 1972; Gramsci 1971).[10]

For Society, Gender Means Difference

The pervasiveness of gender as a way of structuring social life demands that gender statuses be clearly differentiated. Varied talents, sexual preferences, identities, personalities, interests, and ways of interacting fragment the individual's bodily and social experiences. Nonetheless, these are organized in Western cultures into two and only two socially and legally recognized gender statuses, "man" and "woman."[11] In the social construction of gender, it does not matter what men and women actually do; it does not even matter if they do exactly the same thing. The social institution of gender insists only that what they do is *perceived* as different.

If men and women are doing the same tasks, they are usually spatially segregated to maintain gender separation, and often the tasks are given different job titles as well, such as executive secretary and administrative assistant (Reskin 1988). If the differences between

---

[10] The concepts of moral hegemony, the effects of everyday activities (praxis) on thought and personality, and the necessity of consciousness of these processes before political change can occur are all based on Marx's analysis of class relations.

[11] Other societies recognize more than two categories, but usually no more than three or four (Jacobs and Roberts 1989).

women and men begin to blur, society's "sameness taboo" goes into action (Rubin 1975, 178). At a rock and roll dance at West Point in 1976, the year women were admitted to the prestigious military academy for the first time, the school's administrators "were reportedly perturbed by the sight of mirror-image couples dancing in short hair and dress gray trousers," and a rule was established that women cadets could dance at these events only if they wore skirts (Barkalow and Raab 1990, 53).[12] Women recruits in the U.S. Marine Corps are required to wear makeup — at a minimum, lipstick and eye shadow — and they have to take classes in makeup, hair care, poise, and etiquette. This feminization is part of a deliberate policy of making them clearly distinguishable from men Marines. Christine Williams quotes a twenty-five-year-old woman drill instructor as saying, "A lot of the recruits who come here don't wear makeup; they're tomboyish or athletic. A lot of them have the preconceived idea that going into the military means they can still be a tomboy. They don't realize that you are a Woman Marine" (1989, 76–77).[13]

If gender differences were genetic, physiological, or hormonal, gender bending and gender ambiguity would occur only in hermaphrodites, who are born with chromosomes and genitalia that are not clearly female or male. Since gender differences are socially constructed, all men and all women can enact the behavior of the other, because they know the other's social script: " 'Man' and 'woman' are at once empty and overflowing categories. Empty because they have no ultimate, transcendental meaning. Overflowing because even when they appear to be fixed, they still contain within them alternative, denied, or suppressed definitions" (Scott 1988, 49). Nonetheless, though individuals may be able to shift gender statuses, the gender boundaries have to hold, or the whole gendered social order will come crashing down. . . .

Gender as Process, Stratification, and Structure

As a social institution, gender is a process of creating distinguishable 20 social statuses for the assignment of rights and responsibilities. As

---

[12] Carol Barkalow's book has a photograph of eleven first-year West Pointers in a math class, who are dressed in regulation pants, shirts, and sweaters, with short haircuts. The caption challenges the reader to locate the only woman in the room.

[13] The taboo on males and females looking alike reflects the U.S. military's homophobia (Bérubé 1989). If you can't tell those with a penis from those with a vagina, how are you going to determine whether their sexual interest is heterosexual or homosexual unless you watch them having sexual relations?

part of a stratification system that ranks these statuses unequally, gender is a major building block in the social structures built on these unequal statuses.

As a *process*, gender creates the social differences that define "woman" and "man." In social interaction throughout their lives, individuals learn what is expected, see what is expected, act and react in expected ways, and thus simultaneously construct and maintain the gender order: "The very injunction to be a given gender takes place through discursive routes: to be a good mother, to be a heterosexually desirable object, to be a fit worker, in sum, to signify a multiplicity of guarantees in response to a variety of different demands all at once" (Butler 1990, 145). Members of a social group neither make up gender as they go along nor exactly replicate in rote fashion what was done before. In almost every encounter, human beings produce gender, behaving in the ways they learned were appropriate for their gender status, or resisting or rebelling against these norms. Resistance and rebellion have altered gender norms, but so far they have rarely eroded the statuses.

Gendered patterns of interaction acquire additional layers of gendered sexuality, parenting, and work behaviors in childhood, adolescence, and adulthood. Gendered norms and expectations are enforced through informal sanctions of gender-inappropriate behavior by peers and by formal punishment or threat of punishment by those in authority should behavior deviate too far from socially imposed standards for women and men.

Everyday gendered interactions build gender into the family, the work process, and other organizations and institutions, which in turn reinforce gender expectations for individuals.[14] Because gender is a process, there is room not only for modification and variation by individuals and small groups but also for institutionalized change (Scott 1988, 7).

As part of a stratification system, gender ranks men above women of the same race and class. Women and men could be different but equal. In practice, the process of creating difference depends to a great extent on differential evaluation. As Nancy Jay (1981) says: "That which is defined, separated out, isolated from all else is A and pure. Not-A is necessarily impure, a random catchall, to which nothing is external except A and the principle of order that separates it from

---

[14] On the "logic of practice," or how the experience of gender is embedded in the norms of everyday interaction and the structure of formal organizations, see Acker 1990; Connell 1987; Smith 1987.

Not-A" (45). From the individual's point of view, whichever gender is A, the other is Not-A; gender boundaries tell the individual who is like him or her, and all the rest are unlike. From society's point of view, however, one gender is usually the touchstone, the normal, the dominant, and the other is different, deviant, and subordinate. In Western society, "man" is A, "woman" is Not-A. (Consider what a society would be like where woman was A and man Not-A.)

The further dichotomization by race and class constructs the gra- 25 dations of a heterogeneous society's stratification scheme. Thus, in the United States, white is A, African American is Not-A; middle class is A, working class is Not-A, and "African-American women occupy a position whereby the inferior half of a series of these dichotomies converge" (Collins 1990, 70). The dominant categories are the hegemonic ideals, taken so for granted as the way things should be that white is not ordinarily thought of as a race, middle class as a class, or men as a gender. The characteristics of these categories define the Other as that which lacks the valuable qualities the dominants exhibit.

Societies vary in the extent of the inequality in social status of their women and men members, but where there is inequality, the status "woman" (and its attendant behavior and role allocations) is usually held in lesser esteem than the status "man." Since gender is also intertwined with a society's other constructed statuses of differential evaluation — race, religion, occupation, class, country of origin, and so on — men and women members of the favored groups command more power, more prestige, and more property than the members of the disfavored groups. Within many social groups, however, men are advantaged over women. The more economic resources, such as education and job opportunities, are available to a group, the more they tend to be monopolized by men. In poorer groups that have few resources (such as working-class African Americans in the United States), women and men are more nearly equal, and the women may even outstrip the men in education and occupational status (Almquist 1987).

As a structure, gender divides work in the home and in economic production, legitimates those in authority, and organizes sexuality and emotional life (Connell 1987, 91–142). As primary parents, women significantly influence children's psychological development and emotional attachments, in the process reproducing gender. Emergent sexuality is shaped by heterosexual, homosexual, bisexual, and sadomasochistic patterns that are gendered-different for girls and boys, and for women and men — so that sexual statuses reflect gender statuses.

When gender is a major component of structured inequality, the devalued genders have less power, prestige, and economic rewards than the valued genders. In countries that discourage gender discrimination, many major roles are still gendered; women still do most of the domestic labor and child rearing, even while doing full-time paid work; women and men are segregated on the job and each does work considered "appropriate"; women's work is usually paid less than men's work. Men dominate the positions of authority and leadership in government, the military, and the law; cultural productions, religions, and sports reflect men's interests.

Gender inequality — the devaluation of "women" and the social domination of "men" — has social functions and a social history. It is not the result of sex, procreation, physiology, anatomy, hormones, or genetic predispositions. It is produced and maintained by identifiable social processes and built into the general social structure and individual identities deliberately and purposefully. The social order as we know it in Western societies is organized around racial ethnic, class, and gender inequality. I contend, therefore, that the continuing purpose of gender as a modern social institution is to construct women as a group to be the subordinates of men as a group. The life of everyone placed in the status "woman" is "night to his day — that has forever been the fantasy. Black to his white. Shut out of his system's space, she is the repressed that ensures the system's functioning" (Cixous and Clement [1975] 1986, 67) . . .

There is no core or bedrock human nature below these endlessly 30 looping processes of the social production of sex and gender, self and other identity and psyche, each of which is a "complex cultural construction" (Butler 1990, 36). For *humans, the social is the natural.* Therefore, "in its feminist senses, gender cannot mean simply the cultural appropriation of biological sexual difference. Sexual difference is itself a fundamental — and scientifically contested — construction. Both 'sex' and 'gender' are woven of multiple, asymmetrical strands of difference, charged with multifaceted dramatic narratives of domination and struggle" (Haraway 1990, 140).

References

Acker, Joan. 1990. "Hierarchies, Jobs, and Bodies: A Theory of Gendered Organizations." *Gender and Society* 4, 139–58.

Almquist, Elizabeth M. 1987. "Labor Market Gendered Inequality in Minority Groups." *Gender and Society* 1, 400–414.

Amadiume, III. 1987. *Male Daughters, Female Husbands: Gender and Sex in an African Society.* London: Zed Books.

Barkalow, Carol, with Andrea Raab. 1990. *In the Men's House.* New York: Poseidon Press.

Beauvoir, Simone de. 1953. *The Second Sex,* translated by H. M. Parshley. New York: Knopf.

Bem, Sandra Lipsitz. 1981. "Gender Schema Theory: A Cognitive Account of Sex Typing." *Psychological Review* 88, 354–64.

——. 1983. "Gender Schema Theory and Its Implications for Child Development: Raising Gender-Aschematic Children in a Gender-Schematic Society." *Signs: Journal of Women in Culture and Society* 8, 598–616.

——. 1993. *The Lenses of Gender Transforming the Debate on Sexual Inequality.* New Haven: Yale University Press.

Bérubé, Allan. 1989. "Marching to a Different Drummer: Gay and Lesbian GIs in World War II." In Duberman, Vicinus, and Chauncey, eds., *Hidden from History: Reclaiming the Gay and Lesbian Past.* New York: New American Library.

Bettelheim, Bruno. 1962. *Symbolic Wounds: Puberty Rites and the Envious Male.* London: Thames and Hudson.

Blackwood, Evelyn. 1984. "Sexuality and Gender in Certain Native American Tribes: The Case of Cross-Gender Females." *Signs: Journal of Women in Culture and Society* 10, 27–42.

Bolin, Anne. 1987. "Transsexualism and the Limits of Traditional Analysis." *American Behavioral Scientist* 31, 41–65.

Butler, Judith. 1990. *Gender Trouble: Feminism and the Subversion of Identity.* New York: Routledge.

Chodorow, Nancy. 1974. "Family Structure and Feminine Personality." In Rosaldo and Lamphere, eds., *Women, Culture and Society.* Stanford, Calif.: Stanford University Press.

Cixous, Hélène, and Catherine Clement. [1975] 1986. *The Newly Born Woman*, translated by Betsy Wing. Minneapolis: University of Minnesota Press.

Collins, Patricia Hill. 1990. *Black Feminist Thought: Knowledge, Consciousness, and the Politics of Empowerment.* Boston: Unwin Hyman.

Connell, R[obert] W. 1987. *Gender and Power: Society, the Person, and Sexual Politics.* Stanford, Calif.: Stanford University Press.

Durova, Nadezhda. 1989. *The Cavalry Maiden: Journals of a Russian Officer in the Napoleonic Wars*, translated by Mary Fleming Zirin. Bloomington: Indiana University Press.

El Dareer, Asma. 1982. *Woman, Why Do You Weep? Circumcision and Its Consequences.* London: Zed Books.

Faderman, Lillian. 1991. *Odd Girls and Twilight Lovers: A History of Lesbian Life in Twentieth-Century America.* New York: Columbia University Press.

Foucault, Michel. 1972. *The Archeology of Knowledge and the Discourse on Language*, translated by A. M. Sheridan Smith. New York: Pantheon.

Freeman, Lucy, and Alma Halbert Bond. 1992. *America's First Woman Warrior: The Courage of Deborah Sampson.* New York: Paragon.

Frye, Marilyn. 1983. *The Politics of Reality: Essays in Feminist Theory.* Trumansburg, N.Y.: Crossing Press.

Garber, Marjorie. 1992. *Vested Interests: Cross-Dressing and Cultural Anxiety.* New York and London: Routledge.

Garfinkel, Harold. 1967. *Studies in Ethnomethodology.* Englewood Cliffs, NJ.: Prentice-Hall.

Goffman, Erving. 1977. "The Arrangement between the Sexes." *Theory and Society* 4, 301–33.

———. 1983. "Felicity's Condition." *American Journal of Sociology* 89, 1–53.

Gordon, Tuula. 1990. *Feminist Mothers.* New York: New York University Press.

Gould, Lois. 1972. "X: A Fabulous Child's Story." *Ms.*, December, 74–76, 105–106.

Gramsci, Antonio. 1971. *Selections from the Prison Notebooks*, translated and edited by Quintin Hoare and Geoffrey Nowell Smith. New York: International Publishers.

Groce, Stephen B., and Margaret Cooper. 1990. "Just Me and the Boys? Women in Local-Level Rock and Roll," *Gender and Society* 4, 220–29.

Haraway, Donna. 1990. "Investment Strategies for the Evolving Portfolio of Primate Females." In Jacobus, Keller, and Shuttleworth, eds., *Body/Politics: Women and the Discourses of Science.* New York: Routledge.

Jacobs, Sue-Ellen, and Christine Roberts. 1989. "Sex, Sexuality, Gender, and Gender Variance." In *Gender and Anthropology*, ed. Sandra Morgen. Washington, D.C.: American Anthropological Association.

Jay, Nancy. 1981. "Gender and Dichotomy." *Feminist Studies* 7, 38–56.

Lightfoot-Klein, Hanny. 1989. *Prisoners of Ritual: An Odyssey into Female Circumcision in Africa.* New York: Harrington Park Press.

Matthaei, Julie A. 1982. *An Economic History of Women's Work in America.* New York: Schocken.

Nanda, Serena. 1990. *Neither Man nor Woman: The Hijiras of India.* Belmont, Calif.: Wadsworth.

New York Times. 1989. "Musician's Death at 74 Reveals He Was a Woman." February 2.

Paige, Karen Ericksen, and Jeffrey M. Paige. 1981. *The Politics of Reproductive Ritual.* Berkeley and Los Angeles: University of California Press.

Papanek, Hanna. 1990. "To Each Less Than She Needs, From Each More Than She Can Do: Allocations, Entitlements, and Value." In Tinker, ed., *Persistent Inequalities: Women and World Development.* New York: Oxford University Press.

Reskin, Barbara J. 1988. "Bringing the Men Back In: Sex Differentiation and the Devaluation of Women's Work." *Gender and Society* 7, 58–81.

Rubin, Gayle. 1975. "The Traffic in Women: Notes on the Political Economy of Sex." In *Toward an Anthropology of Women*, edited by Rayna R[app] Reiter. New York: Monthly Review Press.

Scott, Joan Wallach. 1988. *Gender and the Politics of History.* New York: Columbia University Press.

Smith, Dorothy E. 1987. *The Everyday World as Problematic: A Feminist Sociology.* Toronto: University of Toronto Press.

van der Kwaak, Anke. 1992. "Female Circumcision and Gender Identity: A Questionable Alliance?" *Social Science and Medicine* 35, 777–87.

Walker, Alice. 1992. *Possessing the Secret of Joy.* New York: Harcourt Brace Jovanovich.

West, Candace, and Don Zimmerman. 1987. "Doing Gender." *Gender and Society* 1, 125–51.

Wheelwright, Julie. 1989. *Amazons and Military Maids: Women Who Cross-Dressed in Pursuit of Life, Liberty and Happiness.* London: Pandora Press.

Wikan, Unni. 1982. *Behind the Veil in Arabia: Women in Oman.* Baltimore, Md.: Johns Hopkins University Press.

Williams, Christine L. 1989. *Gender Differences at Work: Women and Men in Nontraditional Occupations.* Berkeley: University of California Press.

Williams, Walter L. 1986. *The Spirit and the Flesh: Sexual Diversity in American Indian Culture.* Boston: Beacon Press.

Understanding the Text

1. How does Lorber distinguish between "sex" and "gender"?

2. What does Lorber mean by the "social construction of gender"?

3. Lorber claims that transsexuals and transvestites do not fundamentally challenge the dualistic nature of social understandings of gender. Why is cross-dressing or assuming the role of the opposite gender seen *not* to be a challenge to gender codes?

4. Lorber writes that "social statuses are carefully constructed through prescribed processes of teaching, learning, emulation, and enforcement" (p. 22). Give some examples of how gender is constructed through each of the four categories, teaching, learning, emulation, and enforcement.

Reflection and Response

5. Lorber writes that the structure of social life demands that gender statuses be clearly differentiated. Even when men and women are doing the same task, they will be distinguished from one another in terms of gender (as in the formulation "secretary" for a woman and "administrative assistant" for a man). Can you think of other aspects of social life in which the same or similar task, activity, or behavior is differentiated according to gender? Why do you think these distinctions exist?

6. Sex is only one biological difference among many found in the human species. What other biological differences among people are thought to produce differences in social behaviors and status? What biological differences are *not* thought to produce such differences?

7. Lorber claims that children's relationships with same-gendered and different-gendered caretakers structure their identities and personalities. Write a brief paragraph about the impact of one person in your life on your sense of your masculinity or femininity. What values and what behaviors in particular were modeled that shaped your own gender development?

Making Connections

8. Drawing from West and Zimmerman's notion of gender as an ongoing performance, Lorber provides the following formulation: "If we do gender appropriately, we simultaneously sustain, reproduce, and render legitimate the institutional arrangements [of gender]. . . . If we fail to do gender appropriately, we as individuals — not the institutional arrangements — may be called to account (for our character, motives, predispositions)" (p. 26). Consider a case in which someone you know, or someone in the news, or some other public

figure such as a celebrity, performer, or politician "violated" gender codes or otherwise failed to "do gender" appropriately. What was the effect? How was the individual "called to account"?

9. Lorber closes her essay by arguing that "gender ranks men above women" (p. 28) and that "gender is a major component of structured inequality" (p. 29). By looking to outside sources, find at least three statistics that demonstrate inequities between men and women. These can range from "equal pay for equal work" issues, to "rates of infidelity," "to "life-span expectation," to "incidents of car accidents between male and female drivers." The important question to apply to your selected statistics is the role of gender (as defined in this chapter) as a contributive factor. What about gender — either the conditions of masculinity and femininity in contemporary society or the assumptions, predilections, and commonplace understandings of gender — help us better understand the reasons for these inequities you found?

Becoming Members of Society: The Social Meanings of Gender

Aaron Devor

Aaron Devor is a professor of sociology and the academic director of the Transgender Archives at the University of Victoria, Canada. His scholarship focuses on gender studies, particularly on transgendered men and women and female-to-male transsexuals. His books include *Gender Blending: Confronting the Limits of Duality* (1989), from which this selection is drawn, and *FTM: Female-to-Male Transsexuals in Society* (1997).

The Gendered Self

The task of learning to be properly gendered members of society only begins with the establishment of gender identity. Gender identities act as cognitive filtering devices guiding people to attend to and learn gender role behaviors appropriate to their statuses. Learning to behave in accordance with one's gender identity is a lifelong process. As we move through our lives, society demands different gender performances from us and rewards, tolerates, or punishes us differently for conformity to, or digression from, social norms. As children, and later adults, learn the rules of membership in society, they come to see themselves in terms they have learned from the people around them.

Children begin to settle into a gender identity between the ages of eighteen months and two years.[1] By the age of two, children usually understand that they are members of a gender grouping and can correctly identify other members of their gender.[2] By age three they have a fairly firm and consistent concept of

> As we move through our lives, society demands different gender performances from us and rewards, tolerates, or punishes us differently for conformity to, or digression from, social norms.

---

[1] Much research has been devoted to determining when gender identity becomes solidified in the sense that a child knows itself to be unequivocally either male or female. John Money and his colleagues have proposed eighteen months of age because it is difficult or impossible to change a child's gender identity once it has been established around the age of eighteen months. John Money and Anke Ehrhardt, *Man and Woman, Boy and Girl: The Differentiation and Dimorphism of Gender Identity from Conception to Maturity* (Baltimore, Md.: Johns Hopkins University Press, 1972), p. 243.

[2] Mary Driver Leinbach and Beverly I. Fagot, "Acquisition of Gender Labels: A Test for Toddlers," *Sex Roles* 15 (1986), pp. 655–66.

35

gender. Generally, it is not until children are five to seven years old that they become convinced that they are permanent members of their gender grouping.[3]

Researchers test the establishment, depth, and tenacity of gender identity through the use of language and the concepts mediated by language. The language systems used in populations studied by most researchers in this field conceptualize gender as binary and permanent. All persons are either male or female. All males are first boys and then men; all females are first girls and then women. People are believed to be unable to change genders without sex change surgery, and those who do change sex are considered to be both disturbed and exceedingly rare.

This is by no means the only way that gender is conceived in all cultures. Many aboriginal cultures have more than two gender categories and accept the idea that, under certain circumstances, gender may be changed without changes being made to biological sex characteristics. Many North and South American native peoples had a legitimate social category for persons who wished to live according to the gender role of another sex. Such people were sometimes revered, sometimes ignored, and occasionally scorned. Each culture had its own word to describe such persons, most commonly translated into English as "berdache." Similar institutions and linguistic concepts have also been recorded in early Siberian, Madagascan, and Polynesian societies, as well as in medieval Europe.[4]

Very young children learn their culture's social definitions of 5 gender and gender identity at the same time that they learn what gender behaviors are appropriate for them. But they only gradually come to understand the meaning of gender in the same way as the adults of their society do. Very young children may learn the words which describe their gender and be able to apply them to themselves appropriately, but their comprehension of their meaning is often different from that used by adults. Five-year-olds, for example,

---

[3] Eleanor E. Maccoby, *The Two Sexes: Growing Up Apart, Coming Together* (Boston: Harvard University Press, 1998), pp. 225–29.

[4] See Susan Baker, "Biological Influences on Human Sex and Gender," in *Women: Sex and Sexuality*, ed. Catherine R. Stimpson and Ethel S. Person (Chicago: University of Chicago Press, 1980), p. 186; Evelyn Blackwood, "Sexuality and Gender in Certain Native American Tribes: The Case of Cross-Gender Females," *Signs* 10 (1984), pp. 27–42; Vern L. Bullough, "Transvestites in the Middle Ages," *American Journal of Sociology* 79 (1974), 1381–89; J. Cl. DuBois, "Transsexualisme et Anthropologie Culturelle," *Gynecologie Practique* 6 (1969), pp. 431–40; Donald C. Forgey, "The Institution of Berdache among the North American Plains Indians," *Journal of Sex Research* 11 (Feb. 1975), pp. 1–15; Walter L. Williams, *The Spirit and the Flesh: Sexual Diversity in American Indian Culture* (Boston: Beacon, 1986).

may be able to accurately recognize their own gender and the genders of the people around them, but they will often make such ascriptions on the basis of role information, such as hair style, rather than physical attributes, such as genitals, even when physical cues are clearly known to them. One result of this level of understanding of gender is that children in this age group often believe that people may change their gender with a change in clothing, hair style, or activity.[5]

The characteristics most salient to young minds are the more culturally specific qualities which grow out of gender role prescriptions. In one study, young school age children, who were given dolls and asked to identify their gender, overwhelmingly identified the gender of the dolls on the basis of attributes such as hair length or clothing style, in spite of the fact that the dolls were anatomically correct. Only 17 percent of the children identified the dolls on the basis of their primary or secondary sex characteristics.[6] Children five to seven years old understand gender as a function of role rather than as a function of anatomy. Their understanding is that gender (role) is supposed to be stable but that it is possible to alter it at will. This demonstrates that although the standard social definition of gender is based on genitalia, this is not the way that young children first learn to distinguish gender. The process of learning to think about gender in an adult fashion is one prerequisite to becoming a full member of society. Thus, as children grow older, they learn to think of themselves and others in terms more like those used by adults.

Children's developing concepts of themselves as individuals are necessarily bound up in their need to understand the expectations of the society of which they are a part. As they develop concepts of themselves as individuals, they do so while observing themselves as reflected in the eyes of others. Children start to understand themselves as individuals separate from others during the years that they first acquire gender identities and gender roles. As they do so, they begin to understand that others see them and respond to them as particular people. In this way they develop concepts of themselves as individuals, as an "I" (a proactive subject) simultaneously with self-images of themselves as individuals, as a "me" (a member of society, a subjective object). Children learn that they are both as they see themselves and as others see them.[7]

---

[5] Maccoby, p. 255.

[6] Ibid., p. 227.

[7] George Herbert Mead, "Self," in *The Social Psychology of George Herbert Mead*, ed. Anselm Strauss (Chicago: Phoenix Books, 1962, 1934), pp. 212–60.

To some extent, children initially acquire the values of the society around them almost indiscriminately. To the degree that children absorb the generalized standards of society into their personal concept of what is correct behavior, they can be said to hold within themselves the attitude of the "generalized other."[8] This "generalized other" functions as a sort of monitoring or measuring device with which individuals may judge their own actions against those of their generalized conceptions of how members of society are expected to act. In this way members of society have available to them a guide, or an internalized observer, to turn the more private "I" into the object of public scrutiny, the "me." In this way, people can monitor their own behavioral impulses and censor actions which might earn them social disapproval or scorn. The tension created by the constant interplay of the personal "I" and the social "me" is the creature known as the "self."

But not all others are of equal significance in our lives, and therefore not all others are of equal impact on the development of the self. Any person is available to become part of one's "generalized other," but certain individuals, by virtue of the sheer volume of time spent in interaction with someone, or by virtue of the nature of particular interactions, become more significant in the shaping of people's values. These "significant others" become prominent in the formation of one's self-image and one's ideals and goals. As such they carry disproportionate weight in one's personal "generalized other."[9] Thus, children's individualistic impulses are shaped into a socially acceptable form both by particular individuals and by a more generalized pressure to conformity exerted by innumerable faceless members of society. Gender identity is one of the most central portions of that developing sense of self. . . .

Gender Role Behaviors and Attitudes

The clusters of social definitions used to identify persons by gender 10 are collectively known as femininity and masculinity. Masculine characteristics are used to identify persons as males, while feminine ones are used as signifiers for femaleness. People use femininity or masculinity to claim and communicate their membership in their assigned, or chosen, sex or gender. Others recognize our sex or gender more on the basis of these characteristics than on the basis of sex characteristics, which are usually largely covered by clothing in daily life.

---

[8] G. H. Mead.

[9] Hans Gerth and C. Wright Mills, *Character and Social Structure: The Psychology of Social Institutions* (New York: Harcourt, Brace and World, 1953), p. 96.

These two clusters of attributes are most commonly seen as mirror images of one another with masculinity usually characterized by dominance and aggression, and femininity by passivity and submission. A more even-handed description of the social qualities subsumed by femininity and masculinity might be to label masculinity as generally concerned with egoistic dominance and femininity as striving for cooperation or communion.[10] Characterizing femininity and masculinity in such a way does not portray the two clusters of characteristics as being in a hierarchical relationship to one another but rather as being two different approaches to the same question, that question being centrally concerned with the goals, means, and use of power. Such an alternative conception of gender roles captures the hierarchical and competitive masculine thirst for power, which can, but need not, lead to aggression, and the feminine quest for harmony and communal well-being, which can, but need not, result in passivity and dependence.

Many activities and modes of expression are recognized by most members of society as feminine. Any of these can be, and often are, displayed by persons of either gender. In some cases, cross-gender behaviors are ignored by observers, and therefore do not compromise the integrity of a person's gender display. In other cases, they are labeled as inappropriate gender role behaviors. Although these behaviors are closely linked to sexual status in the minds and experiences of most people, research shows that dominant persons of either gender tend to use influence tactics and verbal styles usually associated with men and masculinity, while subordinate persons, of either gender, tend to use those considered to be the province of women.[11] Thus it seems likely that many aspects of masculinity and femininity are the result, rather than the cause, of status inequalities.

Popular conceptions of femininity and masculinity instead revolve around hierarchical appraisals of the "natural" roles of males and females. Members of both genders are believed to share many of the

---

[10] Egoistic dominance is a striving for superior rewards for oneself or a competitive striving to reduce the rewards for one's competitors even if such action will not increase one's own rewards. Persons who are motivated by desires for egoistic dominance not only wish the best for themselves but also wish to diminish the advantages of others whom they may perceive as competing with them. See Maccoby, p. 217.

[11] Judith Howard, Philip Blumstein, and Pepper Schwartz, "Sex, Power, and Influence Tactics in Intimate Relationships," *Journal of Personality and Social Psychology* 51 (1986), pp. 102–09; Peter Kollock, Philip Blumstein, and Pepper Schwartz, "Sex and Power in Interaction: Conversational Privileges and Duties," *American Sociological Review* 50 (1985), pp. 34–46.

same human characteristics, although in different relative proportions; both males and females are popularly thought to be able to do many of the same things, but most activities are divided into suitable and unsuitable categories for each gender class. Persons who perform the activities considered appropriate for another gender will be expected to perform them poorly; if they succeed adequately, or even well, at their endeavors, they may be rewarded with ridicule or scorn for blurring the gender dividing line.

The patriarchal gender schema currently in use in mainstream North American society reserves highly valued attributes for males and actively supports the high evaluation of any characteristics which might inadvertently become associated with maleness. The ideology which the schema grows out of postulates that the cultural superiority of males is a natural outgrowth of the innate predisposition of males toward aggression and dominance, which is assumed to flow inevitably from evolutionary and biological sources. Female attributes are likewise postulated to find their source in innate predispositions acquired in the evolution of the species. Feminine characteristics are thought to be intrinsic to the female facility for childbirth and breastfeeding. Hence, it is popularly believed that the social position of females is biologically mandated to be intertwined with the care of children and a "natural" dependency on men for the maintenance of mother-child units. Thus the goals of femininity and, by implication, of all biological females are presumed to revolve around heterosexuality and maternity.[12]

Femininity, according to this traditional formulation, "would result in warm and continued relationships with men, a sense of maternity, interest in caring for children, and the capacity to work productively and continuously in female occupations."[13] This recipe translates into a vast number of proscriptions and prescriptions. Warm and continued relations with men and an interest in maternity require that females be heterosexually oriented. A heterosexual orientation requires women to dress, move, speak, and act in ways that men will find attractive. As patriarchy has reserved active expressions of power as a masculine attribute, femininity must be expressed through modes of dress, movement, speech, and action which communicate weakness,

---

[12] Nancy Chodorow, *The Reproduction of Mothering: Psychoanalysis and the Sociology of Gender* (Berkeley: University of California Press, 1978), p. 134.

[13] Jon K. Meyer and John E. Hoopes, "The Gender Dysphoria Syndromes: A Position Statement on So-Called 'Transsexualism,'" *Plastic and Reconstructive Surgery* 54 (Oct. 1974), pp. 444–51.

dependency, ineffectualness, availability for sexual or emotional service, and sensitivity to the needs of others.

Some, but not all, of these modes of interrelation also serve the demands of maternity and many female job ghettos. In many cases, though, femininity is not particularly useful in maternity or employment. Both mothers and workers often need to be strong, independent, and effectual in order to do their jobs well. Thus femininity, as a role, is best suited to satisfying a masculine vision of heterosexual attractiveness.

Body postures and demeanors which communicate subordinate status and vulnerability to trespass through a message of "no threat" make people appear to be feminine. They demonstrate subordination through a minimizing of spatial use: people appear feminine when they keep their arms closer to their bodies, their legs closer together, and their torsos and heads less vertical than do masculine-looking individuals. People also look feminine when they point their toes inward and use their hands in small or childlike gestures. Other people also tend to stand closer to people they see as feminine, often invading their personal space, while people who make frequent appeasement gestures, such as smiling, also give the appearance of femininity. Perhaps as an outgrowth of a subordinate status and the need to avoid conflict with more socially powerful people, women tend to excel over men at the ability to correctly interpret, and effectively display, nonverbal communication cues.[14]

Speech characterized by inflections, intonations, and phrases that convey nonaggression and subordinate status also make a speaker appear more feminine. Subordinate speakers who use more polite expressions and ask more questions in conversation seem more feminine. Speech characterized by sounds of higher frequencies are often interpreted by listeners as feminine, childlike, and ineffectual.[15] Feminine styles of dress likewise display subordinate status through greater restriction of the free movement of the body, greater exposure of the bare skin, and an emphasis on sexual characteristics. The more gender distinct the dress, the more this is the case.

---

[14] Erving Goffman, *Gender Advertisements* (New York: Harper Colophon Books, 1976); Judith A. Hall, *Non-Verbal Sex Differences: Communication Accuracy and Expressive Style* (Baltimore: Johns Hopkins University Press, 1984); Nancy M. Henley, *Body Politics: Power, Sex and Non-Verbal Communication* (Englewood Cliffs, N.J.: Prentice Hall, 1979); Marianne Wex, *"Let's Take Back Our Space": "Female" and "Male" Body Language as a Result of Patriarchal Structures* (Berlin: Frauenliteraturverlag Hermine Fees, 1979).

[15] Karen L. Adams, "Sexism and the English Language: The Linguistic Implications of Being a Woman," in *Women: A Feminist Perspective*, 3rd edition, ed. Jo Freeman (Palo Alto, Calif.: Mayfield, 1984), pp. 478–91; Hall, pp. 37, 130–37.

Masculinity, like femininity, can be demonstrated through a wide variety of cues. Pleck has argued that it is commonly expressed in North American society through the attainment of some level of proficiency at some, or all, of the following four main attitudes of masculinity. Persons who display success and high status in their social group, who exhibit "a manly air of toughness, confidence, and self-reliance" and "the aura of aggression, violence, and daring," and who conscientiously avoid anything associated with femininity are seen as exuding masculinity.[16] These requirements reflect the patriarchal ideology that masculinity results from an excess of testosterone, the assumption being that androgens supply a natural impetus toward aggression, which in turn impels males toward achievement and success. This vision of masculinity also reflects the ideological stance that ideal maleness (masculinity) must remain untainted by female (feminine) pollutants.

Masculinity, then, requires of its actors that they organize themselves and their society in a hierarchical manner so as to be able to explicitly quantify the achievement of success. The achievement of high status in one's social group requires competitive and aggressive behavior from those who wish to obtain it. Competition which is motivated by a goal of individual achievement, or egoistic dominance, also requires of its participants a degree of emotional insensitivity to feelings of hurt and loss in defeated others, and a measure of emotional insularity to protect oneself from becoming vulnerable to manipulation by others. Such values lead those who subscribe to them to view feminine persons as "born losers" and to strive to eliminate any similarities to feminine people from their own personalities. In patriarchally organized societies, masculine values become the ideological structure of the society as a whole. Masculinity thus becomes "innately" valuable and femininity serves a contrapuntal function to delineate and magnify the hierarchical dominance of masculinity.

Body postures, speech patterns, and styles of dress which demonstrate and support the assumption of dominance and authority convey an impression of masculinity. Typical masculine body postures tend to be expansive and aggressive. People who hold their arms and hands in positions away from their bodies, and who stand, sit, or lie with their legs apart — thus maximizing the amount of space that they physically occupy — appear most physically masculine. Persons who communicate an air of authority or a readiness for aggression by

---

[16] Elizabeth Hafkin Pleck, *Domestic Tyranny: The Making of Social Policy against Family Violence from Colonial Times to the Present* (Cambridge: Oxford University Press, 1989), p. 139.

standing erect and moving forcefully also tend to appear more masculine. Movements that are abrupt and stiff, communicating force and threat rather than flexibility and cooperation, make an actor look masculine. Masculinity can also be conveyed by stern or serious facial expressions that suggest minimal receptivity to the influence of others, a characteristic which is an important element in the attainment and maintenance of egoistic dominance.[17]

Speech and dress which likewise demonstrate or claim superior status are also seen as characteristically masculine behavior patterns. Masculine speech patterns display a tendency toward expansiveness similar to that found in masculine body postures. People who attempt to control the direction of conversations seem more masculine.[18] Those who tend to speak more loudly, use less polite and more assertive forms, and tend to interrupt the conversations of others more often also communicate masculinity to others. Styles of dress which emphasize the size of upper body musculature, allow freedom of movement, and encourage an illusion of physical power and a look of easy physicality all suggest masculinity. Such appearances of strength and readiness to action serve to create or enhance an aura of aggressiveness and intimidation central to an appearance of masculinity. Expansive postures and gestures combine with these qualities to insinuate that a position of secure dominance is a masculine one.

Gender role characteristics reflect the ideological contentions underlying the dominant gender schema in North American society. That schema leads us to believe that female and male behaviors are the result of socially directed hormonal instructions which specify that females will want to have children and will therefore find themselves relatively helpless and dependent on males for support and protection. The schema claims that males are innately aggressive and competitive and therefore will dominate over females. The social hegemony of this ideology ensures that we are all raised to practice gender roles which will confirm this vision of the nature of the sexes. Fortunately, our training to gender roles is neither complete nor uniform. As a result, it is possible to point to multitudinous exceptions to, and variations on, these themes. Biological evidence is equivocal about the source of gender roles; psychological androgyny is a widely accepted concept. It seems most likely that gender roles are the result of systematic power imbalances based on gender discrimination.[19]

---

[17] Goffman, *Gender Advertisements;* Hall; Henley; Wex.
[18] Adams; Hall, pp. 37, 130–37.
[19] Howard, Blumstein, and Schwartz; Kollock, Blumstein, and Schwartz.

Understanding the Text

1. Consider the importance of Devor's title, "Becoming Members of Society," in terms of the social imperative to uphold the conventions of gender behavior and display. What does it mean to "become a member of society" by conforming to gender codes?

2. What is the "generalized other" and how does it help shape children's growing sense of gender identity?

3. Devor looks at a number of characteristics having to do with how people carry and use their bodies in masculine and feminine ways. What are some of these characteristics, and how do they suggest in general Devor's basic distinction between masculine/dominance and feminine/submission?

Reflection and Response

4. Devor suggests that clothing and dressing styles often serve to accentuate notions of masculinity and femininity. Consider some clothing items, adornment items, or fashion trends that seem to highlight cultural predispositions about masculinity and femininity.

5. While certain clusters of attributes seem to be primary in designating people either masculine or feminine, most people exhibit characteristics of both genders at different times as situations change. Reflect upon your own "masculine" and "feminine" traits and how you (or others) respond to them.

6. Because, as Devor points out, femininity and masculinity are often conceived as "natural," people who perform activities designated as appropriate for another gender will be expected to perform those activities poorly. Think of some examples of how this may play out in real life, in your own life, on television, or otherwise. In short, support this claim from your experiences or observations of the world.

Making Connections

7. Devor writes that "dominant persons *of either gender* tend to use influence tactics and verbal styles usually associated with men and masculinity, while subordinate persons, *of either gender*, tend to use those considered to be the province of women" (p. 39) (emphasis added). Look at examples of well-known public figures who exemplify (or challenge) this claim; that is, locate either two male figures who are more and less "masculine" or two female figures who are more and less "feminine" and examine the attributes that allow us to make this judgment accurately.

8. Devor writes, "As we move through our lives, society demands different gender performances from us and rewards, tolerates, or punishes us differently for conformity to, or digression from, social norms" (p. 35). How do the demands of gender display change over the life course for women, men, or both? How do the codes of gender change (or stay the same) for individuals at different ages or stages of life?

9. Consider the readings in this book on rituals, such as Amy Best's article about the prom (p. 128) or Stephanie Rosenbloom's article on Halloween costumes (p. 164). How does Devor's analysis of body postures, speech patterns, and styles of dress relate to gendered rituals? Do you think he would say that our daily habits of gender are ritualistic, or is there a difference between daily habits and special occasion rituals?

Rethinking Women's Biology

Ruth Hubbard

Ruth Hubbard is a professor emerita of biology at Harvard University. She has been an important researcher in the fields of biochemistry and photochemistry, though in recent years her work has focused on challenging the biological theory of women's inequality. Her books include *The Politics of Women's Biology* (1990) and *Profitable Promises: Essays on Women, Science, and Health* (1995).

Women's biology is a social construct, and a political concept, not a scientific one, and I mean that in at least three ways. The first can be summed up in Simone de Beauvoir's (1953) dictum "One isn't born a woman, one becomes a woman." This does not mean that the environment shapes us, but that the concept, woman (or man), is a socially constructed one that little girls (or boys) try to fit as we grow up. Some of us are better at it than others, but we all try, and our efforts have biological as well as social consequences (a false dichotomy because our biological and social attributes are related dialectically). How active we are, what clothes we wear, what games we play, what we eat and how much, what kinds of schools we go to, what work we do, all affect our biology as well as our social being in ways we cannot sort out. So, one isn't born a woman (or man), one becomes one.

The concept of women's biology is socially constructed, and political, in a second way because it is not simply women's description of our experience of our biology. We have seen that women's biology has been described by physicians and scientists who, for historical reasons, have been mostly economically privileged, university-educated men with strong personal and political interests in describing women in ways that make it appear "natural" for us to fulfill roles that are important for their well-being, personally and as a group. Self-serving descriptions of women's biology date back at least to Aristotle. But if we dismiss the early descriptions as ideological, so are the descriptions scientists have offered that characterize women as weak, overemotional, and at the mercy of our raging hormones, and that construct our entire being around the functions of our reproductive organs. No one has suggested that men are just walking testicles, but again and again women have been looked on as though they were walking ovaries and wombs.

In the nineteenth century, when women tried to get access to higher education, scientists initially claimed we could not be educated because our brains are too small. When that claim became untenable, they granted that we could be educated the same as men but questioned whether we should be, whether it was good for us. They based their concerns on the claim that girls need to devote much energy to establishing the proper functioning of their ovaries and womb and that if they divert this energy to their brains by studying, their reproductive organs will shrivel, they will become sterile, and the race will die out.

This logic was steeped in race and class prejudice. The notion that women's reproductive organs need careful nurturing was used to justify excluding upper-class girls and young women from higher education but not to spare the working-class, poor, or black women who were laboring in the factories and homes of the upper class. If anything, these women were said to breed too much. In fact, their ability to have many children despite the fact that they worked so hard was taken as evidence that they were less highly evolved than upper-class women; for them breeding was "natural," as for animals.

Finally, and perhaps most importantly, our concept of ourselves is 5 socially constructed and political because our society's interpretation of what is and is not normal and natural affects what we do. It therefore affects our biological structure and functioning because . . . what we do and how our bodies and minds function are connected dialectically. Thus norms are self-fulfilling prophecies that do not merely describe how we are but prescribe how we should be.

Body Build and Strength

Let us consider a few examples. We can begin with a few obvious ones, such as height, weight, and strength. Women and men are physically not very different. There are enormous overlaps between women and men for all traits that are not directly involved with procreation.

For example, there is about a two-foot spread in height among people in the United States, but a difference of only three to five inches between the average heights of women and men. When we say men are taller than women, what we really mean is that the abstraction *average (or mean) height* is a few inches greater for men than women. Overall, women and men are about the same height, with many women as tall as, or taller than, lots of men. The impression that women are shorter than men is enhanced by our social convention that when women and men pair off, it is considered preferable for the man to be taller than the woman. In some countries, such as Bali, differences in height and, indeed, overall body build are much smaller than in the United States (Lowe, 1982).

Clearly, height is affected by social factors, such as diet. In the early part of this century, English working-class men were significantly

shorter, on average, than men from the upper class, and this difference in height was due to differences not just in the adequacy but in
the composition of their diets — proportions of carbohydrates, pro-
teins, fats, vitamins. In the United States we are familiar with a similar phenomenon when comparing the heights of immigrants and their
U.S.-born children. We have tended to think that the U.S.-born children are taller than their immigrant parents because they get a better
diet. But now that we are learning more about the health hazards of
the typical U.S. diet, with its excessive fat and·protein content, we
should probably defer value judgments and just acknowledge that the
diets are different.

Sex differences in height probably also arise from the differences in
growth patterns between girls and boys. Until early adolescence, girls,
on average, are taller than boys, but girls' growth rates tend to de-
crease after they begin to menstruate, whereas, boys continue to
grow throughout their teens. It is generally assumed that this difference is due to the fact that the increase in estrogen levels after the onset of menstruation tends to slow the growth of girls' long bones. But
the age of onset of menstruation, hence of increased estrogen secre-
tion, depends on a number of social factors, such as diet, exercise and
stress (Frisch, 1988). For example, female swimming champions, who,
because of their intense, early training, tend to begin to menstruate
later than most girls, tend also to be taller than average. We might
therefore expect factors that delay the onset of menstruation to de-
crease the difference in average height between women and men,
those that hasten the onset of menstruation to increase it.

It is probably not that simple because the factors that affect the on- 10
set of menstruation may also affect height in other ways. All I want
to suggest is that height, in part, is a social variable and that differences in the average height of women and men vary with the social
environment.

Weight clearly has considerable social components. Different societies have different standards of beauty for women, and many of these
involve differences in desirable weight. Today we call the women in
Rubens's paintings fat and consider Twiggy anorexic. In our society
changes in style not just of clothing but of body shape are generated,
at least in part, because entire industries depend on our not liking
the way we look so that we will buy the products that promise to
change it. To some extent this is true also for men: Padded shoulders
are not that different from padded bras. But there is more pressure
on women to look "right," and what is "right" changes frequently and
sometimes quite drastically. At present, U.S. women are obsessed by
concerns about their weight to the point where girls and young

women deliberately eat less than they need for healthy growth and development.

Although we may inherit a tendency toward a particular body shape, most women's weight can change considerably in response to our diets, levels of physical activity, and other patterns of living. These also affect physical fitness and strength. When women begin to exercise or engage in weight training and body building, we often notice surprisingly great changes in strength in response to even quite moderate training. Here again, what is striking is the variation among women (and among men).

People ask whether there are "natural" limits to women's strength and therefore "natural" differences in strength between women and men. In Europe and the United States women and men are far more similar in lower body strength than in the strength of our upper bodies. This fact is not surprising when we consider the different ways girls and boys are encouraged to move and play from early childhood on. We tend to use our legs much more similarly than our arms. Both girls and boys tend to run a lot, and hopscotch and skipping rope are considered girls' games. But when it comes to carrying loads, playing baseball, and wrestling and other contact sports, all of which strengthen the arms and upper body, girls are expected to participate much less than boys are. In general, male/female comparisons are made between physically more highly trained men and less trained women so that so-called sex differences at least in part reflect this difference in activity levels. More and less active men also differ in strength, and so do more and less active women. . . .

Women's Biology in Context

Clearly we need to think about women's biology in its social context and consider how it interacts with culture. We need to get information directly from women and not rely on so-called experts, who are often male and whose knowledge tends to be based on the experience of "patients" — that is, of women with problems. Only when women have the opportunity to share experiences and when scientists collect the experiences of women of different ages and from different classes, races, and cultural groups can we get a sense of the texture and variety of women's biology (Martin, 1987).

We need to pay attention to the obvious contradictions between 15 stereotypic descriptions of women's biology and the realities of women's lives. For example, women's reputed "maternal instinct" needs to be looked at in light of some women's desperate efforts to avoid having children, while society persuades or forces them to have children against their wills. Similarly, descriptions of women's frailty, passivity, and weakness need to be juxtaposed with the reality of women as providers and workers who in most societies, including our own, tend to work harder and for longer hours than most men.

Women's work histories are often obscured by the fact that work has been defined so that it excludes much of their daily work load. Indeed, whereas most of what men do is called work, much of what women do has been interpreted as the natural manifestation of our biology. How often do we hear people say, "My mother didn't work when I was growing up"? If she didn't work, how did we manage to grow up? Even women usually refer to what we do as work only when we get paid for it, implying that what we do at home and in our neighborhoods and communities is not work. This misrepresentation of work sets up the vicious circle whereby women are thought to be less good workers in the workplace when we have family and community obligations and less good housewives and mothers when we work outside the home.

No question, we are biological organisms like other animals, and women and men have different procreative structures and functions. But to try to find the biological basis of our social roles or to sort people by sex when it comes to strength, ability to do math, or other intellectual or social attributes is a political exercise, not a scientific one.

The Meaning of Difference

That said, I want to stress that we need have no ideological investment in whether women and men exhibit biological differences, aside from the obvious ones involved with procreation. I have argued that we cannot know whether such biological differences exist because biology and society (or environment) are interdependent and cannot be sorted out. And in any gender-dichotomized society, the fact that we are born biologically female or male means that our environments will be different: We will live different lives. Because our biology and how we live are dialectically related and build on one another, we cannot vary gender and hold the environment constant. Therefore, the scientific methodology of sex-differences research is intrinsically flawed if scientists try to use it to sort effects of biology and society. Scientists can catalog similarities and differences between women and men but cannot establish their causes.

There are other problems with research on differences. One is that it is in the nature of scientific research that if we are interested in differences, we will go on looking until we find them. And if we do not find any, we will assume that our instruments were wrong or that we looked in the wrong place or at the wrong things. Another problem is that most characteristics vary continuously in the population rather than placing us into neat groups. To compare groups, however defined, we must use such concepts as the "average," "mean," or "median" in order to characterize each group by a single number. Yet these constructed, or reified, numbers obscure the diversity that exists within the groups (say, among women and among men) as well as the overlaps between them. That is why statisticians have invented the concept of the standard deviation from the mean to reflect the spread of the actual numbers around the reified average. This problem is obvious when we think about research into differences between blacks and whites. Just to do it, we have to agree on social definitions of who will count as black and who as white because after several centuries of mixing, the biological characteristic, skin color, varies continuously. Research comparing blacks and whites must first generate the group differences it pretends to catalog or analyze.

> Differences, be they biological or psychological, become scientifically interesting only when they parallel differences in power.

Differences, be they biological or psychological, become scientifically interesting only when they parallel differences in power. We do not frame scientific questions about differences between tall people and short people, although folk wisdom suggests there may be some. Nor do we, in this society, pursue differences between blue-eyed, blond people and dark-haired, dark-eyed ones. Yet the latter were scientifically interesting differences under the Nazis. [20]

Sex differences are interesting in sexist societies that value one group more highly than the other. Because the overlaps are so large for all the characteristics that are not directly involved with procreation, it is easy to find women and men to perform any task we value. The existence of average sex differences is irrelevant to the way we organize society. To achieve an egalitarian division of labor requires political will and action, not changes in our biology. There is enough variability among us to let us construct a society in which people of both sexes contribute to whatever activities are considered socially useful and are rewarded according to their talents and abilities.

References

de Beauvoir, Simone. 1953. *The Second Sex.* Translated and edited by H. M. Parshley. New York: Alfred A. Knopf.

Frisch, Rose. 1988. "Body Fat, Menarche, Fitness and Fertility." *Human Reproduction* 2: 421–533.

Lowe, Marian. 1982. "Social Bodies: The Interaction of Culture and Women's Biology." In *Biological Woman — The Convenient Myth*, edited by Ruth Hubbard, Mary Sue Henifin, and Barbara Fried. Cambridge, MA: Schenkman.

Martin, Emily. 1987. *The Woman in the Body.* Boston: Beacon Press.

Understanding the Text

1. In discussing one common assumption about male and female biological difference — height — Hubbard writes, "Overall, women and men are about the same height, with many women as tall as, or taller than, lots of men" (p. 47). Although men are on average taller than women, what factors contribute to our sense that the differential in men's and women's height is greater than it actually is?

2. What other social and cultural factors, according to Hubbard, may affect height and strength? How are these factors significant in terms of Hubbard's broader argument? What other social and cultural factors seem to emphasize or cultivate differences between male and female bodies?

3. To Hubbard, what are some of the "problems" (p. 50) with research done on sex differences?

Reflection and Response

4. One of Hubbard's central points is that bodies — which we often take to be shaped wholly by genetic forces of nature — are socially constructed (p. 46). What does Hubbard mean by this? In what additional ways are men's and women's bodies conditioned, shaped, and otherwise manipulated to display the contemporary assumptions about masculinity and femininity?

Making Connections

5. In everyday life, we often hear people make casual distinctions between men and women on the basis of the supposedly biological differences between male and female bodies and brains: men are stronger than women, women are more emotional than men, and so on. Think of some other purportedly biological differences between women and men, and reconsider those claims by emphasizing the extent to which social and cultural factors create (or widen) those "biological differences."

6. Hubbard's essay ends by arguing that there are many problems with researchers who look for gendered differences. Examine one of the articles in Chapter 2 about childhood gender roles and write about whether Hubbard's critique would apply. Do any of those articles seem to construct differences even as they analyze them? Or would Hubbard perhaps be comfortable with the kinds of analysis that our Chapter 2 authors conduct?

The Tyranny of Gendered Spaces: Reflections from Beyond the Gender Dichotomy

Petra Doan

Petra Doan is a professor of urban and regional planning at Florida State University. Her work focuses on gendered spaces, and her publications include *Queerying Planning: Challenging Heteronormative Assumptions and Reframing Planning Practice* (2011) and "Safety and Urban Environments: Transgendered Experiences of the City" (2009).

Tyranny refers to the exercise of power which is cruelly or harshly administered; it usually involves some form of oppression by those wielding power over the less powerful. John Stuart Mill (1869) warned about the tyranny of the majority since the sheer weight of numbers can never be sufficient to make an unjust act any more just. History gets written by those who claim victory, and the winners wield the economic power and social influence that enable them to establish the standards for acceptable political and social behaviors. When these histories and standards routinely exclude minority groups, tyranny flourishes.

In this article I argue that transgendered and gender variant people experience the gendered division of space as a special kind of tyranny — the tyranny of gender — that arises when people dare to challenge the hegemonic expectations for appropriately gendered behavior in western society. These gendered expectations are an artifact of the patriarchal dichotomization of gender and have profound and painful consequences for many individuals. For the gender variant, the tyranny of gender intrudes on every aspect of the spaces in which we live and constrains the behaviors that we display. . . .

The term *transgender* is a collective term that refers to people assigned to one gender who do "not perform or identify as that gender, and ha[ve] taken some steps — temporary or permanent — to present in another gender" (D. Valentine 2003, 27–28). Most often included in this category are transsexuals, transvestites, crossdressers, drag queens, drag kings, tranny bois and other gender queer individuals who defy easy categorization. The edges of the category are less clear — i.e. not all intersexed people consider themselves transgendered, though some do (Chase 1998; Kessler 1998; Turner 1999). Even more individuals may identify as their birth sex, but present in such an ambiguous way that their gender is often mistaken (Browne 2004; Lucal 1999). For this entire spectrum of individuals I use the term *gender variant* (Doan 2007), of which the transgendered are one subset. . . .

Coming to Terms with My Transgendered Self

As a child I was powerfully aware that I did not fit into the box marked boy, though I struggled for many years to fit into the gender assigned to me by society. . . . As a young person I understood that I was born in a boy's body, but I also felt a conflict between the inward sense of my gender and the outward expectations for my behavior as a boy. I asked a therapist many years later whether my acquiescence to these gendered rules undermined my authenticity as a transgendered person. He told me that in 1959 gender variance was seen as a severe form of mental illness and if I had told my parents I wanted to be a girl, I might have received electro-shock and aversion therapy as a cure. At that time, my understanding of the gender rules enabled my self-preservation, by opting for self-suppression.

Accordingly, I buried my gender deep in my bodily core and struggled mightily to maintain a bearded façade, the increasingly brittle outer shell designed to project masculinity. After many years of struggle, the lack of authenticity was causing many sleepless nights and much introspection about whether or not I could continue to live my life as the man I was seen to be. At some point the depression became so intense that I experienced a kind of dark night of the soul. After much reflective searching I realized that to keep living, I had to face the world as my "true self" (Brown and Rounsley 1996). Making this change was one of the most difficult experiences of my life. At the age of 42, I "came out" to my family[1] and to my department colleagues, explaining that integrity required that I no longer silence the gender I knew myself to be.

My transition was facilitated by my therapist (a psychiatrist) who eschewed gate-keeping and encouraged me to explore the multi-dimensional and non-dichotomous identity that I was experiencing as gender. However, his questions helped me understand the consequences of displaying my differently gendered identity to the rest of the world. Although I wanted desperately to be a girl since I was young, I came to realize that I could never be "just a girl"; I will always be something more and something less. In most public settings I

---

[1] I had hoped that getting married and fathering two children would silence my gender questioning and anchor my identity as a man, but that is not the way that gender identity works. Though my marriage ended, I remain in close contact with my children and am now in a committed same-sex relationship.

present as and am read as a woman, though often a rather gender variant woman. Because the patriarchal social structure does not tolerate intermediate genders, rejecting the male label meant I had to embrace the label female. Accordingly, I underwent reassignment surgery so that my driver's license and passport indicate that I am female. But I refuse to retreat into that post-operative closet and live in fear that I will be outed as once having had an M on my passport. I choose to live as a visibly queer transgendered person and refuse to re-enter the closet of some post-operative transsexuals who live in fear they will be "outed" as once having lived as some other gender.

My employment as a tenured professor provided me with a relatively "safe" location within which to transform the public presentation of my gender. It also enabled me to begin to shift my research agenda during a one semester sabbatical in which I "discovered" the field of feminist and queer geography. Previously I had researched transgender and transsexual identities, but until I came out as transsexual I was afraid to integrate these insights into my academic work for fear of being marginalized for writing about such a controversial topic. When I encountered the rich research on spatial aspects of queer identity on my sabbatical, it was like finding a vein of unexpected gold.

Part of my intellectual journey has involved coming to grips with the way that the spaces in which I live, work and play are inherently gendered. For many years I literally only expressed the gender of my true self in the most secret spaces within the privacy of my own home — in the very real confines of a large walk-in closet. The closet is both a literary metaphor for gay and lesbian oppression in the US (Sedgwick 1990) and a form of material reality within diverse spatial contexts (Brown 2000). However, for transgendered people it is an essential space in which we live and at times hide the clothing and accoutrements of our identities. I think my fascination with the public or private nature of space is based on this highly personal understanding that for me coming out meant that I had to move from the protective shelter of the closet, to the slightly more risky privacy of my bedroom, to the semi-private space of my living room in the evening with the shades tightly drawn, to the bright glare of daylight where I would be in public view of the neighbors and all the world. . . .

My own experience of meeting other transgendered people suggests that there is a wide diversity in our understanding of what gender is and how it should be displayed. Gender is not a dichotomy but a splendid array of diverse experiences and performances. I resonate with Bondi's (2004, 12) argument that "the binary construct of gender . . . [is] a superfluous and unnecessary distraction from the reality of the human condition." . . .

I recognize that my identity is "contingent and constructed in rela- 10 tion to temporal factors of generation, transitional time span, and social and cultural understandings and practices" (Hines 2006, 64). However, a critical component of that contingency is an awareness of the ways that expressions of non-dichotomous gender are still resisted by the dominant social structure. I understand clearly that gender variant identities challenge gender norms at a significant social cost, namely the "trade-offs in terms of such things as social power, social approval and material benefits" (Mehta and Bondi 1999, 70). The tyranny of gender oppresses those whose behavior, presentation and expression fundamentally challenge socially accepted gender categories. Gendered bodies are subjected to a regulatory regime (Foucault 1978) that enforces the boundaries of properly gendered behaviors. Browne (2004) has called this gender policing "genderism" and argues that the "active contestations of other people's policing of sexed norms draws attention to the attempt to expel that which de-stabilizes self-other dichotomies" (Browne 2006, 122). This disciplining takes place within ourselves, but also in external spaces that permit others to pass judgment on people who transgress the gender dichotomy. From my own experiences I can attest that individuals who persist in violating gender norms are marginalized in both queer and other public spaces (K. Namaste 1996; Doan 2001, 2006, 2007). This article explores some of the mechanisms of that gendered policing in different spatial contexts.

My Transgendered Experience of Gendered Spaces

In the following sections I present my experiences as a transgendered woman across the continuum of spaces ranging from more public to more private locations. I am cognizant that my experiences, difficult as they may have been, are grounded in a complex web of privilege including: my tenured faculty position, my white racial identity and my upper middle class upbringing. I consider myself lucky that I have never been gender-bashed (K. Namaste 1996), though I have certainly experienced blatant genderism (Hill 2003; Browne 2004) and violent trans-phobia (Feinberg 1996) triggered by my gender status. Some transgendered people respond to this tyranny with rage (Stryker 1994), and that anger can lead to a manifesto for change (Stone 1991) and increased gender activism.

We are entitled to our anger in response to this oppression: our anger is a message to ourselves that we need to get active and change something in order to survive. So we resist the oppression, the violence — we resist the tendency of the culture to see us as a joke. (Bornstein 1994, 81)

In my case I have tried to channel my anger along a different path that avoids what Viviane Namaste (2000) has called the powerful silencing of transgendered individuals, rendering them invisible for the most part to North American society. Gender transitions are almost never private affairs; by design they occur in public space and provide a different lens with which to view the gendering of public spaces. The following examples illustrate some of my own experiences with public spaces as a person whose gender does not easily fit into a dichotomous box.

In public spaces the tyranny of gender operates when certain individuals feel empowered to act as heteronormatively constructed gender enforcers in public spaces. These policing behaviors are sometimes exaggerated by the presence of other silent but supportive watchers. At the same time gender variant performance in public spaces that is supported by a wider community can be a powerful statement against the dichotomy.

> In public spaces the tyranny of gender operates when certain individuals feel empowered to act as heteronormatively constructed gender enforcers. . . . These policing behaviors are sometimes exaggerated by the presence of other silent but supportive watchers.

Public Transit

Public spaces such as streets, transportation facilities and elevators contain structural elements that enable the operation of gender tyranny. Gardner (1995) describes the public harassment of women by men as endemic in our society, but it is a more serious problem for those whose expression of gender varies from the heteronormative, as the following experiences illustrate. After my first overseas trip using my new passport with F for a sex designator, I passed through US Customs at JFK airport without so much as a raised eyebrow. Outside the secure area I had a pre-arranged meeting with an airport limo driver. The arrival area was jammed with people and I followed the driver outside to the equally crowded sidewalk to the parking area. When the limo driver asked about my trip, I responded without thinking in my deep bass voice. I was happy to be back in the US and must have relaxed my usual vigilance because I paid no attention to the crowd of people around us. Shortly thereafter I stopped abruptly before crossing an exit for an underground parking garage, causing the man who was right behind me to bump into me. This man immediately began screaming at me and I realized his anger was not because of the bodily collision that had prevented us from being hit by an oncoming car, but because he realized that I was trans. He must have heard me speaking earlier and my sudden stop had ignited his smouldering anger. He started yelling, "I know what you are! You can't fool me! You are disgusting!" I refused to be cowed and asked him point blank what he thought I was. He, in turn, became so agitated that I thought he was going to throw a punch. If the limo driver had not quietly stepped up next to me as a supportive presence, I would have been assaulted on the spot. My gender expression in that public space offended his sense of appropriate public behavior and he acted to sanction that violation in as public a fashion as possible.

Vulnerability in an Elevator

Crowding in public spaces brings people into closer proximity than usual and increases gendered vulnerability in such spaces. Several years ago I experienced this gendering in an up-front and personal way. One evening on a business trip I entered the ground floor entrance of a hotel and entered a reasonably full elevator car. I stood next to a youngish woman and across from an older man who appeared to be her companion for the evening. He was clearly inebriated, and as soon as I entered the space, he began staring at me, obviously disturbed by something about my presentation of gender. Just before we reached the next floor, he stepped up very close to me, and giving a lecherous wink said "Well, look what we have here!" I tried simply staring him down, but as the doors opened, he reached up and grabbed both of my breasts and squeezed, apparently expecting to find the falsies used by drag queens. I was stunned by this unexpected sexual assault and stood there in a speechless state of shock as he turned and walked away. By squeezing my breasts he was objectifying and assaulting what Young (1998) calls the most visible sign of a woman's femininity. In my case he assumed he was attacking my false femininity to expose me for an imposter. Unfortunately his discovery of his error did little to lessen the indignity of the assault. . . .

The Workplace

Coming out at a public university provided many unique experiences of gendered spaces. My first day on the job as a woman was especially memorable. As I entered the building I felt I was entering the eye of a hurricane, at the calm center of a turbulent storm of gendered expectations. As I walked down the hall I could hear conversation in front of me suddenly stop as all eyes turned to look at the latest "freak show." As I passed each office there was a moment of eerie quiet, followed by an uproar as the occupants began commenting on my appearance.

Some people just stared, a few others told me how brave I was and one person told me that I looked "just like a woman." Another gave me a taste of what it means to be objectified by telling me proudly that I was his very first transsexual. These events helped me to realize that my presentation of gender was not just a personal statement, but a co-constructed event. I presented myself, and the academic world watched and passed judgment. I am grateful for the presence of my colleagues and students whose support deflected some of this turbulence.

Classrooms

. . . In my new mode of presentation as a woman, I noticed an undermining of the implicit assumption of my academic competency. When the world perceived me as a man, I found it quite easy to step to the front of a lecture hall and assume the role of a knowledgeable professor. I never had difficulty in keeping or maintaining the attention of any class. After transition, however, this experience changed quite markedly. On the first day of class my students accepted me as an openly transgendered woman, but it slowly dawned on me that I was also no longer automatically perceived as an expert in my field.[2] I perceived a distinct "prove it" attitude on the part of the students. Since my transition I have to work much harder to establish my credentials and maintain control of the classroom than I did when I was perceived as a straight man.

At my university all classes with more than 10 students are required to provide a standardized student evaluation form. Although my overall student evaluations are high, in almost every class there are some who resent being taught by an openly transgendered professor. The mandated evaluation survey includes the following open-ended questions: *What did you like most about the course? What could be improved?* One undergraduate student in my World Cities class responded, "Nothing. Input a new teacher. S/he's a man dressed like a female! It's gross!" In this comment the student critiques my teaching, refutes my gender and expresses disgust typical of trans-phobic comments. A second open-ended question asks: *What did you like best about the instructor?* Another undergraduate respondent answered, "How could a university hire a person who pretends to be female? It's

---

[2] I cannot be certain whether it was my womanhood that caused the issue or my gender variance, but I am sure it was vastly different from the response I received when I was perceived as a man.

horrible! I recently explained to my parents that one of my professors is a man that had a sex change and she about lost it." This comment refutes my gender as well as the possibility of sex change itself and then implies some administrator may get an irate phone call from a parent. These comments are attempts to regulate my behavior or at least to strike back at my gender non-conformance.

These examples from two separate student evaluations do not represent the vast majority of my students, but they do illustrate the vitriol lurking in the back of the classroom. . . .

Only once have I ever felt physically threatened from students who 20 were not known to me. I was proctoring a final exam for my graduate Growth of Cities class when there was suddenly a lot of loud talking just outside the classroom. Since several of my students seemed disturbed by the interruptions, I opened the door and asked the disruptive students to be quiet since I was giving an exam. Several minutes later someone in the hall kicked open the door with a loud bang and yelled at the top of his lungs, "Shemale!" Although this person did not dare show his face, the uproarious laughter suggested that his feelings were widely shared. I was upset and felt very vulnerable after this violation of my classroom space. I stifled the rage that told me to charge into the hall and confront the disruptive students and sat in silence, unsure how to proceed. Eventually, a student loaned me her cell phone to call campus security. When the campus police arrived five minutes later, they cleared the students from the hallway and escorted me back to the safety and privacy of my office. Although I was grateful for the support of my student and the assistance of the police, I was deeply shaken at the public humiliation and sense of violation created by this hate speech. . . .

Public Restrooms

One of the scariest spaces for a person in the midst of a gender transition is a public restroom. The biological urge forces a regular choice between one of two doors with different labels (men/women, gents/ladies, guys/gals, buoys/gulls, etc.). Each excursion for me into the most private of public gendered spaces risked discovery and a potential confrontation with others outraged by my perceived transgression. Browne (2004) has called this "the bathroom problem" and suggests that masculine appearing women regularly experience harassment and difficulties in such places. . . .

At work I had to face the gendered restroom question directly. When I first transitioned, I became temporarily "disabled" since the administration's interim solution was that I use the single access handicapped restroom on a different floor of my building. One day not long after I began using this facility, I was mortified to discover the bathroom had no locking mechanism. I was using the facility when the door opened unexpectedly, exposing me for a moment to some students in the hallway just outside. My gender difference provided a new-found awareness that I too was "not anywhere near the project" (Chouinard and Grant 1996), that I and others like me had fallen between the cracks of a dichotomous world. . . .

The Mall

Shopping malls are enclosed spaces that use private security to provide the appearance of a safer experience than a public street. Some geographers have argued that malls create "a setting for free personal expression and association, for collective cultural expression and transgression, and for unencumbered human interaction and material transaction" (Goss 1993, 25). The transgendered rite of passage known as mall-walking puts this to the test. Frequently novice trans women have not yet grasped that the mundane act of shopping is a highly gendered experience, especially for women whose size (bodily bigness) does not fit normative expectations of attractiveness (Colls 2006). As a transgendered person inhabiting a tall and broad-shouldered body, I was unsure how well I would pass as a woman and so postponed my first mall-walking experience until I was out of town. I was determined to explore my emerging sense that I was a woman by performing that gender in public. In preparation for the excursion, I donned my favorite dress, put on two pair of hose to cover my not yet shaven legs and took extra care with my make-up (to cover evidence of my male beard).

As I entered the mall, it slowly dawned on me that performing gender at home in front of a mirror was nothing like the dance that is gender in a public place. I felt that everyone was staring at me. In hindsight I realize that I was feeling the panoptic (Foucault 1977) nature of shopping malls, both because of the omnipresent but often hidden security guards (Ainley 1998) and also because of the power of the hetero-normative gaze (Pérez 2003; Doan 2007). I experienced an odd sense of "being watched" that was partly a result of my own anxiety about "passing" and partly my rather over-dressed attire for a mall on a Saturday afternoon. I could feel the stares boring into my back as I passed, and decided to skip the shopping and just walk from one end to the other. . . . The gaze of each person I passed was part of the overall "policing practices" that questioned my gender and undermined the tenuousness of the category (Browne 2006).

At Home

The home is often considered a space of safety in which individuals 25
escape the constant surveillance of identity (Saunders 1989), but for
lesbians the home does not always deter heteronormativity that may
infiltrate via neighbors and family (Johnston and Valentine 1995). For
many in the LGBT community, "evocations of home are embedded in
the struggles to create and maintain spaces of belonging and comfort in
the face of adversity without (or within) the lesbian and gay community" (Fortier 2001, 412). Although the home is usually considered a
heteronormative habitation, it can be queered through private interactions with same-sex partners or by supportive family members
(Gorman-Murray 2007, 2008). In my case, after being subjected to the
ever present tyranny of gender across the continuum of public . . .
spaces, my home is a necessary place of refuge, but one that is not un-
contested. The tyranny of gender intrudes via modern communication
systems which allow the home to become "a 'phantasmagoric' place, to
the extent that electronic media of various kinds allow the intrusion of
distant events into the space of domesticity" (Morley 2001, 428).

The telephone constitutes the most significant invasion of my private space. Though I have put my phone number on a Do Not Call list
for telemarketers, I still receive a large number of unsolicited calls. I
do not allow trans-phobic people in my home, but I generally answer
the phone when it rings. Callers who do not know me invariably hear
my voice and assume that I am male. Part of my witness related to
integrity involves telling them patiently that they are speaking to a
woman. However, many callers refuse to disbelieve their ears and
continue this pronoun abuse by calling me Mister and Sir. After a few
attempts to persuade them otherwise I often simply hang up in frustration at this intrusion of the tyranny of gendered pronouns into my
own space. Many people do not understand the power of these little
words and how painful the persistent use of inappropriate pronouns
can be. After a long day of being out in heteronormatively defined
spaces (and getting my share of confused looks and the occasional, yes
sir), it feels like a violation to be subjected to such indignity at home.
As a result I find that I am less likely to answer the phone (no doubt
skewing all those public opinion survey calls). When I need to make a
new contact with someone, I am much less likely to call on the phone
and will use either a face to face meeting or an exchange of email. I do
not mind being visible and even speaking in public spaces as a differently gendered person, but I need a home-place where I can simply be
myself without being subject to the insults of the tyranny of gender.

Conclusions

. . . Different types of gendered spaces have varying potential for confrontation and transformation. There are places in which I never raise my voice above a whisper, such as public restrooms. In addition, when I use public transportation in unfamiliar locations or when I travel the back roads through unfamiliar terrain, I rarely engage those around me in idle conversation until I am able to get a reading on how invested they might be in the dichotomy of gender. I am not shy, just careful. I recognize that my gender performance is simultaneously modulated by the observers of my gender as well as the spaces in which we interact. These modulations do not shift my own sense of gender, but they do shape the visibility and impact of my gender performance. Sometimes I can choose when to perform my gender in ways that might expand the boundaries of the gender dichotomy and sometimes I cannot. I recognize the privilege contained within my subject position as a white middle class transsexual woman and resonate deeply with what Green (2004, 183–4) has written about becoming a visible trans man.

By claiming our identity as men or women who are also transpeople, by asserting that our bodies are just as normal for us as anyone else's is for them, by insisting on our right to express our own gender, to modify our bodies and shape our identities, is as inalienable as our right to know our true religion, we claim our humanity and our right to be treated fairly under the law and within the purviews of morality and culture. To do that we must educate — if we have the ability and emotional energy to do so. That is what visibility is all about.

As more victims of gender tyranny step into the light and become visible, the need to re-conceptualize the relationship between gender and space will also become more evident. In the introduction to the special "Trans" issue of *Women's Studies Quarterly*, Stryker, Currah, and Moore (2008, 12) suggest that

we understand genders as potentially porous and permeable spatial territories (arguably numbering more than two), each capable of supporting rich and rapidly proliferating ecologies of embodied difference. . . . Any gender-defined space is not only populated with diverse forms of gendered embodiment, but striated and crosshatched by the boundaries of significant forms of difference other than gender, within all of which gender is necessarily implicated.

Consequently, a number of questions arise from this work at the intersection of gender and spatial theory. Feminist and queer geographers might usefully explore the parameters of the tyranny of gender as it constrains behavior in a spectrum of spaces and localities. Are there social and spatial contexts that empower the performance of nonbinary genders and how do they operate? How does non-normative gender performance influence others' perception of space and the action they take as a result? How does the spatiality of non-conforming gender performance serve to strengthen or weaken the gender dichotomy?

The time has come to expand our understanding of gender beyond 30 its social construction and include a distinct spatiality within which a range of gendered and other differences can be performed. Gender variance exists throughout the human and natural world and has real consequences for people in their daily lives. Gender strongly influences the ways that spaces are perceived and the kinds of activities that are possible, acceptable, or even safe within them. The tyranny of the gender dichotomy is an artifact of the patriarchal structuring of gendered space and it is time to lay it aside, not just for trans people, but for us all.

Acknowledgments

The author gratefully acknowledges the substantive contributions of Kath Browne, Sally Hines and Catherine Nash whose encouragement and careful critiques helped to hone this article. The article also benefitted from the thoughtful comments and suggestions of the anonymous referees. Finally, the author also wishes to acknowledge the helpful comments of Lori Reid and Margeaux Mutz and the indefatigable support of Elizabeth Kamphausen in sustaining this project.

References

Ainley, Rosa. 1998. Watching the detectors: Control and the panopticon. In *New frontiers of space, bodies, and gender*, ed. Rosa Ainley, 88–100. London: Routledge.

Bondi, Liz. 2004. Tenth anniversary address: For a feminist geography of ambivalence. *Gender, Place and Culture* 11, no. 1: 3–15.

Bornstein, Kate. 1994. *Gender outlaw: On women, men, and the rest of us.* New York: Routledge.

Brown, Michael. 2000. *Closet space: Geographies of metaphor from the body to the globe.* London: Routledge.

Brown, Mildred, and Chloe Ann Rounsley. 1996. *True selves: Understanding transsexualism — for families, friends, coworkers, and helping professionals.* San Francisco: Jossey-Bass.

Browne, Kath. Genderism and the bathroom problem: (Re)materializing sexed sites, (re)creating sexed bodies. *Gender, Place and Culture* 11: 331–46.

———. 2006. "A right geezer bird (man-woman)": The sites and sounds of female embodiment. *ACME: An International E-Journal for Critical Geographies* 5, no. 2: 121–43.

Chase, Cheryl. 1998. Hermaphrodites with attitude: Mapping the emergence of intersex political activism. *GLQ: A Journal of Lesbian and Gay Studies* 4, no. 2: 189–211.

Chouinard, Vera, and Ali Grant. 1996. On being not anywhere near the project: Ways of putting ourselves in the project. In *Body space: Destabilizing geographies of gender and sexuality*, ed. Nancy Duncan, 170–93. New York: Routledge.

Colls, Rachel. 2006. Outsize/outside: Bodily bignesses and the emotional experiences of British women shopping for clothes. *Gender, Place and Culture* 13, no. 5: 529–45.

Doan, Petra. 2001. Are the transgendered the mine shaft canaries of urban areas? *Progressive Planning: Special Issue on Queers and Planning.* New York: Planners Network. http://www.plannersnetwork.org/2001/03/are-the-transgendered-the-mine-shaft-canaries-of-urban-areas/.

———. 2006. Violence and transgendered people. *Progressive Planning: Special Issue on Gender and Violence.* New York: Planners Network. http://www.planners network.org/publications/mag20062spring.html

———. 2007. Queers in the American city: Transgendered perceptions of urban spaces. *Gender, Place and Culture* 14: 57–74.

Feinberg, Leslie. 1996. *Transgendered warriors: From Joan of Arc to Dennis Rodman.* Boston: Beacon Press.

Fortier, Anne-Marie. 2001. "Coming home": Queer migrations and multiple evocations of home. *European Journal of Cultural Studies* 4: 405–24.

Foucault, Michel. 1977. *Discipline and punish: The birth of the prison.* Trans. A. Sheridan. New York: Pantheon.

———. 1978. *The history of sexuality, Volume 1: An introduction.* Trans. R. Hurley. New York: Random House.

Gardner, Carol Brooks. 1995. *Passing by: Gender and public harassment.* Berkeley: University of California Press.

Gorman-Murray, Andrew. 2007. Contesting domestic ideals: Queering the Australian home. *Australian Geographer* 38, no. 2: 195–213.

———. 2008. Queering the family home: Narratives from gay, lesbian and bisexual youth coming out in supportive family homes in Australia. *Gender, Place and Culture* 15, no. 1: 31–44.

Goss, Jon. 1993. The magic of the mall. *Annals of the Association of American Geographers* 83: 18–47.

Green, Jamison. 2004. *Becoming a visible man.* Nashville: Vanderbilt University Press.

Hill, Darryl. 2003. Genderism, transphobia, and gender-bashing: A framework for interpreting anti-transgender violence. In *Understanding and dealing with violence: A multicultural approach*, ed. Barbara Wallace and Robert Carter, 113–36. Thousand Oaks, CA: Sage Publications.

Hines, Sally. 2006. What's the difference? Bringing particularity to queer studies of transgender. *Journal of Gender Studies* 15, no. 1: 49–66.

Johnston, Lynda, and Gill Valentine. 1995. Wherever I lay my girlfriend that's my home: The performance and surveillance of lesbian identities in domestic environments. In *Mapping desire: Geographies of sexualities*, ed. David Bell and Gill Valentine, 99–113. London: Routledge.

Kessler, Suzanne. 1998. *Lessons from the intersexed*. New Brunswick, NJ: Rutgers University Press.

Lucal, Betsy. 1999. What it means to be gendered me: Life on the boundaries of a dichotomous gender system. *Gender and Society* 13, no. 6: 781–97.

Mehta, A., and L. Bondi. 1999. Embodied discourse: On gender and fear of violence. *Gender, Place, and Culture* 16: 67–84.

Mill, John Stuart. 1869. *On liberty.* 4th ed. London: Longman, Roberts and Green.

Morley, David. 2001. Belongings: Place, space and identity in a mediated world. *European Journal of Cultural Studies* 4: 425–48.

Namaste, Ki. 1996. Gender bashing: Sexuality, gender, and the regulation of public space. *Environment and Planning D: Society and Self* 14, no. 2: 221–40.

Namaste, Viviane K. 2000. *Invisible lives: The erasure of transsexual and transgendered people*. Chicago: University of Chicago Press.

Pérez, Emma. 2003. Queering the borderlands: The challenges of excavating the invisible and unheard. *Frontiers* 24: 122–31.

Saunders, Peter. 1989. The meaning of home in contemporary English culture. *Housing Studies* 4: 177–92.

Sedgwick, Eve Kosofsky. 1990. *The epistemology of the closet.* Berkeley: University of California Press.

Stone, Sandy. 1991. The "empire" strikes back: A posttranssexual manifesto. In *Bodyguards: The cultural politics of gender ambiguity*, ed. Katrina Straub and Julia Epstein, 280–304. New York: Routledge.

Stryker, Susan. 1994. My words to Victor Frankenstein above the village of Chamounix: Performing transgender rage. *GLQ: A Journal of Gay and Lesbian Studies* 1: 237–54.

Stryker, Susan, Paisley Currah, and Lise Jean Moore. 2008. Introduction: Trans-, trans, or transgender? *Women's Studies Quarterly* 36, no. 3/4: 11–22.

Turner, Stephanie. 1999. Intersex identities: Locating new intersections of sex and gender. *Gender and Society* 13, no. 4: 457–79.

Valentine, David. 2003. "The calculus of pain": Violence, anthropological ethics, and the category transgender. *Ethnos* 68, no. 1: 27–48.

Young, Iris Marion. 1998. Breasted experience: The look and the feeling. In *The politics of women's bodies: Sexuality, appearance, and behavior*, ed. Rose Weltz, 125–36. Oxford: Oxford University Press.

Understanding the Text

1. What are some types of gender variant identities, and how does the "dichoto-mization of gender" (p. 53) exclude them from some social spaces?

2. After Doan tells about gender exclusion in public spaces, she turns to "the home" (p. 62). How does the "home" become conceived as another kind of "public" space?

Reflection and Response

3. Doan looks at the "geographies" of social space in relation to the "dichotomi-zation of gender." What other places or spaces are "divided" along traditional gender lines, and how are those spaces "policed" or kept exclusive of other genders?

4. According to Doan's description of encountering "policing behaviors" (p. 57), she is met with anger, scorn, derision, and violence in response to her gender variance. What do you think underlies these kinds of responses to gender variant identities?

Making Connections

5. In discussing the "tyranny" of gendered spaces, Doan surveys a number of public and private settings where "policing behaviors" may occur. Consider the differences between the legal, institutional, and social "laws" of gender. What types of gender behavior are illegal? What other kinds of structures impose "rules" related to gender? Finally, what kinds of social codes and modes of "enforcement" (see Lorber, p. 22) regulate gender boundaries?

6. Near the end of Doan's piece, she claims "the tyranny of the gender dichot-omy is an artifact of the patriarchal structuring of gendered space, and it is time to lay it aside, not just for trans people, but for us all" (p. 64). What does Doan mean by "us all"? How are everyday people, women and men, included or excluded from certain social spaces by the dominant understandings and assumptions about gender?

Are We Facing a Genderless Future?

Barbara Kantrowitz and Pat Wingert

Barbara Kantrowitz is a journalist who worked at *Newsweek* for almost 25 years, covering stories on health, education, and women's issues. She is associate director of Continuing Education at Columbia Journalism School. Pat Wingert is also a journalist who has worked at *Newsweek*, and has published numerous articles about health, education, and demographics. Together, Kantrowitz and Wingert wrote *Is It Hot in Here? Or Is It Me? The Complete Guide to Menopause* (2007).

This spring, an Australian named Norrie May-Welby made *headlines* around the world as the world's first legally genderless person when the New South Wales Registry of Births, Deaths and Marriages sent the Sydney resident a certificate containing neither M for male or F for female.

For a few days, it appeared that the 48-year-old activist and performer had won a long legal battle to be declared "sex not specified" — the only category that felt right to this immigrant from Scotland. May-Welby's journey of gender identity can only be characterized as a long and winding road. Registered male at birth, May-Welby began taking female hormones at 23 and had sex-change surgery to become a woman, but now doesn't take any hormones and identifies as genderless. The prized piece of paper May-Welby sought is called a Recognised Details Certificate, and it's given to immigrants to Australia who want to record a sex change.

But the victory was short-lived. After so much publicity, it was perhaps inevitable that the New South Wales government would backtrack — which it *did* a few days later, saying the registry didn't have the legal authority to issue a certificate with anything but male or female. May-Welby (who now goes by the single name Norrie) has filed an appeal with the Australian Human Rights Commission.

It's easy to dismiss this case as just one more bizarre news story from Down Under, but May-Welby's case could also represent the future of gender identity. Although no one is keeping statistics, researchers who study gender say a small but growing number of people (including some who have had sex-change operations) consider themselves "gender neutral" or "gender variant." Their stories vary widely. Some find that even after surgery, they simply can't ignore previous years of experience living as another gender. Others may feel that their gender identity is fluid. Still others are experimenting with where they feel most comfortable on what they see as a continuum of gender. "For some, it's a form of protest because gender is such a strong organizing principle in our society," says Walter Bockting, an associate professor and clinical psychologist at the University of Minnesota Medical School who has been studying transgender health since 1986. "Their identities expand our thinking about gender."

In fact, some researchers compare the evolution in thinking about 5 gender to the struggle that began a generation ago for gay and lesbian rights. Dr. Jack Drescher is a member of an American Psychiatric Association (APA) committee that is currently reviewing changes to the fifth edition of the *Diagnostic and Statistical Manual*, which is used around the world by clinicians, researchers, regulatory agencies, and insurance companies to classify mental disorders. DSM-5, as it's called, won't be published until 2013, but Drescher's committee is reconsidering the diagnosis of gender-identity disorder, which encompasses people who do not identify with the gender assigned to them by biology.

The current debate echoes the controversy over the APA's 1973 decision to modify the second edition of the DSM by declaring that homosexuality could be considered a mental disorder only if it was disturbing to the patient. Drescher's committee thought about dropping the diagnosis of gender-identity disorder altogether, but realized that if it did, people who wanted treatment (sex-change surgery, hormones, or talk therapy) wouldn't be able to get the diagnosis they need for insurance coverage. Instead, Drescher says, the committee is proposing changing the name to "gender incongruence" and making the diagnosis contingent on the person feeling significant distress over their gender confusion. "We didn't want to pathologize all expressions of gender variance just because they were not common or made someone uncomfortable," Drescher says.

But that seemingly simple change of language could help usher in a new era, in which a person's gender could be expressed or experienced as male, female, "in between," or "otherwise." "People who work in this area have very flexible notions of gender," Drescher says. "We don't want to force people to fit into a doctor's categories," even though, he concedes, most cultures "tend to think in binaries."

Bockting predicts that such binary thinking will eventually disappear. Many scientists, he says, see gender as a continuum and acknowledge that some people naturally fall in the middle. Gender, Bockting says, "develops between the biological and the environmental. You can't always detect gender by physical evidence. You have to ask the person how they identify themselves; in that sense, it's psychological."

And gender isn't synonymous with sex, he says, although the distinction may elude the layman. Sex, Bockting says, is assigned at birth based on the appearance of external genitalia. But, he says, "to determine a person's gender identity, you have to wait until they grow up and can describe how they identify their gender." And being genderless or gender-neutral isn't the same thing as being asexual. "If you are asexual," he says, "you are not interested in having sex with other people," while gender-neutral people may be attracted to men, women, both sexes, or other people who are gender-neutral.

And while May-Welby's story may seem out there, Bockting says 10 it's not uncommon for people undergoing sex changes to find that surgery doesn't resolve all their gender-identity issues. "With time," he says, "they accept a certain amount of ambiguity. . . . We have this idea that people take hormones and undergo surgery and become the other gender. But in reality it's more complicated."

Even before the advent of sex-change surgery, there were always people who felt they didn't fit into either gender. In India, a group of people called hijra have existed for centuries. They are typically biological males who dress as women but consider themselves to have neither gender, Bockting says. There is also a long tradition of eunuch culture. Even today, other countries are more comfortable with the idea of gender variance. Drescher says that France has removed transsexuality from its list of psychiatric disorders and put it in the category of rare diseases. The British government has also declared that transsexuality is "not a mental illness," but people who want a sex-change can get treatment under the National Health Service.

How all the debate will play out in this country is still unclear, but college students may be among those leading the charge for change. Many campuses — including Harvard, Penn and Michigan — now offer gender neutral housing and more unisex bathrooms to accommodate students who don't fall neatly into male or female categories. The Common Application, which is used by most college applicants, just announced that it is considering adding voluntary questions that would give students a broader array of choices to describe their gender identity and allow them to state their sexual orientation, after gay advocates urged the change. How long before such changes begin to show up in other parts of society is unclear. But

Drescher says he is certain of one thing after a lifetime of working with gender: "There is no way that six billion people can be categorized into two groups." Now if we could only figure out the pronoun problem.

Understanding the Text

1. Kantrowitz and Wingert report on a person who chooses to identify as "genderless." What is the difference between those who identify as genderless or gender neutral and the DSM-approved category of people living with gender-identity disorder, as described by the authors in paragraph six?

2. The authors quote a clinical psychologist, Walter Bockting, as saying that eventually, binary thinking about gender is likely to disappear altogether. On what basis does he make this prediction?

3. What is the difference between gender neutrality and asexuality? How do the authors explain this difference, and why is it important to include in the article?

Reflection and Response

4. Kantrowitz and Wingert believe that the individual story of Norrie May-Welby is important because it shows us that gender neutrality may be an indicator of the future of gender, and they quote Walter Bockting in support of this idea. Do you agree that this and other stories of people living without a specific gender identity are indicators of the future? Explain why or why not, and use one or two examples to support your position.

5. Why do the authors spend so much time in a short article explaining the context of the American Psychological Association's DSM revision in 1973? What is significant about the medical establishment's role in defining gender identities?

Making Connections

6. Brainstorm about the social and cultural consequences of gender neutrality. What kind of public accommodations might become necessary for gender-neutral people (such as new bathroom spaces or clothing lines)? Would widespread acknowledgment of gender-neutral people affect typically gendered discourses like children's toys, Halloween costumes, and rituals like prom or childbirth? Consult readings from the other chapters in *Composing Gender* to find examples to support your position.

7. Would you say that contemporary culture is more or less accepting of genderless persons than the past two or three generations? Can you think of any examples in popular culture that support gender neutrality, or would you say that most of popular culture today is still invested in traditional gender roles and images?

2 | How Do We Become Boys and Girls?

A s the readings in the previous chapter make clear, the obviously different behaviors, appearances, actions, roles, and symbols we associate with masculinity and femininity do not have as strong a biological basis as commonsense attitudes about gender would suggest. Masculinity and femininity cannot be conceived as clear-cut, wholly independent categories rooted in biological opposition. Gender instead arises from myriad cultural traditions and long-standing assumptions about the supposedly natural differences between men and women — traditions and assumptions inscribed in complex processes and interactions that constitute the social construction of gender.

One logical area in which to begin examining the social construction of gender is childhood and children's culture. Because children must learn how to think and behave in ways appropriate to their society and culture, the experiences of children in acquiring gender illuminate some of the foundational ways the social order separates and constitutes boyhood and girlhood differently, often based on preexisting notions about the correct means and modes of gender display. Even before birth in many cases, the gendering process begins, as expectant parents consider names and bedeck nurseries with gender-appropriate colors, textures, symbols, and toys. As children grow, they come into contact not only with parents and other relatives with whom they identify but also with other adults and children in the community who variously help model and shape their sense of gender identity. Children absorb countless images of men and women interacting in media forms like film, television, and literature. They play with toys and visualize themselves playing adult roles through imaginary play. They are dressed and adorned according to their ascribed gender. And they are inducted even further into the cultural milieu through educational institutions like preschools, kindergartens, and primary schools. The implications of all these are steep for children's growing senses of gender identity as they become aware of their gender status and develop potentialities and capabilities in relation to the opportunities provided to them.

Each reading in this chapter addresses facets of gender construction in childhood. Claire Renzetti and Daniel Curran, in an excerpt from their book *Women, Men, and Society*, look at parent-child interactions to examine differential treatment of boys and girls by parents, and they consider the impact of clothes and toys on children's physical and cognitive development. A short article by Jennifer Goodwin summarizes a recent study of children's toy preferences, highlighting the ongoing debate over whether or not boys are naturally drawn to trucks, and girls to dolls. In " 'No Way My Boys Are Going to Be Like That': Parents' Responses to Children's Gender Nonconformity," sociologist Emily Kane interviews parents about how they respond to their children when their children behave in ways that breach gender boundaries. Mother-daughter team Jane and Hannah Katch, both teachers, dialogue about a case study in gender nonconformity when a male student in Jane's kindergarten class declares himself a "girl." Peggy Orenstein considers the impact of the Disney "princesses" on the psyches of young girls in "What's Wrong with Cinderella?," and Michael Messner examines the salience of male and female role modeling in youth sports organizations. Each of these pieces shows that acquiring and practicing gender imply a complex network of interactions — personal, familial, communal, and institutional. They also ask if gender is a "natural" phenomenon, why does it require so much effort to shape it, and why are so many contradictions to the notion of uniform gender difference so frequently ignored?

From *Women, Men, and Society*

Claire Renzetti and Daniel Curran

Claire Renzetti is a professor of sociology at the University of Kentucky. Her scholarly work focuses on the sociology of gender and violence against women. Her most recent work has been an ethnographic study about the ways that faith-based organizations address the issue of human trafficking. She has also published *Economic Stress and Domestic Violence* (2009) and has coedited the *Sourcebook on Violence against Women* (2010). Daniel Curran is a professor of sociology and is the president of the University of Dayton. He has written several books, including *Dead Laws for Dead Men*, a historical analysis of coal mine health and safety legislation, and has coauthored several sociological books with Dr. Renzetti, including *Women, Men, and Society* (2003) and *Theories of Crime: A Reader* (2000).

Growing Up Feminine or Masculine

If you ask expectant parents whether they want their baby to be a boy or a girl, most will say they don't have a preference (Steinbacher & Gilroy, 1985). The dominance of this attitude, though, is relatively recent; from the 1930s to the 1980s, most Americans expressed a preference for boys as only children and, in larger families, preferred sons to outnumber daughters (Coombs, 1977; Williamson, 1976). In some parts of the world today, boys are still strongly favored over girls. In fact, in some countries this preference has resulted in a population imbalance, with a disproportionate ratio of males to females.

Even though American parents do not express a strong sex preference, research shows that parents do have different expectations of their babies and treat them differently, simply on the basis of sex. It has even been argued by some researchers that gender socialization actually may begin in utero by those parents who know the sex of their child before it is born. As Kolker and Burke (1992, pp. 12–13) explain, "The knowledge of sex implies more than chromosomal or anatomical differences. It implies gender, and with it images of personality and social role expectations." Such a hypothesis is difficult, if not impossible to test, but what currently is known is that gender socialization gets underway almost immediately after a child is born. Research shows, for instance, that the vast majority of comments parents make about their babies immediately following birth concern the babies' sex (Woollett et al., 1982). Moreover, although there are few physiological or behavioral differences between males and females at birth, parents tend to respond differently to newborns on the basis of sex. For example, when asked to describe their babies shortly after birth, new parents frequently use gender stereotypes. Infant boys are described as tall, large, athletic, serious, and having broad, wide hands. In contrast, infant girls were described as small and pretty, with fine, delicate features (Reid, 1994). These findings are quite similar to those obtained in a study conducted twenty years earlier (Rubin et al., 1974), indicating that there has been little change in parental gender stereotyping.

That parents associate their child's sex with specific personality and behavioral traits is further evidenced by the effort they put into ensuring that others identify their child's sex correctly. It's often difficult to determine whether a baby is a boy or a girl because there are no physical cues: Male and female infants overlap more than they differ in terms of weight, length, amount of hair, alertness, and activity level. Parents most often use clothing to avoid confusion (Shakin et al., 1985). Boys are typically dressed in dark or primary colors, such as red and blue. They wear overalls that are often decorated with sporting or military equipment, trucks and other vehicles, or superheroes. Girls are typically dressed in pastels, especially pink and yellow. Their dresses and slacks sets are decorated with ruffles, bows, flowers, and hearts. Parents also often put satiny headbands on their baby daughters (despite their lack of hair) and have their ears pierced. Disposable diapers are even different for girls and boys, not only in the way they are constructed, which arguably might have a rational basis to it, but also in the way they are decorated: Girls' diapers often have pink flowers on them; boys' diapers are embellished with sailboats or cars and trucks. Thus, clothing usually provides a reliable clue for sex labeling, although mistakes do still occur, which often anger parents. As one new mother recently told us in frustration, "I dress her in pink and she always wears earrings, but people still look at her and say, 'Hey, big fella.' What else can I do?"

Clothing, then, plays a significant part in gender socialization in two ways. First, as children become mobile, certain types of clothing encourage or discourage particular behaviors or activities. Girls in frilly dresses, for example, are discouraged from rough-and-tumble play, whereas boys' physical movement is rarely impeded by their clothing. Boys are expected to be more active than girls, and the styles of the clothing designed for them reflect this gender stereotype. Second, by informing others about the sex of the child, clothing sends implicit messages about how the child should be treated. "We know . . . that when someone interacts with a child and a sex label is available, the label functions to direct behavior along the lines of traditional [gender] roles" (Shakin et al., 1985, p. 956).

Clothing clearly serves as one of the most basic ways in which par- 5
ents organize their children's world along gender-specific lines. But
do parents' stereotyped perceptions of their babies translate into differential treatment of sons and daughters? If you ask parents whether
they treat their children differently simply on the basis of sex, most
would probably say "no." However, there is considerable evidence
that what parents *say* they do and what they *actually* do are frequently
not the same.

Parent-Child Interactions

The word *interaction* denotes an ongoing exchange between people.
This meaning is important to keep in mind when discussing parent-
child interaction, for the relationship is not one-way — something parents do to their children — but rather two-way, a give-and-take between
the parent and the child. Parents sometimes raise this point themselves when they are questioned about the style and content of their
interactions with their children. Parents report that male infants and
toddlers are "fussier" than female infants and toddlers; boys, they
say, are more active and anger more easily than girls. Girls are better
behaved and more easy going. So if we observe parents treating their
sons and daughters differently, is it just because they are responding
to biologically based sex differences in temperament? Perhaps, but research by psychologist Liz Connors (1996) indicates that girls may be
better behaved than boys because their mothers expect them to be.
In observing girls and boys three-and-a-half to fourteen months old,
Connors found few differences in the children's behavior. However,
she also found that the mothers of girls were more sensitive to
their children, while the mothers of boys were more restrictive of
their children. Connors reports that fourteen-month-old girls are more
secure in their emotional attachment to their mothers than fourteen-
month-old boys, and she attributes this difference to mothers' differential treatment of their children.

Additional research lends support to Connors's conclusion. For
example, Fagot and her colleagues (1985) found that although thirteen-
and fourteen-month-old children showed no sex differences in their
attempts to communicate, adults tended to respond to boys when they
"forced attention" by being aggressive, or by crying, whining, and
screaming, whereas similar attempts by girls were usually ignored.
Instead, adults were responsive to girls when they used gestures or
gentle touching, or when they simply talked. Significantly, when Fagot
and her colleagues observed these same children just eleven months
later, they saw clear sex differences in their styles of communication;
boys were more assertive, whereas girls were more talkative.

In studies with a related theme, researchers have found that parents communicate differently with sons and daughters. Parents use a greater number and variety of emotion words when talking with daughters than sons. They also talk more about sadness with daughters, whereas they talk more about anger with sons (Adams et al., 1995; Fivush, 1991; Kuebli et al., 1995). One outcome of this differential interaction is that by the age of six, girls use a greater number of and more specialized emotion words than boys (Adams et al., 1995; Kuebli et al., 1995). Researchers have found that preschoolers whose mothers engaged in frequent emotion talk with them are better able to understand others' emotions (Denham et al., 1994), and by first grade, girls are better at monitoring emotion and social behavior than boys (Davis, 1995). Certainly, it is not unreasonable to speculate that through these early socialization experiences, parents are teaching their daughters to be more attentive to others' feelings and to interpersonal relationships, while they are teaching boys to be assertive, but unemotional except when expressing anger. Is it any wonder that among adults, women are better able than men to interpret people's facial expressions and are more concerned about maintaining social connections (Erwin et al., 1992; Goleman, 1996; Schneider et al., 1994)?

Are there other ways in which parent-child interactions differ by sex of the child? Research indicates that parents tend to engage in rougher, more physical play with infant sons than with infant daughters (MacDonald & Parke, 1986). Interestingly, the sex of the parent also appears to be significant. Fathers usually play more interactive games with infant and toddler sons and also encourage more visual, fine-motor, and locomotor exploration with them, whereas they promote vocal interaction with their daughters. At the same time, fathers of toddler daughters appear to encourage closer parent-child physical proximity than fathers of toddler sons (Bronstein, 1988). Both fathers and mothers are more likely to believe — and to act on the belief — that daughters need more help than sons (Burns et al., 1989; Snow et al., 1983). In these ways, parents may be providing early training for their sons to be independent and their daughters dependent. Moreover, Weitzman and her colleagues (1985) found that mothers tend to teach and question boys more than girls, thereby providing their sons with more of the kind of verbal stimulation thought to foster cognitive development.

In their study, Weitzman and her colleagues included mothers who [10] professed not to adhere to traditional gender stereotypes. Although the differential treatment of sons and daughters was less pronounced among these mothers, it was by no means absent. This is an important point because it speaks to the strength of gender bias in our culture, reminding us that gender stereotypes are such a taken-for-granted part of our everyday lives that we often discriminate on the basis of sex without intentionally trying. "Even when we don't think we are behaving in gender stereotyped ways, or are encouraging gender-typed behavior in our children, examination of our actual behavior indicates that we are" (Golombok & Fivush, 1994, p. 26; see also Lewis et al., 1992; Weisner et al., 1994). . . .

Toys and Gender Socialization

Say the word "toys" in the company of children and you are likely to generate a good deal of excitement. Children will eagerly tell you about their favorite toy or about a "cool" new toy they'd like to have. Toys are, without a doubt, a major preoccupation of most children because, as any child will tell you, they're fun. However, toys not only entertain children, they also teach them particular skills and encourage them to explore through play a variety of roles they may one day occupy as adults. Are there significant differences in the toys girls and boys play with? If so, are these different types of toys training girls and boys for separate (and unequal) roles as adults?

More than twenty years ago, two researchers actually went into middle-class homes and examined the contents of children's rooms in an effort to answer these questions (Rheingold & Cook, 1975). Their comparison of boys' and girls' rooms is a study of contrasts. Girls' rooms reflected traditional conceptions of femininity, especially in terms of domesticity and motherhood. They contained an abundance of baby dolls and related items (e.g., doll houses) as well as miniature appliances (e.g., toy stoves). Few of these items were found in boys' rooms, where, instead, there were military toys and athletic equipment. Boys also had building and vehicular toys (e.g., blocks, trucks, and wagons). In fact, boys had more toys overall as well as more types of toys, including those considered educational. The only items girls were as likely to have as boys were musical instruments and books.

A decade later, another group of researchers (Stoneman et al., 1986) replicated Rheingold and Cook's study and obtained similar findings: Toys for girls still revolved around the themes of domesticity and motherhood, while toys for boys focused on action and adventure. A quick perusal of most contemporary toy catalogs reveals that little has changed in this regard during the 1990s as well. The toys for sale in the catalogs are usually pictured with models, which can be taken as an indication of the gender appropriateness of the toy. In the catalogs we examined (Childcraft, 1997; F. A. O. Schwarz, 1997; and Just Pretend,

A sign in a toy shop in London.

1997), most of the toys were obviously gender-linked. We found, for instance, that little girls were most frequently shown with dolls or household appliances. The "dolls" boys were pictured with were referred to as "action figures" and included superheroes (Superman, Batman), G.I. Joe (in a variety of roles, such as General Patton and the Golden Knight army paratrooper), characters from the *Star Wars* film series, and monsters (Spawn Vandalizer, with "real jaw-chomping action," and Deathlock, who is "half-man and half-cyborg"). Costumes for dressing up were also gender-specific. Boys were shown modeling the "Bold and Brave Collection," for the child with "the soul of an explorer" and "the heart of a hero." The set included costumes for a knight, a ninja, a cyborg, a pirate, and even a vampire. Girls were shown modeling the "Satin and Lace Collection," which was "designed to honor those timeless fantasies of girls." This set contained costumes for a ballerina, a princess, a fairy, an angel, and a bride. Accessories for the bride's costume (sold separately, of course) included a "diamond-look ring" on a heart-shaped pillow, five fill-in-the-blank wedding announcements, and a gift bag with two champagne flutes. On other pages of the catalogs, a little girl was talking on a pink cordless telephone with the sound effects, "As if" and "Whatever" from the film, *Clueless*, while a boy dressed in black and wearing dark glasses talked on a black cordless "spy gear" phone that had a flashlight for "night operations." Girls were shown bathing a doll in an "infant care center," weaving hair extensions and attaching them with barrettes, and serving tea from a "teatime treasures" picnic hamper. Boys drove tractors, a train, and a rocket ship; worked in a fix-it shop; built a "space training center" out of snap-together plastic parts; played hockey and electric football; and hunted dinosaurs. Boys were shown with scientific toys in all but one instance (the "Science in the Kitchen" set) and with athletic equipment.

Of course, it may be argued that toy catalogs are directed primarily to parents, and parents usually claim that they buy gender-typed toys because that's what their children prefer. Research does show that children express gender-typed toy preferences as early as one year of age, but their toy "choices" may have been inspired even earlier by parental encouragement. For example, when adults were given the opportunity to interact with a three-month-old infant dressed in a yellow gender-neutral jumpsuit, they usually used a doll for play when they thought the infant was a girl, but chose a football and a plastic ring when they thought the infant was a boy (Seavy et al., 1975; see also Caldera et al., 1989; Fisher-Thompson et al., 1995). Parental encouragement of gender-typed toy choices are further reinforced by the toy catalogs (which children themselves spend a considerable time looking at), by television commercials, by the pictures on toy packaging, and by the way toy stores often arrange their stock in separate sections for boys and girls (Schwartz & Markham, 1985; Shapiro, 1990).

Toys for boys tend to encourage exploration, manipulation, invention, construction, competition, and aggression. In contrast, girls' toys typically rate high on manipulability, but also creativity, nurturance, and attractiveness.

In considering the toys we've de- 15 scribed, it is not difficult to see that they foster different traits and abilities in children, depending on their sex. Toys for boys tend to encourage exploration, manipulation, invention, construction, competition, and aggression. In contrast, girls' toys typically rate high on manipulability, but also creativity, nurturance, and attractiveness (see also Bradbard, 1985; Miller, 1987; Peretti & Sydney, 1985). As one researcher concluded, "These data support the hypothesis that playing with girls' vs. boys' toys may be related to the development of differential cognitive and/or social skills in girls and boys" (Miller, 1987, p. 485). Certainly, the toy manufacturers think so; the director of public relations for Mattel, Inc. (which makes the Barbie doll) stated in an interview that, "Girls' play involves dressing and grooming and acting out their future — going on a date, getting married —

and boys' play involves competition and conflict, good guys versus bad guys" (quoted in Lawson, 1989, p. C1).

This attitude remains a major premise of the $15 billion-a-year toy industry, as evidenced by the new toys introduced annually at the American International Toy Fair. Among the offerings at the 1996 and 1997 toy fairs were "Tub Warriors," floating action figures armed with water-propelled weapons such as a cannon and missile launcher; and "Melanie's Mall," in which a doll with long, silky hair, dressed in a miniskirt goes shopping in stores ("Beauty World," "Glamour Gowns") that children collect. The stores have their own shopping bags and Melanie has her own gold credit card (Lawson, 1996; 1997). It is not difficult to figure out which of these toys is targeted at the male market and which is intended for the female market.

The most popular toy for girls continues to be Barbie, with annual sales of $1.7 billion. In recent years, Barbie has been given several nontraditional roles, including dentist and astronaut (although her space wardrobe includes silver lingerie). In 1997, Mattel introduced "Talk with Me Barbie," in which Barbie has her own computer work station that can be attached to a real personal computer with a CD-ROM. Although some observers might see this invention as progress since it at least encourages girls to use computers, the game still focuses on shopping, makeup, and parties. More progressive was Mattel's 1997 announcement that Barbie is being redesigned to have more realistic body proportions; for thirty-eight years, Barbie's figure has translated into proportions of 36–20–32 (that is, the bust of an adult woman, the waist of a child, and the hips of a teenager). In 1997, Mattel also introduced "Share a Smile Becky," Barbie's disabled friend in a wheelchair, although the new doll met with mixed reactions from disability groups ("New Friend for Barbie," 1997).

In short, with few exceptions, toys for young children tend to strongly reinforce gender stereotypes. The messages these toys — and the marketing and packaging for the toys — send to children is that what they *may* do, as well as what they *can* do, is largely determined and *limited* by their sex. . . .

. . . Virtually every significant dimension of a child's environment . . . is structured according to cultural expectations of appropriate gendered behavior. If, as the cognitive developmental theorists maintain, young children actively try to organize all the information they receive daily, their parents and other adults are clearly providing them with the means. Despite their claims, even most parents who see themselves as egalitarian tend to provide their children with different experiences and opportunities and to respond to them differently on the basis of sex. Consequently, the children cannot help but conclude that sex is an important social category. By the time they are ready for school, they have already learned to view the world in terms of a dichotomy: his and hers. . . .

References

Adams, S., Kuebli, J., Boyle, P. A., & Fivush, R. (1995). Gender differences in parent-child conversations about past emotions. A longitudinal investigation. *Sex Roles, 33,* 309–323.

Bradbard, M. R. (1985). Sex differences in adults' gifts and children's toy requests at Christmas. *Psychological Reports, 56,* 969–970.

Bronstein, O. (1988). Father-child interaction. In P. Bronstein & C. P. Cowan (Eds.), *Fatherhood today: Men's changing role in the family* (pp. 107–124). New York: John Wiley.

Burns, A. L., Mitchell, G., & Obradovich, S. (1989). Of sex roles and strollers: Female and male attention to toddlers at the zoo. *Sex Roles, 20,* 309–315.

Caldera, Y. M., Huston, A. C., & O'Brien, M. (1989). Social interactions and play patterns of parents and toddlers with feminine, masculine, and neutral toys. *Child Development, 60,* 70–76.

Connors, L. (1996). *Gender of infant differences in attachment: Associations with temperament and caregiving experiences.* Paper presented at the Annual Conference of the British Psychological Society, Oxford, England.

Coombs, L. C. (1977). Preferences for sex of children among U.S. couples. *Family Planning Perspectives, 9,* 259–265.

Davis, T. L. (1995). Gender differences in masking negative emotions: Ability or motivation? *Developmental Psychology, 31,* 660–667.

Denham, S. A., Zoller, D., & Couchoud, E. A. (1994). Socialization of preschoolers' emotional understanding. *Developmental Psychology, 30,* 928–938.

Erwin, R. J., Gur, R. C., Gur, R. E., Skolnick, B., Mawhinney-Hee, M., & Smailis, J. (1992). Facial emotion discrimination: 1. Task construction and behavioral findings in normal subjects. *Psychiatry Research, 42,* 231–240.

Fagot, B. I., Hagan, R., Leinbach, M. D., & Kronsberg, S. (1985). Differential reactions to assertive and communicative acts of toddler boys and girls. *Child Development, 56,* 1499–1505.

Fisher-Thompson, D., Sausa, A. D., & Wright, T. F. (1995). Toy selection for children: Personality and toy request influences. *Sex Roles, 33,* 239–255.

Fivush, R. (1991). Gender and emotion in mother-child conversations about the past. *Journal of Narrative and Life History, 1,* 325–341.

Goleman, D. (1996). *Emotional Intelligence.* New York: Bantam Books.

Golombok, S., & Fivush, R. (1994). *Gender development.* Cambridge: Cambridge University Press.

Kolker, A., & Burke, B. M. (1992). *Sex preference and sex selection: Attitudes of prenatal diagnosis clients.* Paper presented at the Annual Meeting of the American Sociological Association, Pittsburgh, PA.

Kuebli, J., Butler, S. A., & Fivush, R. (1995). Mother-child talk about past emotions: Relations of maternal language and child gender over time. *Cognition and Emotion, 9,* 265–283.

Lawson, C. (1989, June 15). Toys: Girls still apply makeup, boys fight wars. *New York Times*, pp. C1, C10.

———. (1996, Feb. 15). Fun at the toy fair: Babies that fly! *New York Times*, p. C2.

———. (1997, Feb. 13). What the next sled of toys is up to. *New York Times*.

Lewis, C., Scully, D., & Condor, S. (1992). Sex stereotyping of infants: A reexamination. *Journal of Reproductive and Infant Psychology, 10*, 53–63.

MacDonald, K., & Parke, R. D. (1986). Parent-child physical play: The effects of sex and age on children and parents. *Sex Roles, 15*, 367–378.

Miller, C. L. (1987). Qualitative differences among gender-stereotyped toys: Implications for cognitive and social development in girls and boys. *Sex Roles, 16*, 473–488.

Peretti, P. O., & Sydney, T. M. (1985). Parental toy choice stereotyping and its effects on child toy preference and sex-role typing. *Social Behavior and Personality, 12*, 213–216.

Reid, G. M. (1994). Maternal sex-stereotyping of newborns. *Psychological Reports, 75*, 1443–1450.

Rheingold, H. L., & Cook, K. V. (1975). The content of boys' and girls' rooms as an index of parents' behavior. *Child Development, 46*, 459–463.

Rubin, J. Z., Provenzano, F. J., & Luria, Z. (1974). The eye of the beholder: Parents' views on sex of newborns. *American Journal of Orthopsychiatry, 44*, 512–519.

Schneider, F., Gur, R. C., Gur, R. E., & Muenz, L. R. (1994). Standardized mood induction with happy and sad facial expressions. *Psychiatry Research, 51*, 19–31.

Schwartz, L. A., & Markham, W. T. (1985). Sex stereotyping in children's toy advertisements. *Sex Roles, 12*, 157–170.

Seavy, A. A., Katz, P. A., & Zalk, S. R. (1975). Baby X: The effect of gender labels on adult responses to infants. *Sex Roles, 1*, 103–109.

Shakin, M., Shakin, D., & Sternglanz, S. H. (1985). Infant clothing: Sex labeling for strangers. *Sex Roles, 12*, 955–964.

Shapiro, L. (1990, May 28). Guns and dolls. *Newsweek*, pp. 56–65.

Snow, M. E., Jacklin, C. N., & Maccoby, E. E. (1983). Sex-of-child differences in father-child interaction at one year of age. *Child Development, 54*, 227–232.

Steinbacher, R., & Gilroy, F. D. (1985). Preference for sex of child among primiparous women. *The Journal of Psychology, 119*, 541–547.

Stoneman, Z., Brody, G. H., & MacKinnon, C. E. (1986). Same-sex and cross-sex siblings: Activity choices, roles, behavior, and gender stereotypes. *Sex Roles, 15*, 495–511.

Temple, L. (1997, May 30). Is Barbie's new pal an insult or an inspiration? *USA Today*, p. 7D.

Weisner, T. S., Garnier, H., & Loucky, J. (1994). Domestic tasks, gender egalitarian values and children's gender typing in conventional and nonconventional families. *Sex Roles, 30*, 23–54.

Weitzman, N., Birns, B., & Friend, R. (1985). Traditional and nontraditional mothers' communication with their daughters and sons. *Child Development, 56*, 894–896.

Williamson, N. E. (1976). *Sons or daughters*. Beverly Hills, CA: Sage.

Woollett, A., White, D., & Lyon, L. (1982). Fathers' involvement with their infants: The role of holding. In N. Beail & J. McGuire (Eds.), *Fathers: Psychological perspectives* (pp. 72–91). London: Junction.

Understanding the Text

1. Renzetti and Curran argue that gender construction begins at, or even before, birth. What are some reasons that parents focus on gender when children are very young or not yet born?

2. Some people argue that boys and girls have basic differences in temperament and that these biological differences account for why parents treat boys and girls differently. How do Renzetti and Curran respond to this position?

3. How do Renzetti and Curran see the clothes young children wear as affecting the development of their gender identity?

4. Consider the toys that Renzetti and Curran mention. What gender stereotypes do they embody? How do the toys they examine contribute to socializing boys and girls differently?

Reflection and Response

5. Consider the ways children are dressed differently according to their assigned gender, and think beyond Renzetti and Curran's analysis of clothing. For example, think about the textures of clothing, the symbols they display, and how people respond to boys' and girls' appearance. How central is clothing to shaping children's conformity to gender codes?

6. When you were a child, what were some of your favorite toys? Looking back, can you identify how gender codes or expectations determined or influenced your selection of toys or your forms of play?

7. What role do toy manufacturers and retailers play in designating toys as boys' or girls' toys?

8. Like dolls and action figures, many toys are designed and packaged for boys and girls differently but actually encourage the same types of play. Can you think of other examples of toys divided along gender lines that actually encourage the same kind of play? How does gender factor in?

Making Connections

9. Visit a toy store or a toy department in a major retail outlet, or look closely at a toy catalog in print or online, and examine a range of toys designated for girls or boys. What skills or activities do they encourage for boys and girls? What values about masculine and feminine gender roles are suggested by the toys? How might these toys impact children's gender identity? Do any toys challenge traditional or stereotypical gender codes, and if so, how?

10. In 2012, the Danish company Lego, one of the most popular toymakers in the world, unveiled a new line of Legos specifically for girls. By visiting a toy store, or toy department, or looking closely at a toy catalog online, examine the recent "division" of Legos into "boys'" and "girls'" sets. Do these new offerings by Lego represent a positive change toward gender equity in toys, or do the

sets designated for boys and girls further divide and define genders along stereotypical lines? Explain your answer.

11. Renzetti and Curran's conclusions about gender socialization end at age five. How might their analysis extend to adult women and men? Apply Renzetti and Curran's conclusions to one other article in our textbook, such as Rosenbloom's "Good Girls Go Bad, for a Day" (p. 164) or Kimmel's "The Rites of Almost-Men" (p. 140). How well do Renzetti and Curran's conclusions map onto adult behaviors and gender roles?

12. Emily Kane's work interviewing parents about gender nonconformity in children (p. 91) indicates that parents tend to be more concerned with conformity for boys than for girls. Write about how Kane's work helps us understand Renzetti and Curran's observations about boys' gender socialization. What connections do you see between these two articles?

Even Nine-Month-Olds Choose Gender-Specific Toys

Jennifer Goodwin is a freelance journalist who has written widely for *Business Week* and other publications about issues of health and lifestyle.

Jennifer Goodwin

P arents may want their girls to grow up to be astronauts and their boys to one day do their fair share of child care and housework duties, but a new study suggests certain stereotypical gender preferences take root even before most kids can crawl.

When presented with seven different toys, boys as young as 9 months old went for the car, digger and soccer ball, while ignoring the teddy bears, doll and cooking set.

And the girls? You guessed it. At the same age, they were most interested in the doll, teddy bear and miniature pot, spoon and plastic vegetables.

"The boys always preferred the toys that go or move, and the girls preferred toys that promote nurturing and facial features," said study author Sara Amalie O'Toole Thommessen, an undergraduate at City University in London.

So does this mean that boys and girls have an innate preference 5 for certain types of objects? Or does socialization — that is, the influence of parents and the larger culture — impact children's choice of toys very early in life?

It's too soon to rule either out, said Walter Gilliam, director of the Edward Zigler Center in Child Development and Social Policy at Yale University.

"One of the things we've learned about babies over the many years we've been studying them is that they are amazing sponges and learn an awful lot in those nine months," Gilliam said.

In the 1970s and 1980s, there was lots of interest in the "nature" versus "nurture" debate, and developmental researchers did plenty of research on gender differences in play. However, most studies were inconclusive and interest faded, Thommessen said.

At the same time, roles within the home were becoming more fluid, with fathers taking on more child care and women working more and at a greater variety of jobs outside the home, though the marketing of children's toys remained very stereotypical.

This latest study included 83 children aged 9 months to 3 years 10
who were observed playing for three minutes. The time they spent
touching or playing with each object was noted.

Researchers chose the toys by surveying 300 adults about the first
toy that came to mind when they thought of a boy or a girl. About 90
percent said "car" for boy and "doll" for girls, with the remainder
mentioning the other toys.

Children were also offered both a pink teddy bear and a blue teddy
bear. "We were quite interested to see if boys had a color preference,
but boys didn't show any interest in the teddy bears at all," Thommessen said.

Gender-specific preferences became even more pronounced as
the children got older. By about age 27 months to 36 months, girls
spent about 50 percent of their time playing with the doll, and were
no longer much interested in the teddy bear, which had interested
them when they were younger, or any of the other objects. The boys
spent 87 percent of their time with the car and digger, ignoring even
the ball.

The finding raises the possibility of a biological basis for toy
choices. A study from 2001 found even 1-day-old boys spent longer
looking at moving, mechanical options than 1-day-old girls, who spent
more time looking at faces.

Yet the impact of socialization should never be underestimated, 15
Gilliam said. Studies have shown parents and others interact differently with female and male babies from almost the instant they're
born, Gilliam said.

Even when they're infants, fathers
tend to encourage more active play
with boy babies, by playfully tickling
or poking them, while they tend to
hold girl babies closer. Parents have also been observed spending
more time talking to girls than to boys.

> "He's not playing with dolls.
> Those are action figures."

As they get older, studies have shown boys are encouraged to more
actively explore their environment, while girls are encouraged to engage in quieter play.

"Even if your boy prefers playing with a truck, make sure you talk
to him and teach him about nurturing," Gilliam said. "Even if a girl is
playing with a doll, every once in a while throw her a ball or take her
on a run. Expose them to all the different possibilities, and then let
them choose."

And keep in mind just how much you may be dragging your own
stereotypical notions into parenting.

In the study, researchers found no association between parents' [20] reported views on gender-appropriate toys for children, or parental roles at home, and the toys children chose. In other words, dads who did their share of housework and moms who held high-level jobs outside the home were just as likely to have girls who picked dolls and boys who picked cars and trucks.

But Gilliam remembers one family who brought their young son in to see him. There was an assortment of toys scattered on the floor, from which the boy chose a plastic figurine. "The mom said, 'Oh, he wants to play with dolls.' And the father replied, 'He's not playing with dolls. Those are action figures.'"

Reference

Thommessen, S. "Children Less Than a Year Old Already Favor Gender-Typical Toys." Proceedings of the British Psych Society Annual Conference, Stratford-upon-Avon, UK, April 16, 2010.

Understanding the Text

1. Goodwin reports that very young children display gender preferences. What evidence does she cite that these preferences are innate and biological? What evidence does she cite that these preferences are the result of socialization?

2. At the end of the article, Goodwin recounts a story about a father who called dolls "action figures." What is the significance of this story? Why do you think Goodwin chooses to end her article with it?

Reflection and Response

3. Some toys are particularly gendered, and others seem to be genderless. Choose a toy that might be genderless and write about the toy. Is it truly genderless? You might even investigate the marketing materials about that toy — do you see any gender bias in those materials?

Making Connections

4. Do some research in the library or online about parenting styles in which the parents are attempting to raise their children in a gender-neutral environment. What do you find in that research? Does it seem that these approaches to parenting might be successful, or is the jury still out about whether gender-neutral parenting is possible?

5. Choose at least one other article from *Composing Gender* that helps explain why toys might be gendered, even in very young children. What social effects might be impacting the ways that children are attracted to and encouraged to choose certain toys? What article might be best paired with Goodwin's in a research paper about the topic of gendered toys?

"No Way My Boys Are Going to Be Like That": Parents' Responses to Children's Gender Nonconformity

Emily W. Kane

Emily W. Kane is a professor of sociology and women and gender studies at Bates College. She has published widely on issues related to gender and childhood, including articles about parental monitoring of children's gender conformity and parental preferences for sons and daughters. She recently published a book about gender and childhood, *The Gender Trap* (2012). In this excerpt from her earlier research, Kane reports on her interviews with 44 parents about their responses to children's gender nonconformity.

Parents accepted, and often even celebrated, their sons' acquisition of domestic abilities and an orientation toward nurturance and empathy. Of the 25 parents of sons who offered positive/neutral responses, 21 did so in reference to domestic skills, nurturance, and/ or empathy. For example, they reported allowing or encouraging traditionally girl toys such as dolls, doll houses, kitchen centers, and tea sets, with that response often revolving around a desire to encourage domestic competence, nurturance, emotional openness, empathy, and nonviolence as attributes they considered nontraditional but positive for boys. These parents were reporting actions and sentiments oriented toward accomplishing gender in what they considered a less conventional manner. One white, low-income, heterosexual mother taught her son to cook, asserting that "I want my son to know how to do more than boil water, I want him to know how to take care of himself." Another mother, this one a white, working-class, heterosexual parent, noted that she makes a point of talking to her sons about emotions: "I try to instill a sense of empathy in my sons and try to get them to see how other people would feel." And a white, middle-class, heterosexual father emphasized domestic competence when he noted that it does not bother him for his son to play with dolls at his cousin's house: "How then are they going to learn to take care of their children if they don't?" This positive response to domestic activities is consistent with recent literature on parental coding of toys as masculine, feminine, or neutral, which indicates that parents are increasingly coding kitchens and in some cases dolls as neutral rather than exclusively feminine (Wood, Desmarais, and Gugula 2002).

In my study, mothers and fathers expressed these kinds of efforts to accomplish gender differently for their sons with similar frequency, but mothers tended to express them with greater certainty, while fathers were less enthusiastic and more likely to include caveats. For example, this mother described her purchase of a variety of domestic toys for her three-year-old son without ambivalence: "One of the first big toys [I got him] was the kitchen center. . . . We cook, he has an apron he wears. . . . He's got his dirt devil vacuum and he's got his baby [doll]. And he's got all the stuff to feed her and a highchair" (white, low-income, heterosexual mother).

Some mothers reported allowing domestic toys but with less enthusiasm, such as a white, low-income, heterosexual mother who said, regarding her three-year-old son, "He had been curious about dolls and I just said, you know, usually girls play with dolls, but it's okay for you to do it too." But this kind of caution or lack of enthusiasm, even in a response coded as positive or neutral due to its allowance of gender-atypical behavior, was more evident among fathers, as the following quote illustrates: "Occasionally, if he's not doing something, I'll encourage him to maybe play with his tea cups, you know, occasionally. But I like playing with his blocks better anyway" (white, middle-class, heterosexual father).

Thus, evident among both mothers and fathers, but with greater conviction for mothers, was widespread support among parents for working to "undo" gender at the level of some of their sons' skills and values. However, this acceptance was tempered for many parents by negative responses to any interest in what I will refer to as iconic feminine items, attributes, or activities, as well as parental concern about homosexuality.

Icons of Femininity

A range of activities and attributes considered atypical for boys were met with negative responses, and for a few parents (3 of 31 parents of sons) this even included the kind of domestic toys and nurturance noted above. But more common were negative responses to items, activities, or attributes that could be considered icons of femininity. This was strikingly consistent with Kimmel's (1994, 119) previously noted claim that the "notion of anti-femininity lies at the heart of contemporary and historical constructions of manhood," and it bears highlighting that this was evident among parents of very young children. Parents of sons reported negative responses to their sons' wearing pink or frilly clothing; wearing skirts, dresses, or tights; and playing dress up in any kind of feminine attire. Nail polish elicited concern from a number of parents too, as they reported young sons wanting to have their fingernails or toenails polished. Dance, especially ballet, and Barbie dolls were also among the traditionally female activities often noted negatively by parents of sons. Of the 31 parents of sons, 23 mentioned negative reactions to at least one of these icons.

In relation to objects such as clothing and toys, the following responses are typical of the many concerns raised and the many indications of actions parents had taken to accomplish gender with and for their sons:

He's asked about wearing girl clothes before, and I said no. . . . He likes pink, and I try not to encourage him to like pink just because, you know, he's not a girl. . . . There's not many toys I wouldn't get him, except Barbie, I would try not to encourage that. (white, low-income, heterosexual mother)

If we go into a clothing store . . . I try to shy my son away from the Power Puff Girls shirt or anything like that. . . . I would steer him away from a pink shirt as opposed to having him wear a blue shirt. (Asian American, middle-class, heterosexual father)

These quotes are typical of many instances in which parents not only specify the items that strike them as problematic but clearly indicate the actions they take in accomplishing gender. In the first quote, the mother indicates her actions in encouraging and discouraging various outcomes, while in the second, the father reports "shying away" and "steering" his young son.

Playing with nail polish and makeup, although tolerated by some parents, more often evoked negative responses like this one, from a white, upper-middle-class, gay father, speaking about his four-year-old son's use of nail polish: "He put nail polish on himself one time, and I said 'No, you can't do that, little girls put nail polish on, little boys don't.'"

Barbie dolls are an especially interesting example in that many parents reported positive responses to baby dolls, viewing these as encouraging nurturance and helping to prepare sons for fatherhood. Barbie, on the other hand, an icon of femininity, struck many parents of sons as more problematic. Barbie was often mentioned when parents were asked whether their child had ever requested an item or activity more commonly associated with the other gender. Four parents — three mothers and one father — indicated that they had purchased a Barbie at their son's request, but more often parents of sons noted that they would avoid letting their son have or play with Barbie dolls. Sometimes this negative response was categorical, as in the quote above in which a mother of a three-year-old son noted that "there's not many toys I wouldn't get him, except Barbie." A father offers a similar negative reaction to Barbie in relation to his two young sons: "If they asked for a Barbie doll, I would probably say no, you don't want [that], girls play with [that], boys play with trucks" (white, middle-class, heterosexual father).

In other cases, parents reported that they would compromise in ways that strike me as designed to minimize Barbie's iconic status. These instances are particularly pointed examples of carefully crafted parental accomplishment of gender: "I would ask him 'What do you want for your birthday?' . . . and he always kept saying Barbie. . . . So we compromised, we got him a NASCAR Barbie" (white, middle-class, heterosexual mother). 10

Another father reported that his five-year-old son likes to play Barbies with his four-year-old sister and expressed relief that his son's interest is more in Ken than Barbie: "He's not interested in Barbie, he's interested in Ken. . . . He plays with Ken and does boy things with him, he has always made clear that he likes Ken. . . . If he was always playing with dolls and stuff like this then I would start to worry and try to do something to turn it around. But he plays with Ken and it doesn't go much further than that, so I'm fine" (white, upper-middle-class, heterosexual father).

Notable throughout these comments is the sense that parents are carefully balancing an openness to some crossing of gender boundaries but only within limits, as the father in the final quote indicated when he said that he would "do something to turn it around" if his son's interest were in Barbie rather than Ken. A similar balancing act in the accomplishment of masculinity is evident for a white, middle-class, heterosexual father who noted that if his son "really wanted to dance, I'd let him . . . , but at the same time, I'd be doing other things to compensate for the fact that I signed him up for dance."

Along with material markers of femininity, many parents expressed concern about excessive emotionality (especially frequent crying) and passivity in their sons. For example, a white, upper-middle-class, heterosexual father, concerned about public crying, said about his five-year-old son, "I don't want him to be a sissy. . . . I want to see him strong, proud, not crying like a sissy." Another father expressed his frustration with his four-year-old son's crying over what the father views as minor injuries and indicated action to discourage those tears: "Sometimes I get so annoyed, you know, he comes [crying], and I say, 'you're not hurt, you don't even know what hurt is yet,' and I'm like 'geez, sometimes you are such a little wean,' you know?" (white, middle-class, heterosexual father).

Passivity was also raised as a concern, primarily by fathers. For example, one white, middle-class, heterosexual father of a five-year-old noted that he has told his son to "stop crying like a girl," and also reported encouraging that son to fight for what he wants: "You just go in the corner and cry like a baby. I don't want that. If you decide you want [some] thing, you are going to fight for it, not crying and acting like a baby and hoping that they're going to feel guilty and give it to you."

A mother who commented negatively about passivity even more 15 directly connected her concern to how her son might be treated: "I do have concerns. . . . He's passive, not aggressive. . . . He's not the rough and tumble kid, and I do worry about him being an easy target" (white, working-class, heterosexual mother).

Taken together, these various examples indicate clearly the work many parents are doing to accomplish gender with and for their sons in a manner that distances those sons from any association with femininity. This work was not evident among all parents of sons. But for most parents, across racial, class, and sexual orientation categories, it was indeed evident.

Homosexuality

Along with these icons of feminine gender performance, and arguably directly linked to them, is the other clear theme evident among some parents' negative responses to perceived gender nonconformity on the part of their sons: fear that a son either would be or would be perceived as gay. Spontaneous connections of gender nonconformity and sexual orientation were not evident in parents' comments about daughters, nor among gay and lesbian parents, but arose for 7 of the 27 heterosexual parents who were discussing sons. The following two examples are typical of responses that invoked the possibility of a son's being gay, with explicit links to performance of femininity and to the parents' own role in accomplishing heterosexuality:

If he was acting feminine, I would ask and get concerned on whether or not, you know, I would try to get involved and make sure he's not gay. (white, low-income, heterosexual mother)

There are things that are meant for girls, but why would it be bad for him to have one of them? I don't know, maybe I have some deep, deep, deep buried fear that he would turn out, well, that his sexual orientation may get screwed up. (white, middle-class, heterosexual father)

The first comment explicitly indicates that feminine behavior, even in a three-year-old boy, might be an indicator of an eventual nonheterosexual orientation. The second comment raises another possibility: that playing with toys "that are meant for girls" might not indicate but rather shape the son's eventual sexual orientation. In both cases, though, the parent is reporting on actions, either actual or hypothetical, taken to discourage homosexuality and accomplish heterosexuality. Another quote from a father raises a similar concern and further exemplifies parental responsibility for the accomplishment of masculinity as linked to heterosexuality. This father had noted throughout the interview that his five-year-old son tends to show some attributes he considers feminine. At one point, he mentioned that he sometimes wondered if his son might be gay, and he explained his reaction to that possibility in the following terms: "If [he] were to be gay, it would not make me happy at all. I would probably see that as a failure as a dad . . . , as a failure because I'm raising him to be a boy, a man" (white, upper-middle-class, heterosexual father). This comment suggests that the parent does not view masculinity as something that naturally unfolds but rather as something he feels responsible for crafting, and he explicitly links heterosexual orientation to the successful accomplishment of masculinity.

The fact that the connection between gender performance and sexual orientation was not raised for daughters, and that fear of homosexuality was not spontaneously mentioned by parents of daughters whether in connection to gender performance or not, suggests how closely gender conformity and heterosexuality are linked within hegemonic constructions of masculinity. Such connections might arise more by adolescence in relation to daughters, as I noted previously regarding other aspects of parental responses to gender nonconformity. But for sons, even among parents of very young children, heteronormativity appears to play a role in shaping parental responses to gender nonconformity, a connection that literature on older children and adults indicates is made more for males than females (Antill 1987; Hill 1999; Kite and Deaux 1987; Sandnabba and Ahlberg 1999). Martin's (2005) recent analysis also documents the importance of heteronormativity in the advice offered to parents by experts. She concludes that expert authors of child-rearing books and Web sites are increasingly supportive of gender-neutral child rearing. But especially for sons, that expert support is limited by implicit and even explicit invocations of homosexuality as a risk to be managed. As Mc-Creary (1994, 526) argues on the basis of experimental work on responses to older children and adults, "the asymmetry in people's responses to male and female gender role deviations is motivated, in part, by the implicit assumption that male transgressions are symptomatic of a homosexual orientation." This implicit assumption appears to motivate at least some parental gender performance management among heterosexual parents, even for children as young as preschool age. Given the connections between male heterosexuality and the rejection of femininity noted previously as evident in theories of hegemonic masculinity, the tendency for parents to associate gender performance and sexual orientation for sons more than daughters may also reflect a more general devaluation of femininity. . . .

References

Antill, John K. 1987. Parents' beliefs and values about sex roles, sex differences, and sexuality. *Review of Personality and Social Psychology* 7:294–328.

Hill, Shirley A. 1999. *African American children.* Thousand Oaks, CA: Sage.

Kimmel, Michael S. 1994. Masculinity as homophobia. In *Theorizing masculinities,* edited by Harry Brod. Thousand Oaks, CA: Sage.

Kite, Mary E., and Kay Deaux. 1987. Gender belief systems: Homosexuality and the implicit inversion theory. *Psychology of Women Quarterly* 11:83–96.

Martin, Karin A. 2005. William wants a doll, can he have one? Feminists, child care advisors, and gender-neutral child rearing. *Gender & Society* 20:1–24.

McCreary, Donald R. 1994. The male role and avoiding femininity. *Sex Roles* 31:517–31.

Sandnabba, N. Kenneth, and Christian Ahlberg. 1999. Parents' attitudes and expectations about children's cross-gender behavior. *Sex Roles* 40:249–63.

Wood, Eileen, Serge Desmarais, and Sara Gugula. 2002. The impact of parenting experience on gender stereotyped toy play of children. *Sex Roles* 47:39–49.

Understanding the Text

1. Kane writes that, increasingly, boys are provided with, or are permitted to play with, toys previously coded as feminine, such as kitchen sets and dolls. Why do you think these changes are occurring?

2. Despite an increasing openness in parents' perceptions of what it is "okay" for boys to play with, for most of Kane's respondents, some toys and forms of play are not permitted for boys. Explain why some prohibitions still exist when it comes to boys' cross-gender play.

Reflection and Response

3. While most children do engage in cross-gender play, it is apparently more acceptable for girls to cross gender boundaries than it is for boys. Why do you think this is so?

4. Consider your own childhood experiences and reflect upon a singular moment or a dynamic in your family through which appropriate gender display was encouraged, required, or disciplined. What were your perceptions then, and what are your perceptions now?

Making Connections

5. Kane's respondents seemed to agree that managing children's play is part of managing their development of sexual orientation, which Kane reads as "heteronormativity" (p. 96). Define this term, and examine other ways in which children's culture (schools, media, toys, products) is heteronormative.

6. Compare and contrast Kane's analysis of parenting with any one of the articles about gender and media from Chapter 5 of *Composing Gender*. What trends in the media make it difficult for parents to be comfortable with gender nonconformity? Do you think that parents are impacted as strongly as children by the images they see of children in the media?

What's Wrong with Cinderella?

Peggy Orenstein

Peggy Orenstein is a best-selling author on gender issues. Her books include *Cinderella Ate My Daughter: Dispatches from the Front Lines of the New Girlie-Girl Culture* (2011), from which this selection is drawn, and *Flux: Women on Sex, Work, Kids, Love and Life in a Half-Changed World* (2000). In 2012, the *Columbia Journalism Review* named Orenstein one of its "40 women who changed the media business in the past 40 years."

When Daisy was three, I lost her. Or, more precisely, I allowed her to get lost. She dashed off into the crowd at a reception after my niece's bat mitzvah, and I did not stop her. How much trouble could she get into, I reasoned: there were at least fifty Jewish mothers in the room. On the other hand, there was also a steep flight of marble stairs, doors that opened onto a dark parking lot leading to a reedy swamp, and a kitchen full of unattended chefs' knives. So when twenty minutes passed and she hadn't checked in, I began to get a little edgy. Okay, I panicked.

I pushed through the crowd shouting her name, leaving riled-up grandmothers in my wake. Then one of my niece's friends tugged at my sleeve. "She's over there," the girl said, pointing to a knot of ten or so teenagers.

I still did not see my child. So I stepped closer and peered over a boy's shoulder. There was Daisy, lying on the ground, her arms folded corpselike across her chest, her lips pursed, her expression somber.

"What about Isaac?" asked a girl, pushing forward a skinny six-year-old boy.

Without opening her eyes, Daisy shook her head. 5

"Michael?" a second girl tried. Another terse shake.

"Jeff?" Again the wordless dismissal.

I asked the boy in front of me what was going on.

"She's Snow White," he explained. "She ate the poison apple, and now we're trying to find the right prince to wake her."

I had never told Daisy the story of Snow White. I had purposely 10 kept it from her because, even setting aside the obvious sexism, Snow herself is such an incredible pill. Her sole virtue, as far as I can tell, is tidiness — she is forever scrubbing, dusting, nagging the dwarves to wash their filthy mitts. (Okay, the girl has an ear for a catchy melody, I'll give you that. But that's where it ends.) She is everything I imagined my daughter would reject, would not, in fact, ever encounter or even understand if she did, let alone embrace: the passive, personality-free princess swept off by a prince (who is enchanted solely by her beauty) to live in a happily-ever-after that he ultimately controls. Yet here was my girl, somehow having learned the plotline anyway, blissfully lying in wait for Love's First Kiss.

Daisy lifted a hand. *"Harry!"* she announced. *"Harry* has to be the prince."* Two girls instantly peeled off to search for her eleven-year-old cousin, while everyone else remained standing there, gazing at my princess, enthralled.

She was so confident of their presence that she still hadn't opened her eyes.

• • •

God knows, I was a Disney kid. I still have my bona fide mouse ears from 1970, monogrammed with an embroidered, loopy yellow PEGGY. I wore out my Close 'n Play on my Magic Mirror storybook records of *Peter Pan, Alice in Wonderland,* and even *Cinderella.* But until I had a daughter, I had never heard of the Disney Princesses. As a concept, I mean. It turns out there was a reason for that. They did not exist until 2000. That's when a former Nike executive named Andy Mooney rode into Disney on a metaphoric white horse to rescue its ailing consumer products division.

I spoke with Mooney one day in his fittingly palatial office in Burbank, California. In a rolling Scottish burr that was pretty darned Charming, he told me the now-legendary story: how, about a month into his tenure, he had flown to Phoenix to check out a "Disney on Ice" show and found himself surrounded by little girls in princess costumes. Princess costumes that were — horrors! — *homemade.* How had such a massive branding opportunity been overlooked? The very next day he called together his team and they began working on what would become known in-house as "Princess." It was a risky move: Disney had never marketed its characters separately from a film's release, and old-timers like Roy Disney considered it heresy to lump together those from different stories. That is why, these days, when the ladies appear on the same item, they never make eye contact. Each stares off in a slightly different direction, as if unaware of the others' presence. Now that I have told you, you'll always notice it. And let me tell you, it's freaky.

It is also worth noting that not all of the eight DPs are of royal extraction. Part of the genius of "Princess," Mooney admitted, is that its meaning is so broadly constructed that it actually has no meaning. Even Tinker Bell was originally a Princess, though her reign did not last. Meanwhile, although Mulan (the protofeminist young woman who poses as a boy to save China) and Pocahontas (an Indian chief's daughter) are officially part of the club, I defy you to find them in the stores. They were, until late 2009, the brownest-skinned princesses, as well as the ones with the least bling potential. You can gussy up Pocahontas's eagle feathers only so much. As for Mulan, when she does show up, it's in a kimono-like *hanfu*, the one that makes her miserable in the movie, rather than in her warrior's gear. Really, when you're talking Princess, you're talking Cinderella, Sleeping Beauty, Ariel, and Belle (the "modern" Princess, whose story shows that the right woman can turn a beast into a prince). Snow White and Jasmine are in the pantheon, too, though slightly less popular.

The first Princess items, released with no marketing plan, no focus groups, no advertising, sold as if blessed by a fairy godmother. Within a year, sales had soared to $300 million. By 2009, they were at $4 billion. Four *billion* dollars! There are more than twenty-six thousand Disney Princess items on the market, a number which, particularly when you exclude cigarettes, liquor, cars, and antidepressants, is staggering. "Princess" has not only become the fastest-growing brand the company has ever created, it is the largest franchise on the planet for girls ages two to six.

To this day, Disney conducts little market research on the Princess line, relying instead on the power of its legacy among mothers as well as the instant-read sales barometer of the theme parks and Disney Stores (Tiana, the much-ballyhooed "first African-American Princess," was somewhat of an exception, but we will get to her in a later chapter). "We simply gave girls what they wanted," Mooney said of the line's success, "although I don't think any of us grasped how much they wanted this. I wish I could sit here and take credit for having some grand scheme to develop this, but all we did was envision a little girl's room and think about how she could live out the princess fantasy. The counsel we gave to licensees was: What type of bedding would a princess want to sleep in? What kind of alarm clock would a princess want to wake up to? What type of television would a princess like to see? It's a rare case where you find a girl who has every aspect of her room bedecked in Princess, but if she ends up with three or four of these items, well, then, you have a very healthy business." Healthy, indeed. It has become nearly impossible for girls of a certain age *not* to own a few Princess trinkets. Even in our home, where neither Steven nor I have personally purchased a Princess item, several coloring books, a set of pencils, a Snow White doll, and a blow-up mattress have managed to infiltrate.

Meanwhile, by 2001, Mattel had brought out its own "world of girl" line of princess Barbie dolls, DVDs, toys, clothing, home decor, and myriad other products. At a time when Barbie sales were declining domestically, they became instant best sellers. Even Dora the Explorer, the intrepid, dirty-kneed adventurer, ascended to the throne: in 2004, after a two-part episode in which she turns into a "true princess," the Nickelodeon and Viacom consumer products division released a satin-gowned Magic Hair Fairytale Dora with hair that grows or shortens when her crown is touched. Among other phrases the bilingual doll utters: "Vámonos! Let's go to fairy-tale land!" and "Will you brush my hair?"

I do not question that little girls like to play princess: as a child, I certainly availed myself of my mom's cast-off rhinestone tiara from time to time. But when you're talking about 26,000 items (and that's just Disney), it's a little hard to say where "want" ends and "coercion" begins. Mooney was prepared for that concern and for my overall discomfort with the Princesses, who, particularly in his consumer products versions, are all about clothes, jewelry, makeup, and snaring a handsome husband.

"Look," he said, "I have friends whose son went through the Power 20 Rangers phase who castigated themselves over what they must've done wrong. Then they talked to other parents whose kids had gone through it. The boy passes through. The girl passes through. I see girls expanding their imagination through visualizing themselves as princesses, and then they pass through that phase and end up becoming lawyers, doctors, mothers, or princesses, whatever the case may be."

He had a point. I have never seen a study proving that playing princess *specifically* damages girls' self-esteem or dampens other aspirations. And trust me, I've looked. There is, however, ample evidence that the more mainstream media girls consume, the more importance they place on being pretty and sexy. And a ream of studies shows that teenage girls and college students who hold conventional beliefs about femininity — especially those that emphasize beauty and pleasing behavior — are less ambitious and more likely to be depressed than their peers. They are also less likely to report that they enjoy sex or insist that their partners use condoms. None of that bodes well for Snow White's long-term mental health.

Perhaps you are now picturing poor, hapless girls who are submissive, low-achieving, easily influenced: the kind whose hair hangs in front of their faces as they recede into the background. I know I have a hard time connecting such passivity to my own vibrant, vital daughter. Yet even can-do girls can be derailed — and surprisingly quickly —

by exposure to stereotypes. Take the female college students, all good at math, all enrolled in advanced calculus, who were asked to view a series of television commercials: four neutral ads (showing, say, cell phones or animals) were interspersed with two depicting clichés (a girl in raptures over acne medicine; a woman drooling over a brownie mix). Afterward they completed a survey and — *bing!* — the group who'd seen the stereotyped ads expressed less interest in math- and science-related careers than classmates who had seen only the neutral ones. Let me repeat: the effect was demonstrable after watching *two ads*. And guess who performed better on a math test, coeds who took it after being asked to try on a bathing suit or those who had been asked to try on a sweater? (Hint: the latter group; interestingly, male students showed no such disparity.)

Meanwhile, according to a 2006 survey of more than two thousand school-aged children, girls repeatedly described a paralyzing pressure to be "perfect": not only to get straight As and be the student body president, editor of the newspaper, and captain of the swim team but also to be "kind and caring," "please everyone, be very thin, and dress right." Rather than living the dream, then, those girls were straddling a contradiction: struggling to fulfill all the new expectations we have for them without letting go of the old ones. Instead of feeling greater latitude and choice in how to be female — which is what one would hope — they now feel they must not only "have it all" but *be* it all: Cinderella *and* Supergirl. Aggressive *and* agreeable. Smart *and* stunning. Does that make them the beneficiaries of new opportunities or victims of a massive con job?

> [Girls] now feel they must not only "have it all" but *be* it all: Cinderella *and* Supergirl. Aggressive *and* agreeable. Smart *and* stunning. Does that make them the beneficiaries of new opportunities or victims of a massive con job?

The answer is yes. That is, both are true, and that is what's so insidious. It would be one thing if the goal were more realistic or if girls were stoked about creating a new femininity, but it's not and they aren't. The number of girls who fretted excessively about their looks and weight actually *rose* between 2000 and 2006 (topping their concern over schoolwork), as did their reported stress levels and their rates of depression and suicide. It is as if the more girls achieve the more obsessed they become with appearance — not dissimilar to the way the ideal of the "good mother" was ratcheted up just as adult women flooded the workforce. In her brilliant book *Enlightened Sexism*, Susan Douglas refers to this as the bargain girls and women strike, the price of success, the way they unconsciously defuse the threat their progress poses to male dominance. "We can excel in school, play sports, go to college, aspire to — and get — jobs previously reserved for men, be working mothers, and so forth. But in exchange we must obsess about our faces, weight, breast size, clothing brands, decorating, perfectly calibrated child-rearing, about pleasing men and being envied by other women."

• • •

A new banner unfurled over the entrance of Daisy's preschool when   25
I dropped by one fall morning: a little girl, adorned with a glittering plastic-and-rhinestone tiara and matching earrings, grinned down from it. WELCOME TO OUR CAMPUS, the banner read. The image might have irritated me in any case — even my kid's *school* had bought into the idea that all girls should aspire to the throne — but what was really cringe-making was the fact that this was part of a Jewish temple. When I was growing up, the last thing you wanted to be called was a "princess": it conjured up images of a spoiled, self-centered brat with a freshly bobbed nose who runs to "Daddy" at the least provocation. The Jewish American Princess was the repository for my community's self-hatred, its ambivalence over assimilation — it was Jews turning against their girls as a way to turn against themselves. Was this photograph a sign we had so transcended the *Goodbye, Columbus* stereotype that we could now embrace it?

"What about Queen Esther?" asked Julie, the mother of one of Daisy's classmates, when I questioned the picture's subtext. "She saved the Jewish people. Shouldn't girls try to be like her?"

Julie, a forty-five-year-old owner of a Web consulting company, was among several mothers I had asked to join me after drop-off for a chat about princess culture. Each one had a preschool-aged daughter obsessed with Disney royalty. They also knew I had my qualms about the subject, which they did not necessarily share. I wanted to know, from a mother's perspective, why they allowed — in some cases even encouraged — their girls to play princess. Did they think it was innocuous? Beneficial? Worrisome? Healthy?

"I think feminism erred in the 1960s by negating femininity," announced Mara, a thirty-six-year-old education consultant who was currently home with her kids. Her voice sounded tight, almost defiant. "That was a mistake. I want my daughter to have a strong identity as a girl, as a woman, as a *female*. And being pretty in our culture is very important. I don't want her to ever doubt that she's pretty. So if she wants to wear a princess dress and explore that side of herself, I don't want to stand in the way."

She folded her arms and collapsed back on her chair, as if she had said her piece. But before I could respond, she cocked her head and added, "On the other hand, I also have a son, and we really encourage his intelligence. I worry about that. A reward for her is 'You look so pretty, you look so beautiful.' People tell her that all the time, and we do, too. We tell *him*, 'You're so smart.'"

Dana, a thirty-eight-year-old stay-at-home mom, who had been 30 watching Mara with a slightly awestruck expression, spoke up. "For me it's a matter of practicality," she said. "Having those Disney Princess outfits around the house is really helpful for the endless play-dates. And Eleanor loves to swim, so she identifies with Ariel."

I began to ask Dana how she felt about the rest of the *Little Mermaid* story, but she cut me off. "Oh, I don't let the actual *story* in the house," she said. "Just the *costumes*. Eleanor doesn't know the stories."

That turned out to be Mara's policy, too. The issue to her was not princesses, it was plotlines. "Those stories are horrible," she said, making a face. "Every single one is the same: it's about romance, love, and being rescued by the prince. I *will* protect my daughter from that."

Thinking back on my own girl's inexplicable acquaintance with the Snow White story, I had to wonder whether that was possible. I'd believed I could keep out the tales *and* the toys but had failed on both counts. What were the odds, then, that you could permit one without the other? I had spent a lot of time with Dana's daughter and already knew she could give a full recitation of Ariel's story. Dana shrugged. "Well, yeah, she hears it from her friends," she admitted. "But at least not at home."

What gave those mothers pause, then, was the fantasy the stories promoted that a man would take care of you. Yet the tales also provide the characters with some context, a narrative arc. Cinderella may ride off with the prince, but before that, she spends much of her time dressed in tatters, offering children object lessons about kindness, forbearance, and humility. Without that backstory, what was left? What did they imagine a storyless "princess" represented to the girls?

That's when Julie piped up. "I think it's all about being looked at," 35 she said, "being admired. And about special treatment." She rolled her eyes. "Receiving it, not giving it."

"And it's *fun*," Dana pointed out.

Hell, yeah, it's fun. Who doesn't love nail polish with flower appliqués? Who doesn't like to play dress-up now and again, swoosh about in silk and velvet? Daisy once whispered conspiratorially to me, "Mom, did you know that girls can choose all kinds of things to wear, but boys can only wear pants?" There it was: dressing up fancy, at least for now, was something she felt she *got* to do, not something she *had* to do. It was a source of power and privilege, much like her game of Snow White in which the action revolved around and was controlled by her.

Whereas boys . . . even here in Berkeley, a friend's seven-year-old son was teased so ruthlessly about his new, beloved pink bike that within a week he refused to ride it. It is quite possible that boys, too, would wear sequins if only they could. Isabelle Cherney, a professor of psychology at Creighton University, found that nearly half of boys aged five to thirteen, when ushered alone into a room and told they could play with anything, chose "girls'" toys as frequently as "boys'" — provided they believed nobody would find out. Particularly, their fathers: boys as young as four said their daddies would think it was "bad" if they played with "girls'" toys, even something as innocuous as miniature dishes. Boys were also more likely to sort playthings based on how they perceived gender roles (such as "Dad uses tools, so hammers are for boys"), whereas girls figured that if they themselves enjoyed a toy — *any* toy — it was, ipso facto, for girls. So it seems that, even as they have loosened up on their daughters, dads continue to vigorously police masculinity in their sons. I believe it: consider the progressive pal of mine who proudly showed off the Hot Wheels set he had bought for his girl but balked when his boy begged for a tutu. Who's to say, then, which sex has greater freedom?

I am almost willing to buy that argument: that boys are the ones who are more limited; that little girls *need* to feel beautiful; that being on display, being admired for how they look, is critical to their developing femininity and fragile self-esteem; that princess sets their imaginations soaring; that its popularity is evidence that we've moved past 1970s feminist rigidity. Except that, before meeting with the preschool moms, I had flipped through a stack of drawings each child in Daisy's class had made to complete the sentence "If I were a [blank], I'd [blank] to the store." (One might say, for instance, "If I were a ball, I'd bounce to the store.") The boys had chosen to be a whole host of things: firemen, spiders, superheroes, puppies, tigers, birds, athletes, raisins. The girls fell into exactly four camps: princess, fairy, butterfly, and ballerina (one especially enthusiastic girl claimed them all: a "princess, butterfly, fairy ballerina"). How, precisely, does that, as Disney's Andy Mooney suggested, expand their horizons? The boys seemed to be exploring the world; the girls were exploring femininity. What they "got" to do may have been uniquely theirs, but it was awfully circumscribed. "Yeah, I was surprised," the teacher admitted when I asked about it. "The girls had so little range in their ideas. We tried to encourage them to choose other things, but they wouldn't."

Of course, girls are not buying the 24/7 princess culture all on their own. So the question is not only why *they* like it (which is fairly obvious) but what it offers their parents. Julie may have been onto something on that front: princesses are, by definition, special, elevated creatures. And don't we all feel our girls are extraordinary, unique, and beautiful? Don't we want them to share that belief for as long as possible, to think that—just by their existence, by birthright— they are the chosen ones? Wouldn't we like their lives to be forever charmed, infused with magic and sparkle? I know I want that for my daughter.

Or do I? Among other things, princesses tend to be rather isolated in their singularity. Navigating the new world of friendships is what preschool is all about, yet the DPs, you will recall, won't even *look* at one another. Daisy had only one fight with her best friend during their three years of preschool—a conflict so devastating that, at pickup time, I found the other girl sobbing in the hallway, barely able to breathe. The source of their disagreement? My darling daughter had insisted that there could be only *one* Cinderella in their games— only *one* girl who reigned supreme—and it was she. Several hours and a small tantrum later, she apologized to the girl, saying that from now on there could be *two* Cinderellas. But the truth was, Daisy had gotten it right the first time: there *is* only one princess in the Disney tales, one girl who gets to be exalted. Princesses may confide in a sympathetic mouse or teacup, but, at least among the best-known stories, they do not have girlfriends. God forbid Snow White should give Sleeping Beauty a little support.

Let's review: princesses avoid female bonding. Their goals are to be saved by a prince, get married (among the DP picture books at Barnes & Noble: *My Perfect Wedding* and *Happily Ever After Stories*) and be taken care of for the rest of their lives. Their value derives largely from their appearance. They are rabid materialists. They *might* affect your daughter's interest in math. And yet . . . parents cannot resist them. Princesses seem to have tapped into our unspoken, nonrational wishes. They may also assuage our fears: Cinderella and Sleeping Beauty may be sources of comfort, of stability in a rapidly changing world. Our daughters will shortly be tweeting and Facebooking and doing things that have yet to be invented, things that are beyond our ken. Princesses are uncomplicated, classic, something solid that we can understand and share with them, even if they are a bit problematic. They provide a way to play with our girls that is similar to how we played, a common language of childhood fun.

That certainly fits into what Disney found in a survey of preschool girls' mothers: rather than "beautiful," the women more strongly associate princesses with "creating fantasy," "inspiring," "compassionate."

And "safe." That one piqued my interest. By "safe," I would wager that they mean that being a Princess fends off premature sexualization, or what parents often refer to as the pressure "to grow up too soon." There is that undeniable sweetness, that poignancy of seeing girls clomp off to the "ball" in their incongruous heels and gowns. They are so gleeful, so guileless, so delightfully delighted. The historian Gary Cross, who writes extensively on childhood and consumption, calls such parental response "wondrous innocence." Children's wide-eyed excitement over the products we buy them pierces through our own boredom as consumers and as adults, reconnecting us to our childhoods: it makes us *feel* again. The problem is that our very dependence on our children's joy erodes it: over time, they become as jaded as we are by new purchases — perhaps more so. They rebel against the "cuteness" in which we've indulged them — and, if we're honest, imposed upon them — by taking on the studied irony and indifferent affect of "cool."

Though both boys and girls engage in that cute-to-cool trajectory, for girls specifically, being "cool" means looking hot. Given that, then, there may indeed be, or at least *could* be, a link between princess diadems and Lindsay Lohan's panties (or lack thereof). But in the short term, when you're watching your preschooler earnestly waving her wand, it sure doesn't feel that way. To the contrary: princess play feels like proof of our daughters' innocence, protection against the sexualization it may actually be courting. It reassures us that, despite the pressure to be precocious, little girls are still — and ever will be — little girls. And that knowledge restores our faith not only in wonder but, quite possibly, in goodness itself. . . .

Understanding the Text

1. Explain Orenstein's reservations about allowing her daughter to hear the "Snow White" fairy tale. What about Snow White and the Disney princesses makes her imagine that they could be detrimental to her daughter's understanding of femininity?

2. How does Orenstein conceptualize the role of more powerful, independent characters created for girls? Do these kinds of characters offset the impact of the princesses?

3. What is Orenstein's problem with Andy Mooney's explanation that in marketing the Disney princesses the company simply "gave girls what they wanted" (p. 101)?

4. What does Orenstein claim that "princess play" (p. 108) offers to parents, and what are the risks she identifies in parental encouragement of "princess play"?

Reflection and Response

5. What about "princesses" in general seems to suggest negative stereotypes about femininity to Orenstein? What characteristics do princesses embody that make Orenstein uncomfortable with them as icons of femininity?

6. For Orenstein, why might the emphasis on glamour and beauty (in the Disney princesses and in the media at large) be "bad" for young girls, even while they might perceive these activities as "fun"?

7. Orenstein suggests that the "princesses" cannot be held solely responsible for constructing girls' beliefs about femininity. What other kinds of characters appear on television and film that might support or contradict Orenstein's claims about media impact on young girls?

Making Connections

8. Visit a toy store and look for toys that are specifically aimed at girls that are not princess-themed. What trends do you see? What is the latest and newest way to appeal to young girls other than princess toys?

9. One of the most recent toy inventions is an engineering toy specifically aimed at girls called GoldieBlox, in which girls can use pink ribbons, wheels, pegs, and animal figurines to construct small machines. The inventor, a female engineer from Stanford University, hopes that this toy will encourage young girls to consider a career in the STEM (science, technology, engineering, and mathematics) fields. One of the toy's taglines is "Gold is the new pink." Look at the GoldieBlox Web site or find a similar engineering- or science-based toy aimed at girls and write about whether these kinds of toys might be counteracting some of what Orenstein notices about the princess toy market. Are these valuable additions to girls' toys, or are they doing the same old thing by using pink and other "girly" things to trick girls into using a construction set?

10. Orenstein only touches on the sexualization of girls' toys. A valuable project, then, would be to connect Orenstein's insights about girls' toys with the readings in *Composing Gender* about the sexualization of girls in the media, such as those by Adler (p. 281) and Dines (p. 250). What connections do you see? How are toys affected by the larger trend toward the sexualization of girls?

"Looking for a Team Mom": Separating the Men from the Moms

Michael Messner

Michael Messner is a professor of sociology and gender studies at the University of Southern California. His work has long focused on men, masculinity, and sports, and his books include *Politics of Masculinities: Men in Movements* (1997), *Taking the Field: Women, Men, and Sports* (2002), and the book from which this selection is drawn, *It's All for the Kids: Gender, Families and Youth Sports* (2009). His current scholarship focuses on male activists working to prevent gender-based violence.

February 14: A winter chill lingers and the field is soggy from recent rains. But here we are at the baseball field, starting another Little League Baseball season, so it must be spring. It's the first practice of the season for this 11- and 12-year-old boys' team. In addition to myself, three more dads have volunteered to assist Coach Dean. The practice drills are all ones that we learned at the coaches' clinic the previous day. I overhear one assistant coach say to Dean, "So, are the women still laying low?" Dean, with a chuckle, replies, "Yes! So far no team mom!" The assistant coach quips, "I guess nobody wants to do it, huh?"

February 23: Coach Dean, in his almost daily e-mails to the team's parents, continues to include a set-off note that reads: "Still looking for a Team Mom . . ."

It strikes me that if it were worded as "team parent," this would at least theoretically expand the potential pool times two!

February 26: At the team's first practice game, I'm standing alone by the dugout, and behind me sitting in the stands are three moms. One of them says, in hushed tones, "I hear they are still looking for a team mom." Another giggles and whispers conspiratorially, "I'm laying low on that one." Another laughs and says, more loudly, "Me too. I'm sure they can find a dad to do it." They all laugh.

By the second game, the "team mom" is Tina, Coach Dean's wife.

When we asked a longtime Little League Softball manager, Albert Riley, why he thinks most of the head coaches are men while nearly all of the team parents are women, he said with a shrug, "They give opportunities to everybody to manage or coach and it just so happens that no women volunteer, you know?" Soccer coach Shelley Parsons saw a certain inevitability to this adult division of labor: "The women always volunteer to be the team moms, the women have always volunteered to make the banners, and the dads have always volunteered to be the refs and the assistant coaches." Riley's and Parsons' statements were typical for head coaches, who generally offered up explanations grounded in individual choice: faced with equal opportunities to volunteer, men just *choose* to be coaches while women *choose* to be team parents.

But . . . the gendered division of labor among men and women volunteers in youth coaching results not simply from an accumulation of individual choices; rather, it is produced through a profoundly *social* process. I will draw from interviews with head coaches to illustrate how gender divisions of labor among adult volunteers are shaped by gendered language and belief systems and are seen as "natural" extensions of gendered divisions of labor in families and workplaces. I will also draw from field observations to illustrate how the gendered organizational context of youth sports shapes people's expectations, ideas, and choices about men's and women's roles as coaches or team parents. . . .

Recruiting Dads and Moms to Help

There is a lot of work involved in organizing a successful youth soccer, baseball, or softball season. A head coach needs help from two, three, even four other parents who will serve as assistant coaches during practices and games. Parents also have to take responsibility for numerous support tasks like organizing snacks, making team banners, working in the snack bar during games, collecting donations for year-end gifts for the coaches, and organizing team events and year-end parties. In AYSO [American Youth Soccer Organization], parents also serve as volunteer referees for games. When we asked head coaches how they determined who would help them with these assistant coaching and other support tasks, a very common story resulted: the coach would call a beginning-of-the-season team meeting, sometimes preceded by a letter or e-mail to parents, and ask for volunteers. Nearly always, they said, they ended up with dads volunteering to help as assistant coaches and moms volunteering to be team parents. Soccer coach Wendy Lytle told a typical story:

At the beginning of the season I sent a little introductory letter [that said] I really badly need an assistant coach and referee and a team mom. You know anyone that is keen on that, let's talk about it at the first practice. And this year one guy picked up the phone and said, "Please can I be your assistant coach." And I spoke to another one of the mums who I happen to know through school and she said, "Oh, I can do the team mum if you find someone to help me." And by the first practice, they'd already discussed it and it was up and running.

We can see from Lytle's statement how the assistant coach and team-parent positions are sometimes informally set up even before the first team meeting, and how a coach's assumption that the team parent will be a "team mom" might make it more likely that women end up in these positions. When asked how he selected a team parent, Soccer coach Gilbert Morales said, "I just generally leave it to a volunteer issue. I ask for volunteers." When asked who normally volunteers, he replied, "Usually female. Usually female. I've found that most of the team parents are usually team moms." Even coaches who consciously try to emphasize that "team parent" is not necessarily a woman's job, like softball coach Rosa Ramirez, find that only women end up volunteering to do this:

Before the season started we had a team meeting and I let the parents know that I would need a team parent, and I strongly stressed parent, *because I don't think it should always be a mother. But we did end up with the mom doing it, and she assigns snacks and stuff like that.*

None of the head coaches we interviewed said that they currently had a man as the team parent, but four recalled that they had once had a man as a team parent (though one of these four coaches said, "Now that I think about it, that guy actually volunteered his wife to do it"). When we asked if they had ever had a team parent who was a man, nearly all of the coaches said never. Many of them laughed at the very thought. Soccer coach Joan Ring exclaimed with a chuckle, "I just can't imagine! I wonder if they've *ever* had a team mom who's a dad. I don't know. Same with the banner. That would be funny to see: has a man ever made a banner? I don't know (laughs)." Soccer coach Doug Berger stammered his way through his response, punctuating his words with sarcastic laughter: "Ha! In fact, that whole concept — I don't think I've ever *heard* of a team dad [*laughs*]. Uh — there *is* no team dad. I've never heard of a team dad. But I don't know why that would be." A few coaches, like softball coach Lisette Taylor, resorted to family metaphors to explain why they think there are few if any men volunteering to be team parents: "Oh, it's always a mom [*laughs*]. Team mom. That's why it's called team *mom.* You know, the coach is a male. And the mom — I mean, that's the *housekeeping* — you know: assign the snack." 5

Gendered Language

In the late 1970s, a popular riddle made the rounds that went something like this:

A man is driving along in his car when he accidentally hits a boy on a bike. He gets out of the car, looks down and sees the injured boy, and says, "Oh, God! I've hit my own son!" He rushes the boy to the hospital, and in the emergency room, the doctor walks in, looks at the boy, and exclaims: "Oh God! I can't do surgery on this boy! He's my son!" How is this possible?

The answer, of course, is that the doctor is the boy's *mother*, and the point of the riddle is to illustrate the automatic assumption in the mind of the listener that *doctor* always implies a *man*. Another way to put this is to say that there are gendered assumptions in the language that we link to certain professions, so much so that often, when the person holding the position is in the statistical minority, we attach a modifier, such as *male* nurse, *male* secretary, *woman* judge, *woman* doctor. Or, *woman* head coach.

As feminist linguists have shown, language is a powerful element of social life—it not only reflects social realities like gender divisions of labor, it also helps to construct our notions of what is "normal" and what is an "aberration."

Over and over, in interviews with coaches, during team meetings, and in interactions during games, practices, and team parties, I noticed this gendered language. Most obvious was the frequent slippage from official term "team parent" to the commonly used term "team mom." But I also noticed that a man coach was normally just called a "coach," while a woman coach was often gender-marked as a "woman coach." As feminist linguists have shown, language is a powerful element of social life — it not only reflects social realities like gender divisions of labor, it also helps to construct our notions of what is "normal" and what is an "aberration."[1] Joan Ring's statement, "I wonder if they've *ever* had a team mom who's a dad," illustrates how gendered language makes this whole idea of a male team parent seem incongruous, even laughable, to

---

[1] Barrie Thorne, Cheris Kramarae, and Nancy Henley, *Language, Gender, and Society* (Rowley, MA: Newbury House, 1983). For an application of theories of gendered language to sport, see Michael A. Messner, Margaret Carlisle Duncan, and Kerry Jensen, "Separating the Men from the Girls: The Gendered Language of Televised Sports," *Gender and Society* 7 (1993), pp. 121–137.

many. In youth sports, this gendered language supports the notion that a team is structured very much like a "traditional" heterosexual family: the head coach — nearly always a man — is the leader and the public face of the team; the team parent — nearly always a woman — is working less visibly behind the scenes, doing the "housekeeping" support work; assistant coaches — mostly men, but including the occasional woman — help the coach on the field during practices and games.

Teams are even talked about sometimes as "families," and while we never heard a head coach referred to as a team's "dad," we did often and consistently hear the team parent referred to as the "team mom." This gendered language, drawn from family relations, gives us some good initial hints as to how coach and team-parent roles remain so sex-segregated. Gendered language, in short, helps structure people's thoughts in ways that shape and constrain their actions. Is a man who volunteers to be a team parent now a "team mom?"

Gender Ideology and Gendered Organizations

When we pressed the coaches to consider why it is nearly always 10
women who volunteer to be the team parent, many seemed never to have considered this question before. Some of the men coaches seemed especially befuddled by this question, and appeared to assume that women's team-parenting work is a result of an almost "natural" decision on the part of the woman to volunteer to help in this way. Some men, like soccer coach Carlos Ruiz, made sense of this volunteer division of labor by referring to the ways that it reflected divisions of labor in their own families and in their community: "In this area, we have a lot of stay-at-home moms, so it seems to kind of fall to them to take over those roles." Similarly, baseball coach Albert Riley, whose wife served as the team parent, explained: "I think it's because they probably do it at home. You know, I mean, my wife — even though she can't really commit the time to coach, I don't think she would *want* to coach — uh, she's very good with that [team parent] stuff." Soccer coach Al Evans explained the gender divisions on youth sports teams in terms of people's comfort with a nostalgic notion of "the classical family":

I suppose unconsciously, on that sort of Freudian level, it's like you got the dad and he's the boss and you got the mom and she's the support, and then you got all the little siblings, so in a sense you're making this picture that, without really drawing too much attention to it — that's sort of the classical family, you know, it's like the Donna Reed family is AYSO, right? They have these assigned gender roles, and people in San Marino and South

Pasadena, probably all over the United States, they're fairly comfortable with them, right? It's, uh, maybe insidious, maybe not, [but] framed in the sort of traditional family role of dad, mom, kids — people are going to be comfortable with that.

Ted Miller, a Little League baseball coach, broadened the explanation, drawing connections to divisions of labor in his workplace:

It's kinda like in business. I work in real estate and most of your deal makers that are out there on the front lines, so to speak, making the deals, doing the shuckin' and jivin', doing the selling, are men. It's a very good ol' boys' network on the real estate brokerage side. There are a ton of females who are on the property management side, because it's housekeeping, it's managing, it's like running the household, it's behind the scenes, it's like cooking in the kitchen — [laughs] — I mean I hate to say that, but it's that kind of role that's secondary. Coach is out in the front leading the squad, mom sitting behind making sure that the snacks are in order and all that. You know, just the way it is.

Having a male coach and a team mom just seemed normal to Evans ("You know, just the way it is") because it seemed to flow naturally from divisions of labor in his household and in his workplace — gendered divisions of labor that have the good ol' boys operating publicly as the leaders, "on the front lines . . . shuckin' and jivin'," while the women are offering support "behind the scenes, . . . like cooking in the kitchen." Echoing this view, soccer coach Paul Leung said, "I hate to use the analogy, but it's like a secretary: you got a boss and you've got a secretary, and I think that's where most of the opportunities for women to be active in the sports is, as the secretary."

It was striking to me how several of the men's explanations for divisions of labor between women and men were offered somewhat apologetically — "I hate to say that," "I hate to use the analogy," — as though they suspected that their beliefs might be considered politically incorrect. When explaining why it is that team parents are almost exclusively women, a small number of women coaches also seemed to see it as natural, like most of the men coaches saw it. Pam Burke, a soccer coach who also served as a "team mom" for her daughter's team, held conservative views on gender. A homemaker, Burke disagreed with the woman coaches who, for feminist reasons, disapproved of the gendered nature of the "team mom" position. In her view, women's support and nurturance needs to be respected and valorized, though she too admitted to some ambivalence about these issues:

I think we have to be careful in making that a negative, because more often than not, at least in this community, the father is the primary breadwinner, so he's working forty to fifty hours a week, and those are his responsibilities. We have lots of stay-at-home moms here in this community, and those are the people who have the time [to serve as a team parent], and these are typically mothering-woman sorts of skills. I mean, you can call it a stereotype and you can call it bad, but it's true: if it weren't for me, my daughter's coach would be a disaster. He's doing soccer [and] he doesn't want to do this other stuff. And it takes like five minutes, and it's not a lot of work, and it's what we do as women, and mothers certainly, and for the most part we do it well, so I don't take offense to that. I have a sort of strange view actually of women and men in the world. I don't think women should be in positions of leadership over men, so I'm, I kind of have this struggle inside of me because I recognize the many differences between men and women, and I take kind of a controversial stand over it, because I don't think we should make us equal in ways that I don't think that we are. I don't think we are the same, and I think we should celebrate the differences.

Many women coaches, however, saw the gendering of the "team-parent" position as a problem, and made sense of its persistence, as did many of the men, by referring to the ways that it reflects family- and work-related divisions of labor. But several of the women coaches added an additional dimension to their explanations, by focusing on *why they think the men don't or won't* consider doing team-parent work. Soccer coach Wendy Lytle said, "I think it's because the dads want to be involved with the action. And they are not interested in doing paperwork and collecting money for photos or whatever it is. They are not interested in doing that sort of stuff." Jessica Torres, another soccer coach, extended this point: "I think it's probably, well, identity, which is probably why not many men do it. You know, they think, that is a woman's job, like secretary or nurse or, you know." In short, many of the women coaches were cognizant of the ways that the "team-parent" job was viewed by men, like all "women's work," as non-masculine and thus undesirable. Jessica Torres found it ironically funny that her husband, in fact, does most of the cooking and housework at home but won't take on the role of team parent for his daughter's team. When asked if changing the name to "team dad" might get more men to volunteer, she replied with a sigh,

I don't know. I wish my husband would be a team dad because he's just very much more domesticated than I am [laughs]. You know, "Bring all the

snacks, honey, hook us up," you know. I think there's a lot of men out there, but they don't want to be perceived as being domesticated.

    Torres's comment illustrates how — even for a man who does a sub-   15
stantial amount of the family labor at home — publicly taking on a job
that is defined as "feminine" threatens to saddle men with a "domesticated" public image that would be embarrassing or even humiliating to them. That some women coaches speculated as to why men
would *not* consider being team parents, while the men coaches relegated their responses to considering merely why women *do* volunteer
as team parents, indicates that at least some of the women coaches
have a more nuanced (and critical) understanding of gender than do
most of the men coaches. As Ellen Lessing observed, her voice drip-
ping with sarcasm, "All the [support] jobs are [done by] women, except for the assistant coach. That's the — the *man's* job." From these
explanations, we can see that many coaches — both women and men —
believe that men become coaches and women become team parents
largely because these public roles fit with their domestic proclivities
and skills. But the women add an important dimension to this explanation: women do the team-parent work because it has to be done . . .
and because they know that the men won't do it. . . .

Challenges and Resistance

The head coach's common assumption that fathers will volunteer to
be assistant coaches and mothers to be team moms creates a context
that powerfully channels men and women into these directions.
Backed by these "commonsense" understandings of gendered divisions of labor, many men and women just "go with the flow" of this
channeling process. Their choices and actions help to reproduce the
existing gendered patterns of the organization. But some don't, choosing instead to swim against the tide. Ellen Lessing already had several seasons of experience as a head soccer coach when she attended
the first team meeting for her youngest child's team:

*At our first team meeting the coach announced, "I'm looking for a couple of
you to help me out as assistant coaches," and he looked directly at the men,
and only at the men. None of them volunteered. And it was really amazing because he didn't even look at me or at any of the other women. So
after the meeting I went up to him and said, "Hey, I've coached soccer for
like ten seasons; I can help you out, okay?" And he agreed, so I'm the assistant coach for him.*

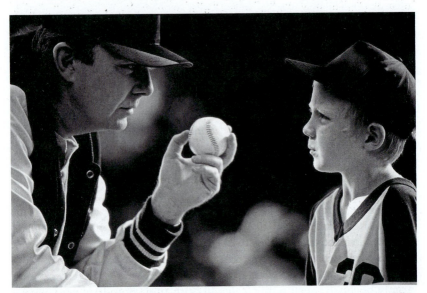

Predominantly, coaching in boys' youth sports organizations is done by men, while women play supporting roles.

This first team meeting, as Ellen Lessing described it, is an example of a normal gendered interaction that, if it had gone unchallenged, would have served to reproduce the usual gender divisions of labor on the team. It's likely that many women in these situations notice the ways that men are, to adopt sociologist Pat Martin's term, informally (and probably unconsciously) "mobilizing masculinities" in ways that serve to reproduce men's positions of centrality.[2] But Lessing's ten years of coaching experience gave her the confidence and the "capital" that allowed her not only to see and understand, but also to challenge the very gendered selection process that was taking place at this meeting. Many — perhaps most — mothers do not have this kind of background, and so when faced with this sort of moment, they just go with the flow. On another occasion, as the following story from my field notes describes, I observed a highly athletic and coaching-inclined woman assertively use her abilities in a way that initially *seemed* to transcend this kind of sex-segregation process, only to be relegated symbolically at season's end as a "team mom":

---

[2] Patricia Yancy Martin, "Mobilizing Masculinities: Women's Experiences of Men at Work," *Organization* 8 (2001), pp. 587–618.

*A new baseball season, the first team meeting of the year; a slew of dads
volunteer to be assistant coaches. Coach George combs the women for a
team mom, and gets some resistance; at first nobody will do it, but then
he finds a volunteer. At the first few practices, few of the fathers who had
volunteered to assistant coach actually show up. Sandra, a mom, clearly
is into baseball, very knowledgeable and athletic, and takes the field. She
pitches to the kids, gives them good advice. On the day when George is
passing out forms for assistant coaches to sign, he hands her one too. She
accepts it, in a matter-of-fact way. It appears to me that her work with the
kids at the practices is being acknowledged by Coach George with assistant coach status.*

*At a later practice, there are three dads (including me) filling in for
Coach George, who had to work. Sandra is there, but hangs on the mar-
gins, almost as though she's waiting to be invited to help. As no invitation
seems forthcoming, she eventually finds a niche, backing up fielders, giving them pointers. I am struck again at how knowledgeable she is, a good
teacher.*

*Though few dads show up for many of the practices, there never seems
to be a shortage of dads to serve as assistant coaches at the games. Coach
George invites Sandra to coach third base once, but beyond that she is
never included in an on-field coaching role during a game.*

*End of season, team party. Coach George hands out awards to all the
kids. Then he hands out gift certificates to all the assistant coaches, but
does not include Sandra. Then he hands out gift certificates to the "team
moms," and includes Sandra here, even though I don't recall her doing any
team-parent tasks. Amazing! She had clearly been acting as an assistant
coach all season long.*

This story illustrates how, on the one hand, a woman volunteer
can informally circumvent the "sorting process" that pushes her toward the "team mom" role by persistently showing up to practices
and assertively doing the work of a coach (and doing it well). As Barrie Thorne showed in her groundbreaking research on children on
school playgrounds, when children cross gender boundaries (e.g., a
girl who plays football with the boys; a boy who plays jump rope with
the girls), "they challenge the oppositional structure of traditional
gender arrangements."[3] However, Thorne also points out that individual incidences of gender crossing are often handled informally, in

---

[3] Barrie Thorne, *Gender Play: Girls and Boys in High School* (New Brunswick, NJ: Rutgers
University Press, 1993), p. 133, notes that "successful crossers" of gender boundaries
are usually persistent and have certain skills that make their crossing acceptable to
members of the dominant group.

ways that affirm rather than challenge gender boundaries: an individual girl who joins the boys' game gets defined "as a token, a kind of 'fictive boy,' not unlike many women tokens in predominantly male settings, whose presence does little to challenge the existing arrangements."[4] Similarly, Sandra's successful "crossing" led to her becoming accepted as an assistant coach during practices. However, the fact that she was accepted as a practice coach, but rarely recognized as a "real" coach during games, made her (to adapt Thorne's terms) a kind of "token," or "fictive," coach, whose gender transgression was probably unknown to the many adults who never attended practices. So, in the final moment of the season, when adults and children alike were being publicly recognized for their contributions to the team, she was labeled and rewarded for being a "team mom," thus symbolically reaffirming the categorical gender boundaries. . . .

The Sex-Category Sorting Process

. . . I have revealed the workings of what I call the *sex-category sorting process*. Through this process, the vast majority of women volunteers are actively sorted into a team-parent position, and the vast majority of men volunteers are sorted into an assistant coach position, which in turn serves as the key entry point to the pipeline for head coaching positions. To say that people are "sorted" is not to deny their active agency in this process. Rather, it is to underline the fact that what people often think of as "free individual choices" are actually choices that are shaped (both constrained and enabled) by social contexts. In particular, I have shown how women's choices to become "team parents" are constrained by the fact that few, if any, men will volunteer to do this important, but less visible and less honored job. Women's choices are enabled by their being actively recruited — "volunteered" — by head coaches, and sometimes by other parents on the team, to become the "team mom." We have seen how men's choices not to volunteer for team-parent positions, and instead to volunteer as assistant coaches, are shaped by the gendered assumptions of head coaches and by informal interactions at the initial team meeting. Moreover, the terms "coach" and "team mom" are saturated with gendered assumptions that are consistent with most people's universe of meanings. These gendered meanings mesh with — and mutually reinforce — the conventional gendered divisions of labor and power in the organization, in ways that make people's decisions

---

[4] Thorne 1993, 133.

to "go with the flow" appear "natural." And we have seen how having women do the background support work while men do the visible leadership work on the team is also made to appear natural, to the extent that it reiterates the gender divisions of labor that many parents experience in their families and in their workplaces.[5]

In short, people's gendered sense of identity, their informal gendered interactions and language, the gendered divisions of labor in their organizations, and their commonly held beliefs about gender and families together fuel a tremendous inertia that tends mostly to make this profoundly social sex-category sorting process appear to be natural. As sociologists Maria Charles and David Grusky have astutely asserted, "The insidiousness of essentialism" — the belief in natural, categorical differences between men and women — "is that it clothes segregation in voluntarist terms."[6] It seemed to me at times that, despite the evidence around them of a sex-category sorting process at work, many of the people we interviewed held stubbornly to their belief that every individual was doing precisely what she or he had freely chosen to do. People's adherence to an ideology and language of individual choice, as the words of soccer coach Al Evans illustrate, makes it difficult for them to see and understand the social nature of the sex-category sorting process:

In most teams, you've got the team manager or your team mom. I hate to use the — to genderize that position — but generally that is what happens, is the mom gets picked to do that.

[She's picked, or she volunteers?]

She volunteers.

The sex-segregated context of sport is a key to understanding the power of essentialism in this sorting process. Unlike in most other institutions, the move toward equality (e.g., the passage of Title IX, the explosive increase in youth sports for girls, expanded high school and college sports for girls and women) takes a sex-segregated form, backed not by ideas of integration but by a kind of "separate but

---

[5] Marjukka Ollilainen and Toni Calisanti, "Metaphors at Work: Maintaining the Salience of Gender in Self-Managing Teams," *Gender and Society* 21 (2007), pp. 5–27, in their study of self-managing teams that are intended to break down gender divisions in the workplace, show how team members' use of "family metaphors" tends to maintain the salience of gender, and thus helps to reproduce a gendered division of labor.

[6] Maria Charles and David B. Grusky, *Occupational Ghettos: The Worldwide Segregation of Women and Men* (Stanford, CA: Stanford University Press, 2004), p. 336.

equal" ethic, which continues always to make gender salient. Time after time, I hear leaders of leagues, and some women coaches, saying that the league leadership works hard to recruit more women coaches but just can't get them to volunteer. The *formal agency* here is to "get more women," but what sociologist Pat Martin calls the *informal practicing of gender* amounts to a collective and (mostly) nonreflexive sorting system that, at the entry level, puts most women and men on separate paths.[7] . . . The mechanisms of this collective practicing of gender are individually embodied and displayed, given voice through informal interactions, made to seem normal through their congruence with family and workplace divisions of labor, and supported by essentialist ideologies. These mechanisms are embedded in youth sports in taken-for-granted ways. . . .

---

[7] Patricia Martin's work has been foundational in showing how gender works in organizations in informal, non-reflexive ways that rely on people's "tacit knowledge" about gender (2006). In particular, she points out "how and why well-intentioned, 'good people' practise gender in ways that do harm" (255). See also Martin 2001; and Patricia Yancy Martin, "'Said and Done' versus 'Saying and Doing': Gendering Practices, Practicing Gender at Work," *Gender and Society* 17 (2003), 342–366.

Understanding the Text

1. How does the language of youth sports teams' organization predispose people to volunteer according to assumptions about "natural" gender roles? How is this reflected in the parents' responses to Messner's questions about "team moms"?

2. Why don't more men volunteer to perform the organizational duties of youth sports teams' operations?

3. What values about femininity and masculinity seem to predispose people's thinking about men and women's roles in organizing youth sports teams?

4. How do the stereotypes about gender roles keep Sandra, the coaching-inclined mother, unrecognized as a coach even though her role during the season was to pitch in on the field?

Reflection and Response

5. If you have ever participated in youth sports, reflect upon the gender divisions you witnessed, encountered, or experienced.

6. Over and over again, respondents to Messner's questions apologize for their responses that seem to suggest the gendered division of volunteer labor on youth sports teams — "I hate to say it, but . . . ," "I hate to use the analogy." Why do you think these apologies are made so frequently?

Making Connections

7. Youth sports represent a fertile ground where the social construction of gender occurs. Write about how boys and girls become acclimated to gender difference and gender segregation in youth sports. Consider different levels at which this occurs, ranging from the organization of leagues, to the assignment of team names and colors, to the community and player expectations about the differences between boys' and girls' play.

8. When Messner discusses the "sex-category sorting process" (p. 120) he observed in youth sports, he shows how what people consider "free individual choice" in volunteering is actually highly circumscribed by assumptions about appropriate and practical gender segregation. He claims that this sorting process structures the "pipeline" through which men and women keep and maintain traditional gender roles within the organization as kids grow. He cites sociologist Pat Martin's term *the informal practicing of gender*, which, at the entry level, puts men and women on different paths. Consider the other readings from this chapter. What other "pipelines" or "paths" are established "at the entry level" for boys and girls — or men and women — that may structure their future courses based on the "informal practicing of gender"? Explore other places where sex segregation occurs based on assumptions about the proper roles for men and women to play, and speculate about its future consequences.

3

What Rituals Shape Our Gender?

O ne of the most powerful ways societies establish, maintain, and affirm the values of their culture is through *rituals* and *rites of passage*. Rituals, according to anthropologist Robbie Davis-Floyd, are fundamentally "patterned, repetitive, and symbolic enactments of cultural belief or value."[1] All three elements here are important: rituals suggest repeatability and relative consistency across a culture, and the performance of rituals typically involves actions that support through symbolic displays what a culture or group holds to be important. Rituals may be mundane and performed almost daily (showering, brushing teeth, shaking hands), or they may be less frequent but more significant in terms of symbolizing group membership and solidarity (visiting the Washington, D.C., monuments, singing the national anthem, reciting the Pledge of Allegiance). Some rituals help express group sentiment or shared experience (holding a candlelight vigil, memorializing a historical event). Other rituals, such as "watching football with Dad" or "baking cookies with Mom," are more dispersed across the population but are also routinely and collectively practiced examples of the ways social values are communicated, enacted, and preserved in American culture — in these cases, values about family, leisure time, and of course gender. Rituals secure group identity through repeated performances of specific actions that symbolically represent the ideologies of culture and, in doing so, align the individual with the common beliefs and activities of the wider population.

A *rite of passage* differs from an everyday ritual in terms of its relative significance in the life course. A rite of passage is a ceremony or event consisting of numerous rituals that, together, mark the transition of an individual from one social state or status to another. Rites of passage are typically organized around an individual's matriculation into a new group, accompanying the conferral of a new identity for the individual within a group. Sometimes, however, they mark the passage from one embodied state to

---

[1] Robbie Davis-Floyd, "Gender and Ritual: Giving Birth the American Way," in *Gender in Cross-Cultural Perspective,* ed. Caroline B. Brettell and Carolyn F. Sargeant (Englewood, NJ: Prentice Hall, 2005), pp. 450–451.

another, as with funerary rites of passage (which often serve to pay homage to the deceased while assisting in his or her spiritual transformation after death) and with those that surround childbirth (which welcome the new member into the social world). Arguably, in all cultures, birth, adulthood, and death are ceremoniously recognized through rites of passage, though those rites can be quite diverse across cultures. Rites of passage may also include weddings, graduation ceremonies, inaugurations, and other initiation rituals that signify a new membership position within a group. Military basic training, fraternity and sorority rituals, and team sports rituals, for example, may be considered rites of passage.

Gender is clearly part of most kinds of rituals and rites of passage, and some rituals and rites of passage are directly focused on affirming gender status, such as circumcision rituals, bar and bat mitzvahs, quinceañera celebrations, and "sweet 16" or "princess" parties. The readings in this chapter each address different rituals and rites of passage in American culture and inspect the ways they contribute to the social construction of gender. An excerpt from Amy Best's book *Prom Night: Youth, Schools and Popular Culture* looks at the high school prom as a ritualized, prescribed event in which young men and women rehearse adult gender display and gender interactions. Michael Kimmel's "The Rites of Almost-Men: Binge Drinking, Fraternity Hazing, and the Elephant Walk" interrogates the sometimes danger-ous rituals of college fraternity hazing to show what he sees as a mistaken vision of adult masculinity being incepted into American collegiate cultures. Jaclyn Geller, in "Undercover at the Bloomingdale's Registry," focuses on one portion of the wedding ritual — the engagement — to analyze messages about femininity and matrimony wrapped up in the consumer culture. Stephanie Rosenbloom looks briefly at Halloween costumes to speculate about gender messages in this holiday costuming ritual. And Joseph Zoske criticizes the controversial ritual of infant circumcision to highlight what he sees as a human rights violation — a primitive blood ritual affecting more than half of U.S. males. In each of the selections, the authors are concerned to read in the activities of specific rituals the "cultural beliefs and values" about masculinity and femininity that are performed and affirmed through the ceremonies.

From *Prom Night: Youth, Schools and Popular Culture*

Amy Best

Amy Best is a professor of sociology at George Mason University. Her scholarship focuses on youth culture, cultural and social inequality, and the intersections among gender, ethnicity, sexuality, race, and class. Her books include *Fast Cars, Cool Rides: The Accelerating World of Youth and Their Cars* (2006) and *Representing Youth: Methodological Issues in Critical Youth Studies* (an edited collection from 2007). This selection is from her 2000 book *Prom Night: Youth, Schools and Popular Culture.*

Before the twentieth century, girls simply did not organize their thinking about themselves around their bodies. Today, many young girls worry about the contours of their bodies — especially shape, size, and muscle tone — because they believe the body is the ultimate expression of the self. The body is a consuming project for contemporary girls because it provides an important means of self-definition, a way to visibly announce who you are to the world. From a historical perspective, this particular form of adolescent expression is a relatively recent phenomenon.

—JOAN JACOBS BRUMBERG, *THE BODY PROJECT*

The popular 1999 teen prom films *She's All That* and *Never Been Kissed* are Cinderella-inspired tales of transformation. As the narratives unfold, the central female characters, both wallflowers, submit to a series of changes culminating in their emergence as beauty queens at the prom. Each wins the adulation of her peers, and best of all, each gets the man of her dreams. In these Hollywood productions, the process of getting ready for the prom is a privileged space in which bodies are magically reworked and identities completely refashioned.

Predictably, the popular construction of the prom as a moment in which to reinvent the self is a gendered one; this narrative is almost always told through the voice of a girl and the transformation that occurs is mapped fundamentally through her body. This is because the prom belongs to "the feminine." The prom is a feminine space, conventionally thought to be the domain of girls. Constructed as such, it is a site where girls are expected to be heavily invested because they can use this space to solidify and display their feminine identities. Such expectations are inscribed in both popular culture forms and everyday talk. Girls are repeatedly told that going to the prom is a fundamentally important part to their being and becoming feminine. In prom magazines, "making a statement" is the very promise of the prom: "the prom is your night to shine." "Dare To Stand Out" and "Be The Babe of the Ball" these magazines tell their readers. One magazine article asks, "On your special night will you steal the social scene?" The message is that a carefully fashioned feminine self is the key to an unforgettable prom. The packaging of the prom in this way virtually ensures girls' participation in the consumption of goods and in feminine body work. And why wouldn't girls want to make a dramatic statement about themselves at the prom? There is tremendous pleasure in the project of self-change.

Yet while girls are expected to take up the work of becoming feminine at the prom, they are also confronted with the inherent contradiction in doing this kind of work. The very practices that girls are expected to invest in and to find pleasurable are also dismissed as trivial. "When I was a freshman I couldn't wait to go. I worked at the postprom party at my school but by the time senior year came around it all seemed so irrelevant and unimportant to the future," one young woman wrote. The basic paradox lies in the following: the project of becoming feminine is defined as frivolous, and that which is frivolous is also feminine.[1]

So profound is this contradiction for girls that many young women I talked to expressed an initial ambivalence about going to the prom. One white young woman wrote,

I wasn't originally going to attend my prom simply because I was broke and didn't want to get dressed up for one night. But somehow my best friend convinced me to go. So then I went home and told my mom that I was going and she didn't believe me until two weeks later when I shelled out $50 for two tickets.

Elise, a biracial, bisexual student at Woodrow, originally rejected the 5 prom because she felt it reflects a space ordered by a set of gendered practices that privilege consumption and heterosexuality. "At first I was like, screw the prom, you know. It's kind of cheesy. Everyone's going parading around, this is my dress, and who's he bringing?" But she also said later in the interview, "You know, I'm kinda getting into it." Elise did end up going, as did many young women who originally thought they might not. Most girls found themselves — for some reason or another — mysteriously "caught up" in the preparations for the prom despite their initial resistance. Only a few girls in this study decided they were not going to attend their proms. One young white woman discussed her decision to not go:

---

[1] Griggers, 1997.

Prom night.

I choose not to attend my junior or senior prom because it was not impor-
tant to me. I had opportunities my sophomore, junior, and senior years to
attend and I worked on the prom committee to organize the event. I think
that the prom is blown completely out of proportion. I came from a small
town and there were some people who became obsessed with the prom.
This was the case with one of my friends. She got mad at me because I
didn't want to go. I think my mom was a little hurt by this too because we
didn't go dress shopping, etc.

Even the marketers of the prom magazines realize the weight of
this contradiction. Consider one article from a 1997 special prom edition of *YM*, which began, "In your opinion, the prom is so, well, not
hip. So though you're majorly excited for the big night, you're saying
'See ya!' to flowing ball gowns and stretch limos — you've got to make
a statement girl!"[2]

The contradictions among delighting in the work of getting ready
for the prom, of wanting to be seen, and of feeling that the prom is an
event having little true social value point to an ongoing tension (significantly beyond that of the prom) that many girls experience when

---

[2] "Discover Your Perfect Prom Look," *YM* special prom edition, 1997: 37.

taking up a position of femininity in a culture organized around consumption in which men and the practices authorized by masculine ideologies are privileged. Leslie Roman and Linda Christian-Smith, in their book *Becoming Feminine*, elaborate the connections between the contradictory nature of popular cultural forms and the struggles girls face in becoming feminine. As they explain, "At stake in the struggles and contestations over these meanings are not only textual representations of femininity and gender relations in particular cultural commodities, but also their place and significance in the lives of actual women and men who consume, use and make sense of them in the context of their daily practices and social relations. The struggle for girls and women, then (whether they are feminist or not), over gendered meanings, representations and ideologies in popular cultural forms is nothing less than a struggle to understand and hopefully transform the historical contradictions of becoming feminine within the context of conflicting sets of power relations."[3] This struggle, a struggle fundamentally formed in relation to the self, was narrated by girls as they prepared for and then attended their proms. While the prom highlights more general dilemmas about the continuing influence of dominant gender meanings on girls' lives and their bodies, it also emerges as a distinct site where context-specific forms of femininity — that surprisingly cut across race and class lines — arise. From hairstyles to dresses, these girls' narratives tell the story of the work and the lessons offered by the prom.

Seeing and Being Seen: The Making of Feminine Bodies

> I want something that makes my dad a little nervous . . . something pretty . . . maybe make him lose a little sleep. I want something that will make me the center of attention . . . I want something the other girls wish they could wear . . . something that makes everyone stop and stare.
>
> —ADVERTISEMENT FOR FLIRTATIONS, *YOUR PROM*, 1996

Despite the tensions some girls initially felt about investing in an event that had been framed as silly and superficial, many young women looked forward to the prom as a place to be seen. As John Berger explains in his important book, *Ways of Seeing.* "A woman must continually watch herself. She is almost continually accompanied by her own image of herself. Whilst she is walking across a room or

---

[3] Roman and Christian-Smith, 1988: 4.

whilst she is weeping at the death of her father, she can scarcely avoid envisaging herself walking or weeping. From earliest childhood she has been taught and persuaded to survey herself continually."[4]

Proms are moments in which girls in particular are on display. The structuring of physical space at the four proms I attended ensured that the prom would be designated in this way: the entrances to the prom sites were situated so that girls could be looked at by others. "Even at the prom, people said it was the best looking dress, I remember," one young white woman offered. Many purposely delay their arrival to the prom so that they can make a grand entrance. As one African-American young woman wrote,

When I stepped out of the limo I remember thinking that I was just the princess of the night. All lights were on me and this was my night. No one and nothing was going to spoil it for me. So we walked in about an hour late. When I made my entrance everyone's eyes were on me. I even remember one of my enemies sitting on the table that was right next to the door. And when she turned around and took a look at me her whole face fell. By the way she looked, it seems like she had just decided at the last minute she was going to the prom.

Though especially pronounced at the prom, being looked at is a normalized and naturalized dimension of life as a girl; as a result, its embeddedness within a gender and heterosexual order usually goes unnoticed.[5] One girl related,

I'm looking forward to seeing everyone in a different dress. Everybody keeps telling everybody else what their dress looks like and you can get an idea but you can't really get an idea until you actually see it. You can get rolls and rolls of film and take lots of pictures.

As this young woman suggests, seeing carries as much significance as being seen in this cultural scene. While suggestive of the agency girls can claim in the space of the prom (being able to look rather than just being looked upon), this agency continues to be

---

[4] Berger, 1977: 46.
[5] McRobbie, 1991; Montgomery, 1998.

lodged in an organization of gender; the practice of seeing chiefly centers on girls' bodies, and in this way offers little room for girls to reject fully their participation in the project of becoming feminine.

> Your 30-Day Beauty countdown. Don't let prom put you in a panic! With one month to go, you've still got tons of time to get perfect skin, beautiful hair and a hot bod. Just follow our head-to-toe guide to getting gorgeous.
>
> —"YOUR 30-DAY BEAUTY COUNTDOWN," ARTICLE IN YM, 1997

The Burdens of Beauty

> Beauty Make Me Over: From Toned-down to Terrific, From Low-key to Luminous; From Sweet to Sophisticated.
>
> —BEAUTY ARTICLE IN *YOUR PROM*, 1996

Some girls, while enjoying the process of getting ready for the prom, were also aware of the extent to which these preparations are distinctly feminine. One white middle-class girl wrote:

This elaborate process of preparation was done by most of the people attending the prom (well, girls). It was ridiculous when you think of all the time and money that went into one night. But it was fun.

Another young white woman wrote,

This whole procedure for preparing for the prom was pretty hectic. That's because, I mean, I don't mean to create more stereotypes for my gender, but, girls who do go to the prom have the tendency to over-exaggerate things. Speaking for most of my friends, we worried too much. There were many questions that ran through my mind as the prom night got closer and closer: what type of dress should I wear? Should I wear long or short? What color dress should I wear? How should I get my hair done? Who should do my hair? Should I do my nails? What type of jewelry should I wear with my dress? What type of shoes? While on the other hand guys have one major question: Should I rent or buy?

Like these two girls above, most took it for granted that boys and girls engaged in a different set of practices as they prepared for the prom. These young women are drawing from a set of social assumptions about what it means to be a "man" or a "woman." Treating gender as simply a matter of social difference and not social power not only works to naturalize a gendered division of labor, it also obscures how this very talk produces and maintains a social organization of gender. Mary and Sarah, two white students from Woodrow, related,

> MD: I don't think they [boys] really care quite as much as the girls do. I mean, like, what they care about is what they're doing before and what they're doing after and with who.
> SJ: They don't really have a lot to get ready.
> MD: "My tux is a double-breasted gray." [she laughs]
> SJ: The girls are — the girls have to do a lot more planning with their dress and their . . .
> MD: Yeah, go through their hair and their nails, their dress.

While many girls were willing to acknowledge that the work required 15 of them was entirely different from the work required of boys to get ready for the prom, few referred to these preparations as burdensome. Exceptions to the rule, two white young women described their experiences as follows:

I'm all through with dress shopping. I'm done. It's tiring. You go from store to store trying on dresses, taking off clothes and putting it on, oh no. It's very tiring shopping for a dress. I'm glad that part is over with.

Shopping for all the prom stuff was a hassle. I went through four dresses and two pair of shoes until I was set on the perfect outfit. The night before the prom I ended up puking my brains out all night and was running a high fever. My mother dragged me to the beauty parlor drugged up, while I had my nails, hair, and makeup done. They had to put extra makeup on me because I was so pale from being sick.

As this last young woman suggests, mothers are central players in the prom, often as invested as these girls in the project of becoming feminine. One young woman laughingly reported to her friends in the bathroom at the prom that her mother had "attacked" her with mascara. In these last two scenes, it is the mothers who enlist their daughters to do the work of looking feminine for the prom. One girl is "dragged" by her mother, while the second had been "attacked." Though clearly expressed in jest, both provide compelling imagery of the ways the practices of femininity are passed from mother to daughter.

While at the prom, a lot of girls talked openly among themselves about the labor-intensive work they do on their bodies to achieve an idealized feminine image. Most common were girls' tales of struggles to find the right dress and their efforts toward having the "perfect" hairstyle. Stories of this kind were exchanged and compared at the prom in the girls' bathroom, a space at the prom reserved exclusively for girls. After observing four proms, I realized that these bathroom discussions about their bodies, dresses, and preparations were not only a source of pleasure, but were also an integral part of the actual prom. In my fieldnotes from Hudson's prom this is most evident:

I watched girls come and go and check themselves out in the mirror as they passed. Three girls came in the bathroom and I started to talk with them as they primped. One girl was wearing a green dress, with a green sheer shawl and a full tulle skirt and I told her how pretty it was. She twirled around for me. I asked her if she'd had it made and she said she had. She told me she wanted it to be fuller on the bottom so that she would get more attention. She also told me that her jewelry came from the makeup artist who did her makeup. She was heavily made up in green eye shadow with her hair pulled up into large ringlets. Her friend, who had also had her dress made to look like a traditional ball gown, with a purse to match, said her sister had done her makeup. The girl in the green dress told me she had only had hers done by a professional because she didn't know how to do it herself. I asked her if she normally wore makeup and she said no. The three of them talked among themselves about their lipstick, comparing prices, mostly. One girl had bought hers for $2.00, while the other had gone and gotten her lipstick from Lancôme for close to $15.00. Another girl walked by showing off her gold shoes and said, "These are toe crackers." Soon after another girl came by whose dress was bursting at the sides. She and her friends were in search of a pin of some sort. They had done a botched job to repair the dress by the bathroom stalls. This led to the three girls' discussion of the mistakes about their own dresses. The girl in the green dress pointed to some gapping around the neckline, while the other pointed to her uneven hemline. (June 1997)

While in many ways this kind of "body talk" represents an articulation of feminine identity and mastery, it also undermines the idealization of feminine display because it exposes it as work that requires money, time, and body alteration. Contrary to the idea that femininity is something girls simply possess, their talk helps to define femininity as something one actively undertakes.[6] I overheard one girl as she rushed up to greet her friend in the beginning of Rudolph's prom, pointing to the top of her head, exclaiming, "Three hours, it took three hours to get my hair to look like this!"

---

[6] See West and Zimmerman, 1987, for a discussion on how gender is actively constructed and reconstructed through day-to-day relations.

More than just a set of frivolous practices of primping, these are fertile sites of identity negotiation and construction, where girls are making sense of what it means to be women in a culture that treats the surface of the body as the consummate canvas on which to express the feminine self. There is also a clear sense that many of these girls enjoyed the attention they received after such significant transformations — their labors were not in vain. Indeed, this is the very promise of the prom, highlighted in girls' talk, and telegraphed in prom films and magazines. The pleasure in being seen in "a new light" helps to gain girls' consent to consume, to ensure their participation in beauty culture and the ongoing creation of gender.

The Politics of Pleasure

The achievement of femininity for the prom depends on an endless 20 consumption of products; makeup, clothing, hair accessories, shoes, lingerie, handbags, and jewelry are all products readily available in a commodity market and heavily marketed as tools for feminine display and self-reinvention at the prom. These are tools that require time, patience, and skill to master. Susan Bordo elaborates on the more lasting effects this kind of exacting and intensive work has on women and how they experience life in their bodies, explaining, "Through the pursuit of an ever-changing, homogenizing, elusive ideal of femininity — a pursuit without a terminus, requiring that women constantly attend to minute and often whimsical changes in fashion — female bodies become docile bodies — bodies whose forces and energies are habituated to external regulation, subjection, transformation, 'improvement.'"[7] But this kind of body work is not just about producing disciplined bodies for consumption; there is more here. The meanings girls themselves attach to this work is significant for understanding why they engage in such practices in the first place.[8]

Engaging in the work of becoming "beautiful" for the prom represents a struggle to stake a claim to one's identity. For many of these girls, participating in beauty work enables them to occupy a position within a public space, a significant fact when considering women's historical relegation to the private sphere. As consumers of beauty culture, these young women are able to possess a sense of power and visibility by claiming public space that often is not experienced in

---

[7] Bordo, 1993: 166.
[8] Carrington, 1989; Craik, 1989; Clark, 1987; Fiske, 1989; McRobbie and Garber, 1981; Radner, 1989, 1995; Radway, 1984; Roman and Christian-Smith, 1988.

their everyday lives in school, with family, or in their relationships with young men. They occupy hair salons, nail salons, and dress shops in a way similar to that of middle-class women in the 1920s who, just after winning the right to vote, proudly (and paradoxically) announced their new freedom by wearing shorter skirts, bobbing their hair, and smoking cigarettes in public.

Not only are these girls able to demonstrate a public commitment to feminine practices, they are also able to express their competence as beauty practitioners. The desire to do so is so significant that girls who were either unable (or sometimes unwilling) to indulge in the extravagances of the beauty/hair salon performed this work in private spaces, most often their homes. These girls created a situation resembling, in remarkable ways, the experience of going to a salon. Friends and female family members were enlisted to perform the beauty work provided to other girls by service workers. Though done in the private setting of home, getting ready signified a public act.

While young women arguably do beauty work for the prom to express their heterosexual desirability, they also do this work to experience a self-pleasure by making themselves feel special.[9] For many of these girls, the prom presents itself as an opportunity to indulge themselves in ways that many of them are simply unable to in their day-to-day school lives. Part of what makes this body work around the prom worth undertaking stems directly from how they experience everyday life as young women.

Teenage girls are often denied control over their bodies, their desire, and their self-definition. Engaging in this elaborate consumption-oriented body work enables them to craft a space of self-control, self-definition, and self-pleasure that is experienced immediately. Many girls perceive adult women as possessing greater control over their lives than they as girls can. Transforming themselves to look more like adult women through these beauty practices allows many of them to feel more like adult women, to possibly experience adult

---

[9] Hillary Radner (1989) suggests in her work on femininity and consumption that women find pleasure in the consumption of beauty culture because it provides a space in which women can be the agents of their own desire. Radner develops a compelling analysis of how feminine pleasure in the production of appearance is tied to beauty and culture industries. In the 1980s, she argues, these industries recognized the influence of women's struggle to articulate an autonomous self-identity on women's patterns of consumption. In so doing, the market repositioned beauty work within a discourse of self-pleasure; the focus shifted from making oneself over for others to doing it simply for oneself. Beauty work at this particular historical moment not only is rooted in the discourses of heterosexual desirability, but in a discourse of feminine desire (e.g., "I'm beautiful and I'm worth it").

freedoms and liberties, even if momentarily, and to negotiate those everyday constraints they experience because of their age and consequent position in society. Of course, the result is that the pleasure of excess conceals the ideological workings of the prom; proms structure girls' investments in both gender and heterosexuality, exacerbate their anxieties about the body, and focus their attention toward the all-consuming project of the body.

References
Berger, John. 1977. *Ways of Seeing*. London: Penguin.

Bordo, Susan. 1993. *Unbearable Weight: Feminism, Western Culture and the Body*. Berkeley and Los Angeles: University of California Press.

Carrington, Kerry. 1989. "Girls and Graffiti." *Cultural Studies* 3 (89–100).

Clark, Ann K. 1987. "The Girl: A Rhetoric of Desire." *Cultural Studies* 1 (195–203).

Craik, Jennifer. 1989. "'I Must Put My Face On': Making Up the Body and Marking Out the Feminine." *Cultural Studies* 3 (1–14).

Fiske, John. 1989. *Understanding Popular Culture*. Boston: Unwin Hyman.

Griggers, Camilla. 1997. *Becoming Woman*. Minneapolis: University of Minnesota Press.

McRobbie, Angela, ed. 1991. *Feminism and Youth Culture: From Jackie to Just Seventeen*. Boston: Unwin Hyman.

McRobbie, Angela and Jennifer Garber. 1981. "Girls and Subcultures." *Feminism and Youth Culture: From Jackie to Just Seventeen*, ed. Angela McRobbie. Boston: Unwin Hyman.

Montgomery, Maureen E. 1998. *Displaying Women: Spectacles of Leisure in Edith Wharton's New York*. New York: Routledge.

Radner, Hilary. 1989. "'This Time's For Me': Making Up and Feminine Practice." *Cultural Studies* 3 (301–21).

———. 1995. *Shopping Around: Feminine Culture and the Pursuit of Pleasure*. New York: Routledge.

Radway, Janice. 1984. *Reading the Romance: Women, Patriarchy and Popular Literature*. Chapel Hill: University of North Carolina Press.

Roman, Leslie G. and Linda Christian-Smith, eds. 1988. *Becoming Feminine: The Politics of Popular Culture*. London: The Falmer Press.

West, Candice and Don Zimmerman. 1987. "Doing Gender." *Gender and Society* 1 (125–51).

Understanding the Text

1. What is the role of the fashion magazine industry and mass media in establishing the significance of the prom as a life event?
2. How is "becoming feminine" (p. 128) embodied in the prom? What specifically "feminine" behaviors and attributes are encouraged in the prom ritual, from "getting ready" for the prom to actually attending it?

3. How does the prom ritual establish heterosexual dating and mating practices as the cultural "norm"?

4. What is the role of parents in encouraging and guiding young women through the process of "becoming feminine" in preparation for the prom?

Reflection and Response

5. Think back to your own high school prom and consider some of the expectations and processes for preparing for the prom that you encountered. How did the expectations and processes you encountered carry messages about gender? How did the prom impact your developing sense of masculinity and femininity?

6. Best claims that "prom is a feminine space" (p. 128), as if the prom were largely constructed by and for women. What elements of masculinity are similarly performed — and thus encultured — through a prom's rituals?

7. Is the prom a significant rite of passage in American culture? Why or why not?

Making Connections

8. The term "compulsory heterosexuality" was coined by feminist scholar Adrienne Rich in 1980 to describe the powerful pressures and institutional norms that produce heterosexuality as the dominant, legitimate form of sexual expression. Consider several ways in which heterosexuality may be construed as "compulsory" in contemporary American culture, beginning with assumptions about gender and sexuality, then as embodied in children's culture, then in the high school prom.

9. One of Best's claims is that the mass media narratives, especially Hollywood films and fashion magazines, structure expectations of the prom in a particular way, outlining its standard rituals and offering models of successful participation. Choose a different rite of passage (mitzvah, quinceañera, wedding, birth), find resources such as instruction guidebooks and magazines that outline the event, and analyze the gender messages included in those resources.

10. Wedding ceremonies are perhaps among the most significant rites of passage in American culture. Examine the numerous rituals that constitute the American wedding ceremony, using Geller's article (p. 151) as a place to start. What culturally significant values about gender are communicated in these rituals? You may also draw from your own experience of a wedding, or draw from one of the many types of wedding-planning magazines or Web sites available to you. How well do Geller and Best provide a framework for understanding the rituals of the wedding ceremony?

11. Compare the prom, wedding, and childbirth rites of passage in the United States with the same ceremonies in a different country or culture. How are the rituals different, and how do these differences reflect cultural differences about gender?

The Rites of Almost-Men: Binge Drinking, Fraternity Hazing, and the Elephant Walk

Michael Kimmel

Michael Kimmel is an author and a scholar on men and masculinity, and he is a distinguished professor of sociology at Stony Brook University. His books include *The Politics of Manhood* (1996), *Manhood in America: A Cultural History* (1996), *The Gendered Society* (2000), and *The History of Men* (2005). He is a founder and spokesperson for the National Organization for Men Against Sexism (NOMAS). This selection is from his acclaimed 2009 book *Guyland: The Perilous World Where Boys Become Men*.

The cab meets the foursome outside of Nick's house at 11:45 p.m. In fifteen minutes, he will turn 21, and Tempe, Arizona's Mill Avenue is waiting for him and his crew. Mill Avenue looks like a lot of avenues near college campuses across the country: a string of bars with names like Fat Tuesday, Margarita Rocks, and The Library. (That way if your parents call you can tell them that you are going to "The Library" and not be lying.) "Let's start out at Fat Tuesday and then go from there," Nick says as the cab drops them off. Tonight is Nick's "power hour," a college ritual where the birthday boy goes out on the eve of his twenty-first birthday to have as much fun as possible (read: drunkenness) between midnight and the closing of the bars. The practice goes by many names on many campuses, but a common theme always emerges: You walk into a bar and stumble out of it.

Nick starts his night by ingesting some vile concoction invented solely for the enjoyment of the onlookers. Tonight the drink of choice is a "Three Wise Men," a shot composed of equal parts Jim Beam, Jack Daniels, and Johnnie Walker. Other variations include the more ethnically diverse (substitute Jose Cuervo for the Johnnie Walker), or the truly vomit-inducing (add a little half-and-half and just a splash of Tabasco). The next drink comes at him fast, a Mind Eraser, another classic of the power hour. It's like a Long Island Iced Tea except more potent, and it is drunk through a straw as quickly as possible. Shot after shot after shot is taken, the guys become all the more loud and obnoxious, and the bar manager brings a trash can over to Nick's side, just in case.

Not surprisingly, the trash can comes in handy. Nick's body finally relents as closing time approaches. He spews out a stream of vomit and the other guys know it's time to go. Fun was had, memories were made, but most importantly . . . he puked. His friends can rest easy; a job well done.

Jason, a freshman at the University of Georgia, has been waiting all semester for this night. He's put up with a lot of humiliating abuse from the brothers, done mountains of their laundry, made their beds, and even written a paper for the pledgemaster. He's mopped up vomit-stained bathrooms at the fraternity house on the morning after parties, done stupid things, and drank a bit more — okay, a lot more — than he ever did in high school. One more night and he's sure he'll be in.

The pledges gather in the rec room at about 10 p.m. Dressed, as 5 instructed, in old T-shirts and jeans, they were told to bring flip flops, a change of clothes, and a jockstrap. (A jockstrap?) An anxious frivolity permeates the room, as brothers drink beer with the pledges. After everyone seems good and drunk the brothers swarm over the pledges, yelling their demands to recite the fraternity's mission statement, rituals, and membership information. Screw it up, the brothers yell, and you might not make it.

Calisthenics, of a sort, follow. Push-ups, then chugging some beers. Sit-ups, and more chugging. Most of the pledges are ready to puke. They are then told to strip naked and stand in a straight line, one behind the other (which is hard enough given how much they have had to drink). Each pledge is ordered to reach his right hand between his legs to the pledge standing behind him and grab that guy's penis, then place his left hand on the shoulder of the guy in front of him. (You have to bend over to make this work.) Forming a circle, they walk around the basement for several minutes, in what is known as the "elephant walk." By now it is nearly 2 a.m. "Okay, you worthless pieces of shit," the pledgemaster screams. "Now let's see if you're willing to give it all for the brotherhood!"

Still naked, the pledges stumble to the second-floor balcony of the house. The brothers measure out lengths of rope, and a cinderblock is tied to the end of each, so that it almost — but not quite — touches the ground. The pledges are blindfolded as the other ends of the ropes are tied to the base of each pledge's penis. "You better have a big enough dick, pledge," the pledgemaster shouts. "If your dick isn't big enough, you aren't getting into this house. This block is gonna rip it the fuck off your body! How do you like that, you little weenies? Our dicks made it! Is yours big enough?"

Each pledge feels a little tug on his rope, and then hears the cinderblocks being lifted up to the edge of the balcony. The next thing he knows, he feels a sharp tug and hears the cinderblock being pushed off the edge and crashing to the ground below. One guy screams and starts to cry. Another pisses. Blindfolds are removed and the brothers are laughing their heads off. Turns out the ropes were not really tied to those blocks after all. They embrace their new "brothers," and it is over: Jason has made it.

These snapshots capture typical events that are taking place at colleges and universities across America. Binge drinking is epidemic, and nowhere near as innocuous as many of us would like to believe. Hazing rituals span the range from the ridiculous to the truly criminal, occasionally becoming lethal as well. There is an impulse — among parents, college administrators, alumni, and the guys themselves — to chalk it all up to harmless fun. College is supposed to be the best years of your life. Yet stories like those above also suggest something important about Guyland that lurks beneath the surface of all that "fun": its chronic insecurity, its desperate need for validation, and the sometimes sadistic cruelty with which that validation is withheld and then conferred.

Here's what guys know. They know that every move, every utter- 10 ance, every gesture is being carefully monitored by the self-appointed gender police, ensuring that everyone constantly complies with the Guy Code — even if they don't want to. They know that if you do go along, you'll have friends for life, you'll get laid, you'll feel like you belong. And if you don't, you won't. If you're lucky, you'll just be ignored. If you're not, you'll be ostracized, targeted, bullied. The stakes are so high, the costs of failure enormous. Many guys — perhaps most — suspect that they might not have what it takes. They feel unable to live up to the Guy Code, yet their fear compels them to keep trying. And so many of the other guys seem to do it so effortlessly.

> Here's what guys know. They know that every move, every utterance, every gesture is being carefully monitored by the self-appointed gender police, ensuring that everyone constantly complies with the Guy Code—even if they don't want to.

And so the initiations begin — initiations that are designed to prove misguided notions of masculinity, with legitimacy conferred by those who have no real legitimacy to confer it. No wonder the rituals become increasingly barbaric, the hazing increasingly cruel. And at the same time the initiations serve another purpose, perhaps less clear than the first. They also reassure the guys that they are not yet men, not yet part of the adult world, and that there's still time to have a little fun before they have to find their way in the real world.

Initiation: Replacing Mother

Initiation is about transition, a moving from one status to another. Its power rests on the instability of one's current identity. A person undergoes initiation in order to stabilize a new permanent identity.

Initiations are centerpieces of many of the world's religions. Sometimes the rituals are arduous, other times they are relatively benign. In Judaism and Islam, circumcision is practiced as a rite of passage that marks the boy's membership in the community. In Judaism, it is performed at birth, signifying the covenant of God with Abraham — that Abraham was willing to sacrifice his only son to his belief in God. In Islam, circumcision takes place at different times, depending on the sect. In Turkey, for example, the *sunnet* takes place at 13, roughly the onset of puberty, and is a certifiable rite of passage to manhood.

In Christianity, ritual circumcision is not required but we can consider Christian baptism as an initiation ritual. In the baptism, the old self is symbolically, ritually, destroyed — drowned — and the new self is reborn into the community of the Church. And though baptism is not gender-specific, as both males and females are baptized, it is nonetheless a meditation about gender. (After all, the original baptisms were for men only.) The old "feminized self," born of a woman, is destroyed and the priest, always a man, brings the new self to life. In a sense, then, the male priest has given birth to the new man. The mother may have given birth, but the child does not become a member of the community until the priest confers that status. Women are pushed aside, and men appropriate their reproductive power.

Freud made such a moment the centerpiece of his theory of child 15 development. Before the Oedipal crisis, Freud argued, the child, male or female, identifies with mother, the source of love, food, and nurturing. To become a man, a boy must leave his mother behind, and come over to his father's side. The successful resolution of the Oedipal complex is identification with the masculine and "dis-identification" with the feminine. Whether or not one subscribes to Freudian theory, all theories of initiation pivot on uncertainty, anxiety, indeterminacy. It is an unstable moment, what anthropologist Victor Turner called a "liminal" stage — a stage of in-between-ness, "neither here nor there; they are betwixt and between the positions assigned and arrayed by law, custom, convention, and ceremony."

Initiations in Guyland are about the passage from boyhood to manhood. Boyhood is the world of women — Mama's boys, wimps, wusses, and losers — or the world of men who are considered women — gays, fags, homos, queers. Or babies. One guy told me of the "Baby

Dinner" at his fraternity house at a large public university in the Northeast. Pledges dressed in diapers, with little white bonnets on their heads. The pledgemaster would put gross previously chewed food on their heads, simulating pabulum, and the pledges would scoop it off with their fingers and eat it. Many fraternities have equally infantalizing rituals. If initiation is going to validate your manhood, first you have to regress to babyhood.

Initiations, then, are all about masculinity — testing it and proving it. It's not that women don't initiate girls into womanhood. But rarely does becoming a woman involve danger, or threats, or testing. A girl might be inducted into womanhood when her mother explains menstruation at puberty. Or she might be briefed by her friends about the hows and whys of sex, or by her roommates about how to navigate the world of men. But a woman doesn't typically feel the need to prove she is a "real woman." In fact, if she feels a need to prove anything, it's usually some misguided notion of being equal to the guys. Katie, a 22-year-old junior at Hobart and William Smith Colleges, explained:

A "real woman"? Hmmm. Yeah, I had to prove it, had to prove I was a real woman. I hooked up with a guy I didn't know after drinking several guys under the table. That sort of showed them. You know, sort of a "anything you can do I can do better" sort of thing. And you know what? They haven't bothered me about it since.

"But," I asked, "how does drinking to excess and having sex with someone you don't know prove your femininity?"

"Uh, I guess it doesn't," she said after a pause. "It meant I was equal to the guys. That's sort of proving it; isn't it?"

Who Does the Validating?

In the United States, proving masculinity appears to be a lifelong project, endless and unrelenting. Daily, grown men call each other out, challenging one another's manhood. And it works most of the time. You can pretty much guarantee starting a fight virtually anywhere in America by questioning someone's manhood. But why must guys test and prove their masculinity so obsessively? Why are the stakes so high? Why so different here than elsewhere? In part it's because the transitional moment itself is so ill-defined. We, as a culture, lack any coherent ritual that might demarcate the passage from childhood to adulthood for men or women. Not surprisingly, it also remains unclear who, exactly, has the authority to do the validating. 20

In non-Western cultures, it is the adult men of the community whose collective responsibility it is to ensure the safe ritual passage of boys into manhood. The older men devise the rituals, they perform the ceremonies, and they confer adult male status as only adults can. They have already passed over to adulthood — as husbands, workers, and fathers, often of the very boys they are initiating. As legitimate adults, they can authentically validate the boys' manhood.

As a result, once initiated, men no longer have identity crises, wondering who they are, if they can measure up, or if they are man enough. It's over, a done deal. There's nothing left to prove.

Not so in Guyland. . . .

. . . In Guyland, it is not men who are initiating boys into manhood. It is boys playing at initiating other boys into something they, themselves, do not even possess — that they *cannot* even possess. In America's fraternities, military boot camps, and military schools, and on athletic teams, it's always peers who are initiating peers. In fact, initiation and hazing are required to take place when adults are not there, *because* adults are not there — not the coaches, nor the professors, nor the administrators. In some cases, this is because the adults want to have "plausible deniability." They want to be able to claim that they didn't know — couldn't have known — what was happening. But they do, of course; odds are that they went through it themselves, and feel powerless or unwilling to stop it. They may even believe in it.

Perhaps that is why initiations in Guyland are so perilous — and so pointless. Maybe it doesn't work because it can't work. Since peers cannot really initiate peers into a new status, the initiations must be made ever more arduous. And because they are trying to prove what cannot be proved, each generation raises the ante, indulges in more cruelty, and extracts greater pain.

The very mechanisms of initiation in Guyland are so distorted that they can never produce a real man—sensible, sober, responsible, a decent father, partner, husband. Initiations in Guyland have nothing to do with integrity, morality, doing the right thing, swimming against the tide, or standing up for what is right despite the odds. In fact, initiations in Guyland are about drifting with the tide, going along with peer pressure even though you know it's both stupid and cruel, enabling or performing sometimes sadistic assaults against those who have entrusted their novice/initiate status into your hands. The process makes initiation into fraternities or athletic teams or the military closer to a cult than a band of brothers.

"Proof-ing it" All Night

Drinking to excess is the lubricant of initiations—but it can be an initiation itself. As we saw with Nick earlier, power hours are a birthday celebration, a rite of passage, and an initiation all rolled into one. Ever since Congress passed the Uniform Drinking Age Act of 1984, turning 21 has become a national birthday party, in every state, in every community. "You go out, hang out with your friends, you drink a shitload, and you throw up," says one 21-year-old. "And if you don't throw up, then your friends didn't do their job."

For most college students, by the time they turn 21, they've already had ample opportunity to work on their tolerance. A recent survey in Montana (a heavy drinking state across all age groups) found that 38 percent of high schoolers had binged in the previous thirty days—higher than the national average of 28 percent. (Yet that national average is pretty significant itself!) Binge drinking — drinking several times during the week and throughout the weekend — has become a staple of college life. Two out of five college students are binge drinkers according to a survey by Henry Wechsler, a professor of public health at Harvard. Among fraternity and sorority members the rate balloons to 80 percent. Wechsler defines binging as consuming five or more drinks in one session for males and four or more in a row for females, at least once in the past two weeks. By Wechsler's count, 6 percent of college students would qualify as alcoholic and nearly one-third would be given a diagnosis of "alcohol abuser." Almost half — 44 percent — reported at least one symptom of either abuse or dependence. . . .

For the parents of college-aged guys, all this extreme drinking is often incomprehensible. It's a waste of time, a waste of money, alarmingly dangerous, and their own hindsight insists that it isn't even actually *fun*. What's fun about vomiting? What they might not understand is that drinking for these guys involves a lot more than just getting drunk. It's also about freedom — or what they think freedom means. It's about being a man.

By the time most young men go off to college, they've been living under the watchful eyes of their parents their entire lives. It is their parents who oversee the college admissions process, their parents who make sure their homework is done before they're allowed to hang out with their friends, their parents who make sure they're home by midnight. In middle-class America, parenting is a full-time job, and it's taken seriously. And this is not necessarily a bad thing. Yet one of the unintended results of overinvolvement is that the child never learns to develop his own internal compass regarding what constitutes appropriate behavior. All his guidelines are imposed from outside. If you get drunk, you'll get in trouble. If you don't do your homework, you'll get in trouble. All their lives they've tested the limits, gone to the edges, only to have their parents say the final "No," or bail them out if they've gone too far.

Then they go off to college. Their parents drop them off, say their tearful goodbyes, and leave — and they are transformed from overinvolved helicopter parents to absentee parents in the space of one afternoon.

As a result, for these guys, freedom is equated with a lack of accountability — not having to answer to anyone — and so being irresponsible becomes a way of declaring your freedom and, hence, your adulthood. And they've never had so much freedom. They are accountable to no one, and as long as they maintain a reasonable GPA, they're free to do as they like. It might not exactly be adulthood, but they certainly aren't kids anymore.

At the same time, college is considered the last hurrah before the real demands of adulthood begin. Most know that when they graduate they'll be expected to get jobs, support themselves, be responsible. As they see it, they've only got four more years of boyhood left, and they're going to make the best of it. And perhaps this is why binge drinking is so attractive. It allows them to prove their manhood and hold onto their boyhood all at the same time. All the freedom and none of the responsibility. . . .

Uncivil Rites

Binge drinking is both ritualized — the expected norm for parties in Guyland — and a specific ritual, often tied to initiation into a club or organization like a fraternity or an athletic team. There it may be coupled with other activities that fall under the heading "hazing."

Hazing takes place everywhere men gather on campus, whether on athletic teams, in fraternity houses, secret societies, or even in clubs and organizations. (Indeed, the very first mention of President George W. Bush in the *New York Times* came on November 8, 1967, when, as a Yale senior, he was asked about a story in the *Yale Daily News* reporting that his fraternity, Delta Kappa Epsilon, was ritually branding its pledges with a hot coat hanger. The newspaper called the practice "sadistic and obscene," but Bush defended it, saying that the resulting wound was "only a cigarette burn.")

Hazing is a broad term, describing behavior that ranges from dumb pranks or silly skits to seriously dangerous and even potentially lethal activities. It can involve things that you are forced to do, from memorizing arcane trivia about your fraternity chapter or singing pornographic songs to doing people's laundry or fetching their mail, from drinking contests to participation in ridiculous, humiliating, or degrading rituals. Or it can involve things being done to you, from being subject to verbal taunts and humiliating yelling to physical assault, sexual assault, branding, torture, and ritual scarification.

On campus today, the overwhelming majority of the nearly half-million men who belong to collegiate fraternities have undergone some form of hazing. Most of the quarter-million women who belong to sororities have as well.

The most recent study of collegiate hazing, released in March 2008, surveyed more than 11,000 students at 53 institutions. Survey directors, University of Maine professors Elizabeth Allan and Mary Madden, found that more than half of students who belonged to campus organizations — from fraternities to the glee club — had experienced some forms of hazing. It was most common on varsity athletic teams (74 percent) and fraternities and sororities (73 percent) but 56 percent of all members of performing arts organizations, 28 percent of academic clubs, and 20 percent of honor societies also reported being hazed. For 31 percent of the men and 23 percent of the women hazing included drinking games; 17 percent of the men and 9 percent of the women drank until they passed out. About one-fourth believe that their coach or advisor knew about it.

Most hazing rituals are just plain stupid. Lots of vulgar refer- 35 ences to body parts, symphonies of farting, belching, and gagging. "The truth is, most of it is just plain dumb," says Jake, a twenty-four-year-old and former pledgemaster at his Michigan State fraternity house:

We'd line 'em up at all hours, yell at them for a while, quiz 'em on chapter history, lore, and make sure they memorized all the brothers' names, hometowns, majors, and favorite beers. Like who cares, really? Dumb shit like that.

"Oh," he adds as an afterthought, "we'd make 'em drink. A lot." Now he smiles for a moment, remembering. "A real lot."

Often, these hazing rituals result in a sort of cat-and-mouse game between the pledges and the brothers. Jared, 20, tells me about his experience as a pledge at Duke:

The brothers were always calling us to do stuff at weird hours, or drinking until we passed out or puked or something. But who can do that shit all the time? I mean, I'm pre-med, and I can't be like staggering into my organic

*chemistry lab with a blinding hangover, can I? So the pledges would do all
sorts of things to sort of get out of it. We'd fake being plastered, I mean so
drunk that they'd stop making us drink. Or we'd conveniently miss a
lineup the night before a test. One time, I went to the infirmary and said I
had a bad stomach ache because I just knew they were going to call us at
like 2 a.m.*

Yet at least some hazing rituals are sufficiently degrading or
humiliating — and dangerous — that they qualify as physical or sexual
assaults. . . .

Why Do Guys Put Up with It?

Why do guys participate in ceremonial degradation? Part of it is simply because they want to be liked, want to be accepted, want to be
one of the cool guys, the in crowd, aligned with the alpha males. "I
went along with all that [hazing] because I wanted to be liked and
couldn't figure out a way to accomplish that except to be all things to
all people. In trying to be something I could not be I prostituted myself," one former pledge told journalist Hank Nuwer.

"By the end of freshman orientation you pretty much know that 40
the fraternities rule here," said Chuck, 21, a junior at the University of
Oregon. "This isn't like Reed or Santa Cruz, where everything is
hippy dippy. This is fucking rah-rah college. The frats have all the
parties, get all the hot girls, and have all the cool guys. You want to
hang around with the athletes and the hot girls, right? Well, they
are the only game in town. I joined even though they seemed sort of
stupid and definitely seemed sort of smug and arrogant, you know.
But they were *it*. There wasn't anything else. And I wanted a social
life."

Dave, 26, recalls his first week in the dorm at Cornell:

*From the second you arrive on campus, the frat guys are everywhere.
During freshman orientation, in the evenings, they come around the guys'
floors, like selling stuff, like school spirit sort of stuff, like beer mugs, and
college jackets and stuff. They're like the concession guys at the ball park.
They come in, socialize a bit, show you what they're selling. But really,
they're selling being frat guys. And all the freshman guys wanted to buy
that.*

"Not to be in a fraternity or sorority was widely regarded as being
nothing at all," writes Larry Lockridge recalling his father's experience in a fraternity at Indiana in the 1930s.

Part of it is the Guy Code — the desperate desire to feel worth, to feel powerful, to be validated as a man. Somehow these almost-men seduce themselves into believing that these guys, a year older and so much cooler, hold the magical key that will open the door to a feeling of confident manhood with nothing left to prove. As Jackson, a senior at Lehigh, explained:

I knew from the moment I accepted a bid to pledge Beta that my fate was sealed. I would be a cool guy. I would be one of them. No, I mean, I would be one of us. It was a really special feeling. Like I could do anything, because the other guys would always have my back. And we could do anything because, well, because we were Betas, and on this campus, Betas rule. No one — and I mean Greek types, administrators, other guys, and, yeah, well, even you professors — would ever be able to touch us.

In reality, of course, going through the torture of hazing doesn't make you a man. In a sense, fraternity hazing is the distorted mirror image of cultural rituals of initiation, where boys actually do become men in the eyes of their culture. In the collegiate fraternity something else is happening. Just at the moment when your entire culture tells you that it's time to grow up — be a man, step up to sober adult responsibilities, declare a professional ambition, pair up romantically, settle down and get married to the person with whom you will spend your entire life "forsaking all others," have kids, a mortgage, a responsible job, bills to pay — just at that sad, depressing moment of the actual transition to adulthood here is a group of slightly older peers who collectively scream "No!" Not so fast. No need to grow up just yet. Be our brother. Remain a boy. Irresponsible and carefree. . . .

As we've seen, the ability *not* to grow up, *not* to become a man, is 45 Guyland's definition of freedom. And guys believe that it's certainly worth undergoing some humiliating rituals, doing gross and stupid things, and even getting sick over. In fact, doing that gross and stupid stuff is what convinces you that you have not crossed over the threshold of adulthood, that you are still just a guy. It's a man's world, all right. It can wait. . . .

Understanding the Text

1. What does Kimmel complain about in relation to "peers . . . initiating peers" (p. 145) in fraternity, military, and sports culture? What is his complaint about the current role of adult supervisors, instructors, and coaches? What is his proposed remedy?

2. If, according to Kimmel, initiations help people transition from one status or identity to a new one, what are the hazards when it comes to taking on an identity as a "man" in the kinds of fraternity culture he discusses? What is Kimmel's alternative conception of manhood?

3. When Kimmel discusses initiation ceremonies for girls' clubs and teams, what does he note about them?

Reflection and Response

4. Kimmel references the "Guy Code" as a set of informal "rules" young adult males must adhere to in order to gain acceptability and credibility among other "guys," who act as "the self-appointed gender police" (p. 142). How do young men learn about the Guy Code? How do kids and young adults become the "enforcers" of the Guy Code? What kinds of rules exist in the Guy Code beyond the ones mentioned by Kimmel?

5. Kimmel generalizes a lot about fraternities, which many people defend as important social organizations that do good work on campuses and in communities. In your experience, is hazing as important an issue as Kimmel makes it out to be? Why or why not?

6. What significant differences do you see between the initiation ceremonies in male and female organizations? What kinds of hazing practices occur in girls' organizations?

7. Why do you think so many initiation rituals involve sexual humiliation and homoerotic overtones?

8. The kinds of rituals Kimmel discusses have to do largely with establishing "brotherhood," or strengthening social bonds among males in fraternities. What kinds of male bonding rituals continue after college, and into adulthood? What other kinds of groups do men seek to belong within?

Making Connections

9. Hazing on college campuses has become an increasingly visible problem met with all kinds of campaigns and efforts to curtail it. Research the problem of hazing on college campuses, and find one, two, or several examples of hazing crimes that Kimmel's article helps to clarify. Analyze the specific incidences in terms of Kimmel's argument about masculinity.

10. Examine another reading (or a set of readings) from this book in terms of rituals, rites of passage, and the "Guy Code," applying Kimmel's ideas to another process in the social construction of gender.

Undercover at the Bloomingdale's Registry

Jaclyn Geller

Jaclyn Geller is a professor of English at Central Connecticut State University. Her scholarship focuses on marriage studies, and she has written about bridal culture and the institution of marriage in scholarly books, popular magazines, and newspapers. Her book *Here Comes the Bride: Women, Weddings, and the Marriage Mystique* (2001), from which this selection is excerpted, was a Barnes & Noble Selected Nonfiction Title.

. . . In 1963 Gloria Steinem went undercover as a Playboy bunny, donning fishnet stockings, a strapless bathing suit, and rabbit ears to work for one month at the Playboy Club in New York City, where she could experience life as a Hefneresque sex symbol. The Smith College graduate, journalist, and activist assumed the persona of an anonymous sex toy, displaying her cleavage for tips so that she could debunk the glamorous image of Playboy women generated by Hugh Hefner's publicity machine. Published in *Show* magazine, her subsequent two-part essay, "A Bunny's Tale" remains one of the most effective exposes of the merger of corporate interests and sexual liberation without women's liberation.[1] For two weeks in 1992 black attorney Lawrence Otis Graham endured a seven-dollar-an-hour job as a busboy in Connecticut, working at the Greenwich Country Club in order to detail the self-indulgence and casual racism and antisemitism of contemporary American suburbia in his article, "Invisible Man."[2] The Princeton graduate, corporate lawyer, and author of eleven books became a polyester-clad minimum-wage employee addressed as "busboy" by the patrons who barked orders at him. These writers temporarily eschewed their own trappings of social and professional status to taste commonplace humiliation firsthand. Today I'm utilizing their method to a different end. Rather than relinquishing social prestige, I'm assuming it. I'm stepping inside the world of the soon to be married. I plan to taste the rewards of wedlock firsthand. I plan to know the admiration and feel the self-satisfaction of the bride-to-be. I plan to experience, if only for one fictitious afternoon, the engaged woman's sense of material entitlement. Selecting one's own

---

[1] Steinem republished the essay under the title "I Was a Playboy Bunny" in *Outrageous Acts and Everyday Rebellions* (New York: Holt, Rinehart and Winston, 1983), 29–69.
[2] Lawrence Otis Graham, "Invisible Man" in *The Best American Essays 1993*, ed. Robert Atwan and Joseph Epstein (New York: Ticknor & Fields, 1993), 114–130.

wedding gifts — household goods such as dishes and bed linen — is
an integral part of the marriage process. At no other point in life does
a middle-class person feel able to ask his or her community for what
he or she needs and wants, and at no other moment does the community reach out with such magnanimity. I've studied the etiquette
of registration in myriad wedding planners, but I feel that I need to
undergo the process in order to truly understand it, so I've come to the
Bloomingdale's registry undercover as a would-be bride.

It's late afternoon on a winter Sunday. The registry is sparsely
populated. It's staffed by a single employee — an elegant West Indian
woman wearing a gray blazer and skirt, a black turtleneck, and pearl
earrings. She appears to be my age — midthirties. Sitting behind the
desk, she speaks to the only other registrant in the office, a petite
woman who is perhaps in her midtwenties and who wears a rumpled
blue trench coat and nervously clutches a clipboard. The wedding
consultant's tone is pious, insistent. "You'll want your champagne
glasses to match your wine glasses and your water goblets," she
intones. "Understand something, very often someone at the table will
drink wine and someone else will have champagne. Or let's say you're
serving both. Someone isn't ready for the champagne yet; they're still
working on the wine. So you have both kinds of glasses on the table,
and you want everything to match."

"I just like two different patterns," insists the woman. "The Cal-
vin Klein goblets and champagne flutes and the Waterford wine
glasses."

"No, no. It's not a good idea. Trust me. I've been doing this a long
time. You're not gonna be happy, and you're gonna get into returns,
which is a mess, and with everything else on your mind right now.
Keep it simple."

"My husband —"

"Forget about him. Don't involve him. Keep it simple. Keep it uniform."

"Okay, but he told me to make sure to register for a full set of demitasse cups. That's the only thing he cares about in the whole business.
He's European."

"Sure, European or not, you need demitasse cups. No question."

Sensing that this dialogue may continue for some time, I signal
the wedding consultant to let her know that I'm waiting to register but
will take a hiatus and be back shortly. I leave the registry and wander
through the floor, soaking in the opulence. Everything in the displays that surround the Bloomingdale's registry conspires to make
one feel that she has entered a magical world, a never never land of
material splendor in which money is no obstacle. The beautifully set

5

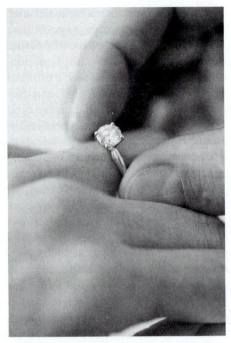

An engagement ring is part of the traditional symbolism of the marriage ritual.

tables that glow with china, silver, and crystal advertise a romantic myth, the gilded fortress in which the bride and groom set up home — the private sanctuary into which Mr. and Mrs. Right retreat from the world to revel in opulent connubial bliss. Delicate porcelain place settings adorn tables draped in white linen. Crystal decanters flank glass champagne buckets. Silver candlesticks line ceramic trays alongside stacks of lace napkins and place mats. These displays announce a mood of abundant self-satisfied domesticity. Bloomingdale's does not merely offer products to shoppers; it demonstrates the tranquility, prestige, and financial comfort that middle-class marriage is supposed to entail. From what I can see, wedlock's social code still dictates female management of the domestic sphere. Wandering among the displays are two or three lone women holding clipboards, deliberating over their selections. There is also a handful of women shopping in pairs and three with older women, aunts or mothers. I do not see one male registrant or couple.

"Should I get the nonstick or the Cuisinart cookware?" I overhear a 10
woman anxiously asking an older companion. "The Cuisinart," the
older woman replies definitively. "The nonstick gets black after a few
washings. The Cuisinart is stainless steel. Take good care of it, and it
will shine like it does when you first buy it."

Nancy Armstrong has written that the eighteenth century, which
saw the rise of a large middle class in England and then in the
United States, also witnessed the emergence of a new archetype of
femininity: the bourgeois domestic woman invested with the power
of educating children, managing a household, and ensuring standards of domestic taste. As Europe industrialized and men established businesses outside of the home, the previously male-centered,
medieval household was feminized. "Thus it was the new domestic
woman rather than her counterpart, the new economic man, who first
encroached upon aristocratic culture and seized authority from
it. . . . She therefore had to lack competitive desires and worldly
ambitions that consequently belonged — as if by some natural principle — to the male. . . . She was supposed to complement his role as
an earner and producer with hers as a wise spender and tasteful
consumer."[3]

Any skepticism about the sweeping nature of Armstrong's claims
or her assertion that eighteenth-century domestic ideals have become more rather than less powerful in the last three hundred years
evaporates upon visiting the Bloomingdale's registry. Here, the domestic woman takes her first faltering steps toward wifely authority.
Here, soothing maternal wedding consultants school female consumers in the art of purchasing. Here, women wander among display
cases accompanied by uxorious aunts, mothers, and mothers-in-law,
selecting items to personalize those shrines of coupledom, their
homes. Although the store has veered toward egalitarianism in short-
ening its name from the "bridal registry" to the "registry," this is a service offered to and utilized by women, an arena in which men clearly
have no place.

After wandering aimlessly among the displays for ten minutes, I
find a china pattern that I do like and would purchase if I were financially able to. (I'm not.) I then return to take my place as a bridal
registrant. I sit on one of the gray, upholstered chairs in the registry
office and introduce myself.

---

[3] Nancy Armstrong, *Desire and Domestic Fiction: A Political History of the Novel* (New
York: Oxford University Press, 1987), 59.

"Hi, I'm Jackie. I'm getting married, and I'm here to register."

"Well, congratulations, Jackie. I'm Jackie too! I'm your wedding 15 consultant." She smiles at me as if to say, "you've arrived," and then continues, "I'm here to help you. We'll work together throughout this whole process. Now, I want you to look over some material."

I don't feel entirely comfortable lying to this friendly stranger. But there's no other way to elicit that smooth knowing smile, that intimate congratulatory handshake, that admiring glance that tells me that I've achieved what is, in the final analysis, most important: the promise of permanent monogamy from a man.

She hands me a thick packet of paper, forms to fill out with my name and address, charts that list registration options: formal china, casual china, formal stemware, casual stemware, barware, formal flatware, casual flatware, giftware, serveware, table linens, cookware, bed linens, small electric appliances, towels, luggage, and decorative home items. I glance over the forms, and she anticipates my reaction:

"Listen, it's very overwhelming at first, setting up a home. I know that. And you can't do it all in one day. You'll want to make several trips to decide what you like and don't like. Don't commit if you're not certain, because as soon as you register for an item, it will be computerized in the system. And, your mother's friends who know that you're getting married, they may stop off here for some other reason and just end up buying, you know, since they're here anyway. And then we send it to you, and you have it, and if you don't like it, you get into returns and making corrections on the computer, which is a nightmare."

"Listen," I interrupt, "I think that I basically know what I want, the Ralph Lauren porcelain — the Academy platinum pattern. And the matching glasses — Glen Plaid I think it's called."

"Beautiful. Good choice. That goes with everything, no matter what 20 your decor is."

"But," I continue, "my friends and relatives aren't wealthy. There are an awful lot of options here — towels, bedding, kitchen stuff. I thought that I would just do dishes and glasses — twelve place settings — and then leave it at that. . . ."

"Why when you can get everything for free?" she asks me earnestly. "This is your time."

"So I should just go for it?"

"Sure. A lot of my brides register for furniture, sofas, rugs. Everyone chips in. That's the point. This is your time to get what you need. And whatever they don't buy you we'll sell to you at a significant discount. Ten percent on the furniture, for instance."

"Are you married?" I ask.   25

"No, not yet. But I'll sure know exactly what to do when it's my turn."

I enter my hypothetical choices — twelve settings of china, twelve settings of crystal wine glasses and water goblets — on the selection sheet and hand it to her, promising to return next week after evaluating my flatware, cookware, and linen options. She shakes my hand and sends me off with a gift, a book entitled, *Inspirations: The Bloomingdale's Home Planner.*

"Any final advice?" I ask, as we both stand up to say goodbye.

"Yeah. I tell all of my brides to get the George Foreman grill. It's the one advertised on television that tilts down to let all of the fat drip off of whatever meat you're cooking. It's excellent. You don't want to be without it."

"I'll think about it."   30

I ride the escalator down two floors, sink into a cream-colored leather sofa, and peruse *The Bloomingdale's Home Planner,* a hardcover volume with a spiral binding that contains page after glossy page of advice to the newly married. The text is enhanced with photographs of domestic plenitude. Like most pieces of popular advice literature, this book combines the banal with the personal, the starkly utilitarian with the poetic. There is a recipe for mushroom frittata, "an easy-to-prepare, one-course meal that's perfect anytime"[4] alongside rhapsodic descriptions of the contemporary home ("Your sanctuary and your showplace. . . . Where you retreat for relaxing times alone").[5] Directions on how to make a bed are juxtaposed with sentimental addresses to the soon to be married reader: "We wish you well on your journey. It is an exciting one."[6] The *Planner* is divided into seven sections, each of which offers a distinct component of the marital promise: "Dining In" (companionship), "Gourmet Kitchen" (hospitality), "Master Suite" (erotic fulfillment), "Personal Pleasures" (leisure time), "Interior Design" (domesticity), "Home Finance" (economic solvency), and "Travel Plans" (romantic isolation). At the bottom of each exquisitely designed page is a drawing of two interlocking, gold wedding bands adjacent to the imperative, "Call 1-899-888-2WED." . . .

As I browse through the pages of *The Bloomingdale's Home Planner,* I begin to detect the phantom bride for whom this frothy concoction

---

[4] Bloomingdale's, *Inspirations: The Bloomingdale's Home Planner* (1997), 79.
[5] Ibid., no page number.
[6] Ibid., no page number.

has been whipped up. She is the perennial, middle-class, "single" woman who yearns for the stable normalcy of married life. Having snagged a man, she must now master the domestic arts, learning how to brew the perfect pot of coffee, toss and dress the exemplary salad, and fold formal napkins. But she simultaneously feels anxious about submitting to wedlock's dicta and becoming part of a homogeneous heterosexual mass. She is the same woman whose wedding invitations — enhanced with Renaissance poetry, self-help cliches, or kitschy show tune lyrics — use a defensively individualistic rhetoric. *The Bloomingdale's Home Planner* is cunningly written to assuage this schizophrenic reader's fears. Each page assures the bride-to-be that while learning the art of home management — ordering wallpaper, sampling paint colors — she will not become a household drone. Her independent spirit, her essence, her personal style will burst through, finding expression in that shrine of self-advertising domesticity, her home. "We'll help to surround you with an ambiance that's uniquely yours," *The Planner* promises.[7]

Another distinct, equally powerful image emerges from the pages of this book: the stressed out, hardworking professional couple retreating from its daily corporate battles at the end of each day to the privacy of gourmet dinners, soothing milk baths, and restful naps on Stearns & Foster mattresses fitted with percale sheets. The wife is no longer envisioned as a full-time homemaker, vacuuming, cooking meat loafs, and fluffing pillows to ready the house for the return of her weary male commuter. Like her husband, she is a high-powered earner, a corporate warrior. Like him, she is vulnerable to the pressures of the external world, the professional and social realm outside the home that is subtly portrayed as hostile. Home is envisioned as a refuge for the overwrought modern couple, a fairy-tale retreat where each stressed out pair can find solace in each other, stirring martinis ("For a ten-to-one drink, use only two teaspoons of dry vermouth"),[8] roasting chicken ("The classic method is to baste the chicken with butter or oil every ten to twenty minutes"),[9] and sipping espresso ("Amazingly enough, cup for cup, espresso has less caffeine than regular coffee").[10] *The Planner* prescribes marital togetherness as the panacea to modern woe, urging couples to cook, clean, eat, bathe,

---

[7] Ibid., no page number.
[8] Ibid., 32.
[9] Ibid., 63.
[10] Ibid., 76.

and sleep together and preaching the value of egalitarian symbiosis: "And remember, women are not the only ones doing the cooking any longer. As more men are discovering the joys of cooking . . . they are preparing many a fine meal. . . . And couples are finding out that cooking as a team is time together well spent."[11]

In the midst of American feminism's third wave, advice literature prescribes complementary heterosexual partnership as the means by which each woman can achieve the good life. Because one's spouse provides ultimate meaning, time with him at home, even if it is spent chopping vegetables or washing dishes, facilitates intimacy and is therefore productive, useful, good. In this stabilizing social vision the conjugal household insulates each pair from worldly anxiety, offering a cornucopia of therapies for the body and mind. It is a zone of endless comfort in which "today's working couples" can enjoy dinner "from a well-set tray in the library or a warm, comfortable bed."[12] Appointed with Karastan rugs and distressed leather sofas, the urban bedroom is a modern day Garden of Eden in which today's Adam and Eve are instructed to recline ("your private corner of the world . . . an intimate room where you can relax, be alone, and be completely yourself").[13] Only at home can men and women shed their stern, adult masks and become themselves; playful kids who indulge in the "grown-up water toys" of hot tubs, jacuzzis, and hand-held shower heads.[14] Readers of *The Bloomingdale's Home Planner* are advised to soak in scented baths (". . . many a young couple has shared a drink and a bath to relax and steal an intimate hour at the end of a long, stressful day")[15] and, in a section entitled "Mastering a Massage," to rub each other's stress away.[16]

The Bloomingdale's Home Planner's glossy magazine version of mar- 35 riage is, of course, no more realistic a presentation of wedlock than *Playboy* magazine is a reliable account of American male sexuality. This document presents an inflated fantasy, a bubble. But fantasies and myths have the power to seduce. Perusing *The Planner*'s pages, I begin to understand why so many highly educated women — independent thinkers in other areas — adhere to marital convention. Despite the recent flurry of articles validating the "single" life, no

---

[11] Ibid., 52.
[12] Ibid., 15.
[13] Ibid., 88.
[14] Ibid., 107.
[15] Ibid., 104.
[16] Ibid., 112.

set of idealizing images exists for unmarried people. There are no equivalent domestic guidebooks for "single" women, no photographs that glamorize the celibate life, no images of a woman burrowing at home with a book and a glass of wine or sitting up with a friend talking. To walk away from the life justified in primers like *The Bloomingdale's Home Planner* is to resist a massive body of cultural propaganda on behalf of wedlock and jump into imaginative nothingness. Most of us are not willing to leap into a cultural void.

The Bloomingdale's Home Planner's glossy magazine version of marriage is . . . no more realistic a presentation of wedlock than *Playboy* magazine is a reliable account of American male sexuality. This document presents an inflated fantasy, a bubble. But fantasies and myths have the power to seduce.

Before leaving Bloomingdale's I head back up to the sixth floor to browse one last time among the Limoges soup tureens, Spode tea sets, and Rosenthal dinner plates. The registry is closed, the floor all but deserted. I stroll past crystal pitchers, Nambe sauce bowls, silver fondue dishes, the famed words of Virginia Woolf's 1927 novel *To the Lighthouse* echoing in my mind: "an unmarried woman has missed the best of life."[17] But this is only because we withhold it from her.

Stepping onto the escalator to leave, I witness a telling vignette. A young blonde woman in jeans and a pea coat is speaking to an older female companion; the physical resemblance is too striking for them not to be mother and daughter. "It's really nice," the young woman gushes, "to be, you know, getting settled, all settled, all married, together, with the stuff we need . . . it just feels right." As I pass the pair I notice the mother nod approvingly, smiling in what appears to be a combination of empathy, admiration, and relief. This, I realize once again, is the myth of wedlock in a nutshell, its "rightness," its "naturalness." The marital ideal rests on its proponents' inability to differentiate emotion (e.g. sexual attraction, trust, love) from institutionalization (e.g. the wedding ceremony, the bridal shower, wedding invitations, the marriage contract, bridal registration). The journey from the initial tense date to the first blush of love to intensifying commitment to betrothal to the registry to the altar is purported to be one of seamless coherence. This is ideology's peculiar power, to alchemize cultural artifice into human experience.

---

[17] Virginia Woolf, *To the Lighthouse* (New York: Harcourt, Brace & World, Inc., 1927), 77.

During the subway ride home I'm in a crowded car surrounded by the usual, heterogeneous pack of New York commuters: Chinese mothers cradling infants, Wall Street commuters working even on Sunday, young black couples completing an afternoon of shopping, Hispanic men reading the sports pages, teenagers huddled in groups, orthodox Jews heading to the far reaches of Brooklyn. I'm especially aware of the women in the car, and I find myself glancing at their left hands to see which ones are wearing a wedding band. Even a group this eclectic is divided along lines of romantic affiliation; the married women on the train share a common set of experiences that separate them even from the "single" women of their own ethnic groups. The Chinese, black, and Hasidic women who wear gold wedding bands have received tangible validation from their respective cultures, no matter how different those cultures may be from each other.

I have a sudden thought; what if each of these cultures pooled its resources toward a different kind of celebration? What if each community established the practice of celebrating a woman's twenty-fifth birthday? Just before the big birthday, friends and relatives could chip in to provide her with some basics: furniture, cookware, linens, cash. A celebration might even occur in which she would walk down an aisle, alone or surrounded by the most important people in her life, one of whom might be a lover. If it was a religious ceremony, a cleric would bless her; a secular event might involve readings, reminiscences, toasts that expressed hopes for her future. The woman would be celebrated as a remarkable entity unto herself, apart from erotic partnership, apart from the fact of having attracted a man, apart from the service that her reproductive organs might render to her community.

She would look forward to this day, as contemporary teenage girls 40 fantasize about their weddings. She would understand the event as a landmark — the day she became someone different, special, adult, in the eyes of others. But she would feel no pressure to find a man in order to secure this celebration. It would be in place, part of the trajectory of her life plan. She would not have to focus obsessively on male attention or ritualized courtship, with all of its snares and contrivances. She would not have to withhold or provide sex in order to secure the relationship that would advertise her validity to the world. Her intrinsic value would be assumed — and acknowledged materially. There is, after all, something touching about the custom of communal support for an individual coming of age. There is something admirable about the older generation's desire to help the younger generation get a start in life. These generous impulses are more expansive than the consumerist vision of domestic bliss offered by a store like Bloomingdale's. But reserving this kind of substantive support for couples is deeply problematic. All women — all people — deserve it, or no one does.

The idea of offering ritualized celebration and support to all adults, regardless of their sexual preference or romantic status, seems impossible, contrived, absurd. But this is only because the notion of wedlock as an unassailable truth is so deeply embedded in our consciousness. It is important to remember that marriage, like institutionalized male dominance itself, is not natural, timeless, or ahistorical, but that it is codified in a specific time (6000–600 B.C.E.) in the near east.[18] Archaic nation states maintained a controlling interest in women as reproductive agents and enforced female subordination through marriage law. Various means of achieving female compliance were used; among the most powerful were the bestowal of class privilege to conforming women and the "artificially created division of women into respectable and not respectable women."[19] After centuries of reform and counterreform and even in the aftermath of the twentieth-century West's mobilization of its female population, these remain wedlock's underlying categories. A woman attached to one man — a wife — is celebrated, applauded, rewarded, while a woman attached to many men or free of all men is still, very often, the subject of fear, ridicule, and contempt. To alter this state of affairs — to shift the balance in the politics of marital entitlement — we must therefore repudiate the delicious package of privilege that is modern middle-class marriage. We must eschew the short-term advantages of wedlock and instead create alternative structures that fulfill our need to ritually mark the passage into adulthood.

'I return from the contrived opulence of the Bloomingdale's registry to my stark studio apartment in Brooklyn determined to do just this. I eye my shelves crammed with books and listen to answering-machine messages from friends anxious to hear about my adventures as an undercover bride. Recalling Virginia Woolf's words once again, I decide that as an unmarried woman, I do in fact have the best in life. . . .

---

[18] Lerner, *Creation of Patriarchy*, 54–75 and 101–122.
[19] Ibid., 9.

Understanding the Text

1. What inspired Geller's attempt to go "undercover" at the Bloomingdale's registry? What does she see as the major difference between her project and those of her predecessors?

2. What, according to *The Bloomingdale's Home Planner,* are the dominant characteristics of the "ideal" wife, and how does Geller respond to this representation?

3. Geller sees the wedding ceremony and nuptials as the dominant form of women transitioning from one identity category ("single") to another ("married"). What does she propose as an alternative?

Reflection and Response

4. Registering for a wedding at a department store is just one of the many rituals that take place with the larger "wedding" rite of passage. What other rituals typically occur in advance of the wedding, and how do these rituals reflect the social construction of gender?

5. One of the statements Geller's wedding planner makes is "forget about [your husband]" (p. 152). Why do you think weddings are often, even typically, coordinated and planned by women, with little or peripheral input from the groom-to-be?

6. The "normal" script for a wedding ceremony is so common that even people who hold progressive beliefs about gender equality in families often abide these expectations of the ceremony, even though they might believe some of the values communicated by those expectations to be "old-fashioned." Why do you think this is?

Making Connections

7. Like in Amy Best's examination of the consumerist dimensions of the prom — that is, in the material and products that young women are encouraged to purchase to perform their role in the rite of passage adequately — so too in Geller's examination of the engagement period the author finds strong currents of materialism. Acquire a prom preparation guidebook or a special edition of a magazine focused on the prom and locate a bridal guidebook or magazine, and look at the advertisements surrounding the content of both publications. What messages about femininity and masculinity are suggested by the advertisements? What kinds of products are advertised the most? What conclusions can you draw about the relationship between these rites of passage and corporate involvement in shaping them?

8. Locate at least two guidebooks or Web sites devoted to wedding planning and execution, one telling women how to plan their wedding ceremony or how to prepare for the event, and one specifically addressing men. What major differences do you see between the messages given to women and those given to men about weddings, and how do these messages contribute to the social construction of gender?

9. Gay marriage has been an important issue in contemporary culture, with some states legalizing it, some recognizing only "civil unions" between same-sex couples, and some not yet permitting it at all. How does gay marriage intersect with any set of readings or ideas present in other readings in this book?

Good Girls Go Bad, for a Day

Stephanie Rosenbloom

Stephanie Rosenbloom is a staff reporter for the *New York Times*, where she is currently writing about travel in a column called *The Getaway*. Before that, she wrote for the Thursday and Sunday sections on American social trends, including fashion, relationships, and Internet culture. She was also a featured writer in *The New York Times Practical Guide to Practically Everything* (2006).

In her thigh-highs and ruby miniskirt, Little Red Riding Hood does not appear to be en route to her grandmother's house. And Goldilocks, in a snug bodice and platform heels, gives the impression she has been sleeping in everyone's bed. There is a witch wearing little more than a Laker Girl uniform, a fairy who appears to shop at Victoria's Secret and a cowgirl with a skirt the size of a tea towel.

Anyone who has watched the evolution of women's Halloween costumes in the last several years will not be surprised that these images — culled from the Web sites of some of the largest Halloween costume retailers — are more strip club than storybook. Or that these and other costumes of questionable taste will be barely covering thousands of women who consider them escapist, harmless fun on Halloween.

"It's a night when even a nice girl can dress like a dominatrix and still hold her head up the next morning," said Linda M. Scott, the author of *Fresh Lipstick: Redressing Fashion and Feminism* (Palgrave Macmillan) and a professor of marketing at the University of Oxford in England.

The trend is so pervasive it has been written about by college students in campus newspapers, and Carlos Mencia, the comedian, jokes that Halloween should now be called Dress-Like-a-Whore Day.

But the abundance of risqué costumes that will be shrink-wrapped 5 around legions of women come Oct. 31 prompts a larger question: Why have so many girls grown up to trade in Wonder Woman costumes for little more than Wonderbras?

"Decades after the second wave of the women's movement, you would expect more of a gender-neutral range of costumes," said Adie Nelson, the author of "The Pink Dragon Is Female: Halloween Costumes and Gender Markers," an analysis of 469 children's costumes and how they reinforce traditional gender messages that was published in the *Psychology of Women Quarterly* in 2000.

This Oktoberfest costume is an example of a trend toward revealing Halloween outfits for women.

Dr. Nelson, a professor of sociology at the University of Waterloo in Ontario, said the trend toward overtly sexualized costumes actually begins with little girls. "Heroic figures for women or considered icons of femininity are very much anchored in the femme fatale imagery," she said, adding that those include an assortment of Disney heroines, witches, cocktail waitresses, French maids and an "interchangeable variety of beauty queens."

While researching "Pink Dragon," Dr. Nelson found that even costumes for little girls were gendered. Boys got to be computers while the girls were cupcakes. Today, there are bride costumes for little girls but one is hard pressed to find groom costumes for little boys. Additionally, Dr. Nelson said, the girls' costumes are designed in ways that create the semblance of a bust where there is none. "Once they're older women it's just a continuation of that same gender trend," she said.

Men's costumes are generally goofy or grotesque ensembles with "Animal House"-inspired names like Atomic Wedgie and Chug-A-Lug

Beer Can. And when they dress up as police officers, firefighters and soldiers, they actually look like people in those professions. The same costumes for women are so tight and low-cut they are better suited for popping out of a cake than outlasting an emergency.

Obviously, however, many women see nothing wrong with making 10 Halloween less about Snickers bars and SweeTarts and more about eye candy.

Rebecca Colby, 28, a library clerk in Milwaukee, said the appeal of sexy costumes lies in escaping the workaday, ho-hum dress code.

"I'm not normally going to wear a corset to go out," said Ms. Colby, who has masqueraded as a Gothic witch with a low-cut bodice, a minidress-wearing bumblebee, a flapper and, this year, most likely, a "vixen pirate."

"Even though you're in a costume when you go out to a party in a bar or something, you still want to look cute and sexy and feminine," she said.

Indeed, many women think that showing off their bodies "is a mark of independence and security and confidence," said Pat Gill, the interim director of the Institute of Communications Research and a professor of gender and women's studies at the University of Illinois at Urbana-Champaign.

It is a wonder gyms do not have "get in shape for Halloween" spe- 15 cials. In her book *Dilemmas of Desire: Teenage Girls Talk About Sexuality* (Harvard University Press), Deborah Tolman, the director of the Center for Research on Gender and Sexuality at San Francisco State University and a professor of human sexuality studies there, found that some 30 teenage girls she studied understood being sexy as "being sexy for someone else, not for themselves," she said.

When the girls were asked what makes them feel sexy, they had difficulty answering, Dr. Tolman said, adding that they heard the question as "What makes you *look* sexy?"

Many women's costumes, with their frilly baby-doll dresses and high-heeled Mary Janes, also evoke male Lolita fantasies and reinforce the larger cultural message that younger is hotter.

> Many women's costumes, with their frilly baby-doll dresses and high-heeled Mary Janes . . . evoke male Lolita fantasies and reinforce the larger cultural message that younger is hotter.

"It's not a good long-term strategy for women," Dr. Tolman said.

But does that mean women should not use Halloween as an excuse to shed a few inhibitions?

"I think it depends on the spirit in which you're doing it," Dr. Tol- 20 man said. "I'm not going to go and say this is bad for all women."

Perhaps, say some scholars, it could even be good. Donning one of the many girlish costumes that sexualize classic characters from books, including *Alice's Adventures in Wonderland, Cinderella* and *The Wizard of Oz,* can be campy, female sartorial humor, said Professor Gill. It can be a way to embrace the fictional characters women loved as children while simultaneously taking a swipe at them, she said. "The humor gives you a sense of power and confidence that just being sexy doesn't," she said.

Dr. Tolman added that it is possible some women are using Halloween as a "safe space," a time to play with sexuality. By taking it over the top, she said, they "make fun of this bill of goods that's being sold to them."

"Hey, if we can claim Halloween as a safe space to question these images being sold to us, I think that's a great idea," Dr. Tolman said.

But it may be only an idea. Or, more fittingly in this case, a fantasy.

"I love to imagine that there's some real social message, that it's 25 sort of the female equivalent of doing drag," Dr. Nelson said. "But I don't think it's necessarily so well thought out."

Tanda Word, 26, a graduate student at Texas Tech University in Lubbock, who wrote a satirical article about the trend for the *Daily Toreador,* agreed. "I think it's damaging because it's not just one night a year," she said. "If it's all the costume manufacturers make, I think it says something bigger about the culture as a whole."

Salacious costumes — the most visible reminder that Halloween is no longer the sole domain of children — have been around longer than plastic Grim Reaper scythes. But there has been an emergence of "ultrasexy" costumes in the last couple of years, according to Christa Getz, the purchasing director for BuyCostumes.com, which sells outfits with names like Little Bo "Peep Show" and Miss Foul Play.

"Probably over 90 to 95 percent of our female costumes have a flirty edge to them," Ms. Getz said, adding that sexy costumes are so popular the company had to break its "sexy" category into three subdivisions this year.

Heather Siegel, the vice president of HalloweenMart.com, said her company's sexy category is among its most popular. (The two best-selling women's costumes are a low-cut skin-tight referee uniform and a pinup-girl-inspired prisoner outfit called Jail Bait.)

"Almost everybody gets dressed up really, really sexy for it," said 30 Carrie Jean Bodner, a senior at Cornell University in Ithaca who wrote about the abundance of skimpy Halloween garb for the *Cornell Daily Sun* last year. "Even the girls who wouldn't dream of going to class without their pearls and pullovers."

Last year Ms. Bodner, 21, dressed up as a sexy pinch-hitter for an imaginary baseball team. This year she and her friends are considering being va-voom Girl Scouts.

Ms. Getz of BuyCostumes.com said far more women are buying revealing costumes than firing off indignant e-mail messages asking, "Why are all of your costumes so sexy?" (though some do).

Still, women may be buying racy outfits because that is all that is available. Ms. Getz said she wished there were more sexy men's costumes on the market and that the lack of them is but further evidence of the gender double standard. "It's just not as socially acceptable," she said, adding that men feel comfortable expressing themselves with Halloween costumes that are "either crude or outrageous or obnoxious."

Ms. Siegel of HalloweenMart.com said the costume industry is merely mirroring the fashion industry, where women have more variety in their wardrobes. Besides, she said, men are less interested in accessorizing. "They're happy grabbing a mask and a robe and being done," she said.

At least they get a robe. Ms. Bodner of Cornell estimated that it will 35
be about 30 degrees in Ithaca on Oct. 31.

"We're not just risking our dignity here," she said. "We're risking frostbite."

Understanding the Text

1. What are the major differences Rosenbloom sees between the costumes designated for boys and those designated for girls?

Reflection and Response

2. Do you think the "sexualized" costumes for young girls and young women represent part of the social construction of feminine gender types as sex objects, or do these costumes simply offer a way for "good girls to go bad for a day" — as simply "play" or experimentation? In other words, do you think it is healthy or unhealthy for girls to experiment in this way? Why or why not?

Making Connections

3. Rosenbloom summarizes the findings of a longer study of children's Halloween costumes. With these findings in mind, visit a costume store or look at a Halloween costume catalog and examine the costumes (and perhaps the language used to describe them). How do the costumes and descriptions mesh with typical expectations or stereotypes of masculinity and femininity?

4. How might the readings in Chapter 5 of *Composing Gender* complement the descriptions of costumes that Rosenbloom describes? Are the commodification and sexualization of young girls directly impacting the Halloween costume market, or do these costumes indicate that young girls have some control over their own images and are not completely subject to Hollywood and other media forces?

Male Circumcision: A Gender Perspective

Joseph Zoske

Joseph Zoske is a social worker whose primary field of practice is health care. He is on the faculty at Siena College, where he administers the Social Work Program and teaches a variety of courses about health care communication, interpersonal communication, and men's health issues. He is also a published poet. This selection was originally published in the *Journal of Men's Studies* in 1998.

. . . Circumcision is . . . more than a benign medical procedure. It is fundamentally an elective amputation of healthy genital tissue driven by the power of tradition and performed without a patient's consent, occurring when he is most vulnerable and completely dependent.

Broad medical, psychological, and ethical debates continue to surround this practice, displaying a perplexing lack of resolution. It continues to be readily authorized and infrequently questioned by parents or hospital personnel and not generally considered by and of the parties to be an act of violence. However, there are strong arguments that support viewing circumcision as a societal act of physical and sexual assault; an event that holds deep significance for men's psychosexual development, reinforces cultural attitudes of disregard for the well-being of men's bodies, and tacitly accepts violence as a part of men's lives. This article intertwines these ideas and presents routine neonatal circumcision as a fundamental men's issue. Framed within a historical context and an ongoing medical debate, circumcision should be seen as the first psychological and somatic wounding of men — a cultural act of gender betrayal and brutality. . . .

Technical Details

To avoid the discussion becoming lost in the abstract, it is important to understand the medical specifics of this surgery. Circumcision requires that a male infant be taken from his parents and placed on a restraint table with his extremities fastened or held down, while a variety of surgical instruments (probes, clamps, scalpel) are used to grasp the foreskin, separate it from the glans, slit it, stretch it, crush it, and amputate it (Cohen, 1992; Gelbaum, 1993). It has, also, most often been performed without anesthesia due to medical contraindications, or with the use of a painful local anesthetic injection (the dorsal nerve block). However, the latter "is not widely used due to concerns of sufficient safety, the additional time required to perform the block, and the continued belief that the pain of neonatal circumcision is insignificant" (Howard, Howard, & Weitzman, 1994, p. 641). Numerous studies have clearly identified traumatic pain responses in infants, and specifically the severe and persistent pain of circumcision (Anand & Hickey, 1987; Stang, Gunner, Snellman, Condon, & Kesterbaum, 1988). While investigators are exploring the efficacy of topical anesthesia (Benini, Johnston, Faucher, & Aranda, 1993), there remains lasting impact from the pain experience of current practice. Taddio, Goldbach, Ipp, Stevens, and Koren (1995) found continuing pain response in baby boys at four to six months, and expressed concern for possible long-term effects of the intense pain of circumcision. Anand and Hickey (1987), concluding their review of more than 200 citations, spoke of the "memory of pain in neonates" and cautioned about circumcision's possible long-term psychological effects (p. 1325). Ritter (1992), an activist anti-circumcision physician, describes the procedure as a "great human and humane transgression" in which the baby's first perception of genital sensation is needless pain (p. 3-1).

Beyond pain, there are many other risks. "Although not technically difficult," Gluckman, Stoller, Jacobs, and Kogan report (1995), "it results in a large number of reported and unreported complications annually. . . . The potential for complications from circumcision is real and ranges from the insignificant to tragic" (p. 778). Among the complications noted we find: bleeding, infections (localized and systemic), excess foreskin removal, glans necrosis or amputation, removal of penile shaft skin, psychosocial problems in adulthood, erectile dysfunction, and death. "The fairly high rate (1.5% to 15%) reflects the fact that the procedure is often performed by an inexperienced individual without attention to basic surgical procedures" (p. 778).

History

One might imagine that an intelligent species like man would leave   5
them (the human genitals) alone. Sadly, this has never been the case.
For thousands of years in many different cultures, the genitals have
fallen victim to an amazing variety of mutilations and restrictions.
For organs that are capable of giving us an immense amount of pleasure, they have been given an inordinate amount of pain (Morris,
1985, p. 218).

Ritual circumcision (as differentiated from modern medical circumcision) has existed throughout history. Among the many 19th and 20th century authors who have studied its historical, religious, and cultural aspects, there is a consensus that its roots originated thousands of years ago, predating Judaism, with depictions of circumcision found even in Stone-Age cave drawings (Bitschai, 1956; Wallerstein, 1980; Wrana, 1939). Rites of initiation, fertility rituals, control of sexual drives, and tribal identification — for men and women — are considered the primary purposes for circumcision's many variations (Campbell, 1988; Zindler, 1990).

Male ritual circumcision involves various degrees of foreskin removal, while female circumcision ranges from clitoridectomy to vulvectomy to infibulation (known as Pharaonic circumcision — the most severe and mutilating form). However, whether past or present, ritual circumcision serves cultural purposes, as opposed to justification as a health promoting practice (Aldeeb Abu Sahlieh, 1994). As James DeMeo (1990) succinctly states, "The ritual [circumcision] has absolutely nothing whatsoever to do with medicine, health, or science in practically all cases" (p. 108). Regrettably, ritual circumcision of females, unlike males, is still extensively performed in many cultures throughout the world — especially within African and Arab Islamic nations — where, for example, 80–90% of Somalian and Sudanese girls are infibulated by age seven or eight (Hicks, 1993; Hosken, 1982; Lightfoot-Klein, 1989; van der Kwaak, 1992). Further cultural/religious discussion of ritual circumcision (male or female), however, is beyond the scope of this article. What is significant is the acknowledgment of the depths of circumcision's origins. It is a practice deeply embedded within global consciousness — interwoven within centuries of cultural myths, values, and customs. All of which contribute to the resistance of 20th century thinking in releasing it from modern U.S. medical practice.

Routine medical circumcision is similarly rooted in neither science nor medicine. Instead, it grew out of the mid-19th century's hysteria and superstition about masturbation. Given the sexual mores of that time, child-rearing practices, and the lack of understanding of much disease etiology, masturbation was blamed for a litany of ills. Insanity, epilepsy, blindness, and even death were its feared results, with circumcision viewed as a "treatment" (Remondino, 1891/1974; Romberg, 1985). As a primary means of controlling masturbation in young children, circumcision peaked between 1850 and 1879 with even physicians recommending its use (deMausse, 1974, p. 49). . . . .

It took about 100 years for a different viewpoint, a more enlightened one, to grow within the medical community, stemming from the

British physician Douglas Gardiner's (1949) critical article "The Fate of the Foreskin." For the first time, a direct challenge was made to the practice of routine circumcision. Physicians were encouraged to delay circumcision for 2–3 years, until its "minor advantages" could be better assessed. The message was heard within the structure of the British National Health Service. Together with its 1948 policy restrictions on elective surgery (Romberg, 1985) the circumcision rate in England — always less than the circumcision rate found in the United States — dropped dramatically (Wallerstein, 1985). In the United States, however, it would take another generation for alternative ideas to take hold. . . .

Though the *Journal of the American Medical Association* published a 10
courageous editorial in 1965, written by Morgan and pointedly titled, "The Rape of the Phallus," it wasn't until the 1970s when formal medical organizations came out with official position statements opposing routine circumcision. The American Academy of Pediatrics (AAP, 1971) formed an Ad Hoc Task Force Committee on Circumcision that reported its objection and reiterated its stand once again in 1975: "There is no absolute medical indication for routine circumcision of the newborn" (Thompson, King, Knox, & Korones, 1975). The American College of Obstetricians and Gynecologists (ACOG, 1983) eventually concurred. Nevertheless, the incidence rate did not change. Instead, the 1980s brought more frequent opinions, studies, and debate in support of the practice. The AAP later reviewed existing data and changed its stance to a neutral position. While acknowledging issues of pain, contraindications of anesthesia, and the role of good hygiene, it concluded with the noncommittal statement that "newborn circumcision has potential medical benefits and advantages as well as disadvantages and risks" (AAP, 1989, p. 390).

With the repudiation of masturbation as an illness, physicians were now citing fears of infectious disease and cancer as justifications. Countless studies and articles were reporting on the protective effect of circumcision relative to: urinary tract infections (with a small projected 1.4% incidence rate), penile cancer (a serious albeit very rare malignancy occurring in 2/100,000 cases), HIV, cervical cancer in female sex partners, STDs, and minor inflammations and/or infections of the foreskin or urethral meatus (i.e., opening at the tip) (Wiswell, 1992; Wiswell & Hachey, 1993). Further, adherence to tradition and custom were raised in arguments of "convenience" in personal hygiene and a need to "look like dad."

. . . Advocates speak of preventive medicine, while opponents call for an end to violence and the teaching of proper hygiene practices. The former group feels they are acting in the child's best interest, while the latter argues that the medical dictum "Primun Non Nocere" (First, do no harm) should guide this issue. Beyond the ongoing medical debate, however, there is a disturbing silence regarding such significant issues as foreskin physiology, the normalcy of the intact penis, loss and grief, and circumcision's impact upon a man's overall psychosexual development.

. . . The impact of circumcision upon the sexual nature of boys and men deserves consideration. A man's foreskin after all is not an anachronistic error by nature, but an important functional aspect of masculine sexuality. . . .

Relevant issues such as low self-esteem, sexual avoidance, trauma reactions, social interactional difficulties, and treatment considerations are more readily articulated about the female experience of circumcision (Bengston & Baldwin, 1993; Miller, 1991; Toubia, 1994). Psychotherapist Miller (1991) discusses the phenomena of women perpetuating the victimization of female circumcision to the next generation. "They were unable to defend themselves as young girls and were forced to repress their feelings. Today, as a result of their repression, they can justify the procedure as harmless and necessary (p. 74). Bengston and Baldwin (1993) specifically recommend counseling strategies for women similar to those used for a victim of sexual assault or for a woman grieving the loss of a female body part as in mastectomy. Toubia (1994), writing in the prestigious *New England Journal of Medicine*, speaks to circumcision's psychological effects on women often being subtle and buried in layers of denial and acceptance of social norms. Voicing the male counterpart to this surgical assault, however, has been much rarer. . . .

Cultural Denial

Through his linguistic studies, Mario Pei (1965) demonstrates language's cultural power in maintaining many ritualized activities over the centuries via its written, spoken, gestural, and symbolic forms. "Language," he writes, "is an all-pervasive conveyor, interpreter and shaper of humankind's social and scientific endeavors" (p. 29). When circumcision, then, is viewed by the culture as a "prophylactic surgical procedure performed by medical personnel as part of standard hospital practice," it creates a narrow framework in which to consider its implications upon the personal life of the boy and man. Boyd (1990) argues for the term "genital mutilation" when speaking about circumcision, as clinical words tend to trivialize and dismiss the depth of emotional and physical implications of foreskin removal. Such a term "is not only scientifically accurate, but also honors the feelings of those who feel they are victims of circumcision" (Boyd, 1990, p. 8). Directly speaking to men, Boyd further writes

If what is routinely done to baby boys started being done to baby girls in the U.S., there would be a great hue and cry and very legitimate charges of child abuse. But we've come to accept male circumcision as normal. The force of tradition has shut our cries at our own violation, our mutilation, and we've adapted to the silent denial. (p. 37)

Such language directly confronts cultural denial, that is, the forgetting that normal male genitalia have been intentionally altered, made unnatural not by the male's choice. This conceptualization is new for men, but not for women.

"If what is routinely done to baby boys started being done to baby girls in the U.S., there would be a great hue and cry and very legitimate charges of child abuse. But we've come to accept male circumcision as normal."

Illegal in the United Kingdom since the Prohibition of Female Circumcision Act of 1985, "female genital mutilation" became the preferred term at the U.K.'s First National Conference on Female Genital Mutilation in 1989 (Webb & Hartley, 1994). Also, at the International Conference on Population and Development held in Cairo in September, 1994, in response to World Health Organization estimates of more than 2 million circumcisions performed on girls and women each year, a uniform condemnation statement read, "Governments are urged to prohibit female genital mutilation wherever it exists" (International Conference on Population and Development, 1994). Both of these progressive international bodies, though, were silent on the same occurring to boys and men.

In 1985, invoking law and judicial case precedent, Brigman labeled "child mutilation through routine neonatal circumcision of males . . . as barbarous as female circumcision," and called for it to be acknowledged as the "most widespread form of child abuse in (U.S.) society" (p. 337). In exploring the constitutionality of parental decision-making rights and the child's rights to privacy and protection, he argues that neither physicians nor parents should be safe from government authority to prohibit non-medically warranted circumcision, and suggests a class-action civil rights suit as an effective societal response to "child mutilation." Farrell's (1986) words similarly confront our denial of the trauma of male circumcision by referring to it graphically as when "their penises are taken to the blade of a knife and cut," and underscores "the subconscious lack of caring about men that is displayed" (p. 231).

Re-framing circumcision into issues of abuse and rights is more than a conceptual shift. A generation ago, noted biologist and species analyst Desmond Morris (1973) called circumcision a form of "adult aggression" (p. 243). Today, however, more radical politicized anti-circumcision statements name it as "a crime" (K, 1995) and an act of "terrorism" (Worth, 1995), and consider it a core link to the perpetuation of fear, rage, and violence within men. It has also become the focus of citizen action. For example, the activist group NOHARMM (i.e., the National Organization to Halt the Abuse and Routine Mutilation of Males) was founded in 1992, and conducts national advocacy and information campaigns in defense of the child's right to an intact body, and in support of the empowerment of men. . . .

Conclusion

In the face of a growing body of opposing scientific evidence and an 20 increasingly vocal anti-circumcision movement by both consumers and professionals, the majority of newborn American males continue to experience non-consensual amputation of healthy genital tissue. Pro-circumcision empiricists pursue a search for scientific evidence that supports prophylactic benefits of surgery; however, their findings remain narrow and ambiguous. Their opponents submit that, as the United States holds a global minority stance on this medical custom, American males do not hold a distinction of being born in need of immediate surgical correction, and that simply good hygiene would allay concerns with medical risks, patient rights, and psychological trauma. Others take a middle ground and defer the issue to the process of informed consent between physician and parents. Finally, activists and victims speak about violence against innocent baby boys, urging that nature and justice prevail over social custom.

This article has attempted to show that beyond the biomedical aspects of routine medical circumcision lie complex societal issues that affect core elements of masculinity. Medical literature tends to avoid or obscure this via its more reductionistic clinical approach.

However, considering the massive scale upon which this elective neonatal surgery is performed, to one particular gender, an integrative cultural-based examination of this issue seems necessary. The broadest, most male-affirming statement found has been made by two female pioneering anti-circumcision advocates and nurses, Milos and Macri (1992). They raise the debate about routine medical circumcision of U.S. boys to a global level, and speak to issues shared by both genders.

Women have struggled to achieve rights of body ownership for themselves. It is imperative that mutual respect for these inalienable human rights be extended, not only to the women in Africa with whom we can identify, but also to men, male children, and male newborns. (p. 94S)

Boyd (1990) summarizes the issue concisely: "For over a hundred years, it has been a surgery in search of a justification" (p. 42). Unless health studies and men's studies combine, this search may continue in its circular fashion.

References

Aldeeb Abu Sahlieh, S. A. (1994). To mutilate in the name of Jehovah or Allah: Legitimation of male and female circumcision. *Medicine and Law,* 13, 575–622.

American Academy of Pediatrics (AAP), Committee on the fetus and newborn. (1971). *Standards and recommendations for hospital care of newborn infants* (5th ed.), 110. Evanston, IL: AAP.

American Academy of Pediatrics. (1989). Report of the ad hoc task force on circumcision. *Pediatrics,* 84, 388–391.

American College of Obstetricians & Gynecologists (ACOG). (1983). *Guidelines for perinatal care.* Washington, D.C.: Committee on Obstetrics, Maternal and Fetal Medicine.

Anand, K. J. S., & Hickey, P. R. (1987). Pain and its effects in the human neonate. *New England Journal of Medicine,* 317, 1321–1329.

Bengston, B., & Baldwin, C. (1993). The international student: Female circumcision issues. *Journal of Multicultural Counseling and Development,* 21(3), 168–173. [Special issue: Multicultural health issues].

Benini, F., Johnston, C., Faucher, D., & Aranda, J. V. (1993, August 18). Topical anesthesia during circumcision in newborn infants. *Journal of the American Medical Association,* 270, 850–853.

Bitschai, J. (1956). *A history of urology in Egypt.* Cambridge, MA: Riverside Press.

Boyd, B. R. (1990). *Circumcision: What it does.* San Francisco: Taterhill Press.

Brigman, W. (1985). Circumcision as child abuse: The legal and constitutional issues. *Journal of Family Law,* 23(3), 337–357.

Campbell, J. (with B. Moyers). (1988). *The power of myth.* New York: Doubleday.

Cohen, M. S. (1992). Circumcision. In J. F. Fowler (Ed.), *Urologic surgery* (pp. 422–428). Boston: Little, Brown.

deMausse, L. (1974). *The history of childhood.* New York: Peter Bedrick Books.

DeMeo, J. (1990). Desertification and the origins of armoring: The Sahasasian connection. *Journal of Orgonomy,* 24, 99–110.

Farrell, W. (1986). *Why men are the way they are.* New York: McGraw-Hill.

Gardiner, D. (1949). The fate of the foreskin: A study of circumcision. *British Medical Journal, 2,* 1433.

Gelbaum, I. (1993, Supplement, March/April). Circumcision: Refining a traditional technique. *Journal of Mid-Wifery, 38,* 18S–30S.

Gluckman, G. R., Stoller, M. I., Jacobs, M. M., & Kogan, B. A. (1995). Newborn penile glans amputation during circumcision and successful reattachment. *Journal of Urology, 153,* 778–779.

Hicks, E. K. (1993). *Infibulation: Female mutilation in Islamic northeastern Africa.* New Brunswick, NJ: Transaction Publishers.

Hosken, F. (1982). *The Hosken report: Genital and sexual mutilation of females* (Revised). Lexington, MA: Women's International Network News.

Howard, C. R., Howard, F. M., & Weitzman, M. L. (1994). Acetaminophen analgesia in neonatal circumcision: The effect on pain. *Pediatrics, 93,* 624–628.

International Conference on Population and Development. (1994, September 17). Knight-Ridder News Service.

K., A. (1995). [Letter to the editor]. *Mentor, 7*(1), 6.

Lightfoot-Klein, H. (Ed). (1989). *Prisoners of ritual: An odyssey into female genital circumcision in Africa.* Binghamton, NY: Haworth Press.

Miller, A. (1991). *Breaking down the wall of silence: The liberating experience of facing painful truth.* New York: Dutton.

Milos, M., & Macri, D. (1992, Supplement, March/April). Circumcision: A medical or a human rights issue? *Journal of Mid-Wifery, 37*(2), 87S–96S.

Morgan, W. (1965, July 19). The rape of the phallus [Commentary]. *Journal of the American Medical Association, 193*(3), 123–124.

Morris, D. (1973). *Intimate behavior.* New York: Bantam Books.

Morris, D. (1985). *Body watching.* New York: Crown.

Pei, M. (1965). *The story of language.* New York: Lippincott.

Remondino, P. C. (1974). *History of circumcision from the earliest times to the present.* New York: AMS Press. (Original work published 1891.)

Ritter, T. (1992). *Say no to circumcision!* Aptos, CA: Hourglass Book Publishing.

Romberg, R. (1985). *Circumcision: The painful dilemma.* South Hadley, MA: Bergen & Garvey Publishers.

Stang, H. J., Gunner, M. R., Snellman, L., Condon, L. M., & Kesterbaum, R. (1988). Local anesthesia for neonatal circumcision: Effects on distress and cortisol response. *Journal of the American Medical Association, 259,* 1507–1511.

Taddio, A., Goldbach, M., Ipp, M., Stevens, B., & Koren, G. (1995, February 4). Effects of neonatal circumcision on pain responses during vaccination in boys. *Lancet, 345,* 291–292.

Thompson, H. C., King, L. R., Knox, E., & Korones, S. B. (1975). Report of the ad hoc task force on circumcision. *Pediatrics, 56,* 610–611.

Toubia, N. (1994). Female circumcision as a public health issue. *New England Journal of Medicine, 331,* 712–716.

van der Kwaak, A. (1992). Female circumcision and gender identity: A questionable alliance? *Social Science and Medicine, 35,* 777–787.

Wallerstein, E. (1980). *Circumcision: An American health fallacy.* New York: Springer Publishing Company.

Wallerstein, E. (1985). Circumcision: The uniquely American medical enigma. *Urology Clinics of North America,* 12, 123–132.

Webb, E., & Hartley, B. (1994). Female genital mutilation: A dilemma in child protection. *Archives of Disease in Childhood,* 70, 441–444.

Wiswell, T. (1992). Circumcision: An update. *Current Problems in Pediatrics,* 22, 424–431.

Wiswell, T., & Hachey, D. O. (1993). Urinary tract infections and the uncircumcised state: An update. *Clinical Pediatrics,* 32, 130–134.

Worth, P. (1995, Fall). Beyond harm: The politics of circumcision. *Man, Alive!: Journal of Men's Wellness,* 8(3), 6–7.

Wrana, P. (1939). Historical review: Circumcision. *Archives of Pediatrics,* 6, 385–392.

Zindler, F. R. (1990, February). Circumcision: The stone age in the steel age. *American Atheist,* 34–40.

Appendix: Organizations against Male Circumcision

Doctors Opposing Circumcision, 2442 N. W. Market Street, Seattle, WA 98107.

National Organization of Circumcision Information Resource Centers, P.O. Box 2512, San Anselmo, CA 94979.

National Organization of Restoring Men, 3205 Northwood Drive, Suite 209, Concord, CA 94520-4506.

National Organization to Halt the Abuse and Routine Mutilation of Males, P.O. Box 460795, San Francisco, CA 94146.

Nurses for the Rights of the Child, 369 Montezuma, #354, Santa Fe, NM 87501.

Understanding the Text

1. Why does Zoske see male infant circumcision fundamentally as a human rights issue?

2. What are some of the reasons parents of newborns still elect to have their male children circumcised?

3. What are some of the risks — physical or emotional — of male infant circumcision?

Reflection and Response

4. Do you personally think circumcision should be performed as a routine elective medical procedure, or should it be banned? Why or why not?

5. Many people cite among their reasons for elective circumcision for newborns a feeling that the child should "look like his father." How does this imitative desire play out in other gender dynamics?

6. Zoske cites sources that call circumcision a "crime." What do you think of criminalizing this practice?

7. Around the world, the practice of female genital circumcision has been widely criticized and has become a central point of global women's rights campaigns. Why do you think the same has not been true for male genital circumcision?

Making Connections

8. Gather some of the statements from recognized bodies of national or international health organizations on the medical and ethical dimensions of male infant circumcision, and use those statements to discuss and contend with Zoske's claims. Is there medical consensus on the issue across countries? What are some of the major points of conflict surrounding the practice of circumcision?

9. In Germany in 2012, controversies erupted after a national high court deemed circumcision a human rights abuse and banned the practice as such. A little over a month later, the practice was reinstituted as "legal." Research this case, and reflect on its connections with Zoske's claims and the claims of others who have written on the issue of circumcision.

10. Infant male circumcision is presented by Zoske as a medical procedure performed without the patient's consent, and without regard to freedom of choice — and therefore he believes it should be illegal. Using other readings from this book, consider the role *laws* play in the social construction of gender. How have laws in the past helped change gender practices, and our understanding of masculinity and femininity?

11. Do some research on the debate about infant male circumcision in the United States. What groups support it, and what groups do not, and why? What are some of the positions and counterpositions taken by these groups in relation to one another's claims? Finally, where do you stand on the issue?

4

How Do We
Define Sexuality?

J ust as commonplace notions of gender see masculinity and femininity as flowing in an unproblematic way from an individual's biological sex category, so too do many people consider there to be an inherent linkage between sex, gender, and sexuality. Gender and sexuality are commonly linked in widespread beliefs about "normal" sexual orientation: the idea that individuals born with male or female anatomy will not only naturally manifest masculine and feminine characteristics but will also be naturally attracted exclusively to the opposite sex. But both sexuality, as a vital part of human experience and pleasure, and sexual orientation are far more complicated than such ideas suggest. First, expressions of sexuality are not simply natural: individuals learn through many social mechanisms what kinds of sexual acts and what kinds of sexual scripts are appropriate and pleasurable. The fundamental sex drive inherent in human beings is shaped and directed in countless ways according to all kinds of social permissions and prohibitions. Furthermore, sexual orientation itself may be construed as a social phenomenon: a division of people into categories dependent on their sexual tendencies toward same-sex, opposite-sex, both, or all kinds of sex partners.

The readings in this chapter address the socially constructed nature of sexuality itself, along with the correlative "identities" associated with "straight," "gay," "bi," and "queer" cultures. At the heart of all the readings are provocative and challenging questions about human sexuality in its "natural" state and about whether or not there is (or should be) any one sexual orientation deemed more correct or legitimate than another. Other questions arise such as whether or not human sexual orientation is shaped by social and cultural forces so powerfully that homoerotic desires, for example, not being deemed "legitimate" and sometimes even branded "immoral," are disciplined out of individuals who develop their sexual orientation according to social codes about proper forms of sexual expression.

Throughout *Composing Gender*, many readings refer to sexuality as an inevitable part of gender construction, and several authors use the terms "heteronormative" and "compulsory heterosexuality" to describe a social structure in which the expression of sexuality is seen as normal only when it is directed toward the opposite sex. The word "compulsory" even suggests that achieving the "proper" display of sexuality is something that society at large encourages if not demands from individuals—which may indicate, as Pepper Schwartz imagines in "The Social Construction of Heterosexuality," that heterosexuality itself in fact is a sort of discipline, a form of sexual identification that must be constantly monitored and kept in check, and may not be as automatic as many people think. Sandra Bem, in "On Judith Butler," summarizes the work of an important feminist scholar in order to demonstrate that instead of attempting to eliminate gender polarization by pointing to overlapping, common interests between masculinity and femininity, Butler and others instead argue for an explosion of new and equally legitimate categories in such a way as to normalize multivalent sexual identities and practices. C. J. Pascoe, in " 'Dude, You're a Fag': Adolescent Male Homophobia," based on her fieldwork at an American high school, attempts to understand how popular usage of the word "fag" helps regulate and police heterosexual identity among young people. Finally, Patricia Hill Collins, in "Hegemonic Masculinity and Black Gender Ideology," explores the social construction of black sexuality as it relates to hegemonic white masculinity and sexuality. These readings all explore the ways that we conceive of sexuality in relation to gender, focusing particularly on the practices, categories, and language we use to define ourselves and others.

The Social Construction of Heterosexuality

Pepper Schwartz

Pepper Schwartz is a noted professor of sociology at the University of Washington in Seattle. She studies human sexuality and has written several books on the subject for both academic and nonacademic audiences, including *The Gender of Sexuality: Exploring Sexual Possibilities* (with Virginia Rutter), *What I've Learned about Sex: Leading Sex Educators, Therapists, and Researchers Share Their Secrets* (with Debra Haffner), and *Prime: Adventures and Advice on Sex, Love, and the Sensual Years.* She has also served as a media expert on sexuality, appearing on television shows such as *Oprah* and *The Today Show*, and writing columns for publications like *Glamour* and the *New York Times.* This selection is an article she published in an anthology edited by Michael Kimmel in 2007 titled *The Sexual Self: The Construction of Sexual Scripts.*

Much of modern sex research has grown from the social constructionist viewpoint articulated by Simon and Gagnon in *Sexual Conduct,* the pathbreaking book that encouraged a generation of young scholars to look beyond the collection of data points and into the cultural construction of sexual norms, values, perceptions, and behaviors. Way ahead of their time, Simon and Gagnon made all things problematic and asked us to at least understand the cultural lens we used to interpret behavior and gender. . . .

I would not be surprised to get a ho-hum reaction to this enterprise. We tend to explain the exotic and problematize the exception. If most people are five foot ten, we try to explain under five feet or over seven. If something is common and normative, we think we understand it, and we certainly feel no need to explain it. But, in fact, that tendency merely constructs a black box, a familiar shape that fools us into thinking we can explain something merely because we come in contact with it every day. This acceptance of the common obfuscates in two ways: we create post hoc justifications about why what exists is supposed to exist (and mistake that for wisdom), and by accepting a "natural order of things" we hide all the nuances of "fact" by inhibiting further investigation or critique. As a result, we have neglected the social construction of heterosexuality as if it was unproblematic—as if we are born, and poof! we are totally and adequately heterosexual, a mere outcome of some natural selection with an invariant program that creates heterosexuality as a uniform product, with no other markers or interesting differences within until other shades of sexual orientation are introduced.

In fact, "doing heterosexuality" is no less problematic than homosexuality—though its punishments are more for failure than for accomplishment—and the norm is enforced and sanctioned differently from exceptional behavior. Reactions to failures of heterosexual enactment are less violently corrected than portrayals of homosexual identity—except, of course, when a failure of adequate enactment causes an attribution of homosexuality, and psychic or physical violence follows in order to preserve normative heterosexual roleplaying along narrowly constructed and strongly idealized stereotypes.

Just what are those stereotypes and idealistic portrayals of heterosexuality? They vary by region of the world, country, and subculture, but they share a common body of work, and those normative expectations are fed to us at the same time we are being breast-fed. Countless research papers have shown that even infants are programmed into adult sexual niches: we are socially constructed as heterosexual as soon as we are propelled out into the world. Hospitals still paste blue or pink bows on babies' heads, and oohs and ahs about the "little man" and baby girl usually quickly include comments on chests, legs, and genitals, creating expectations for the man or woman to be. Baby boys are held less and cooed at less, says the research, not because they are loved less (there is certainly some evidence that they may be loved more in some families) but because they are being handled in a way that preserves their manliness—their heterosexuality—right from the start. Little girls are dressed in brighter colors and frillier outfits because they are supposed to be supremely adorable as part of their core equipment right from the beginning.

> Countless research papers have shown that even infants are programmed into adult sexual niches: we are socially constructed as heterosexual as soon as we are propelled out into the world.

Heterosexuality has its grave expectations. They are not articu- 5 lated all at once—some are never openly articulated—but we all know that a lack of articulation of norms doesn't mean they don't exist. Briefly, I would like to mention some of the presumptions and social scripts that guide our management of heterosexuality, and comment on some of the consequences of our peculiar rules and regulations.

There are several overarching requirements of heterosexuality that I believe organize the major script of being heterosexual in American society. First of all, heterosexuality is confabulated with gender performance. Whatever the culture, its norms about masculinity and femininity are supposed to co-vary with heterosexual enactment, and gender itself is expected to be unambiguous and performed according to the cultural outlines of the moment. Even today, after the sexual and gender revolutions of the late 1960s and 70s, heterosexual dress codes, mannerisms, and body language are still strictly mandated. Although our culture has antiheroes who disdain these conventions (most notably located in the worlds of rock and roll, grunge, heavy metal and other communities of art and counterculture), the majority culture creates cultural icons in its magazines, TV shows, [and] movies, featuring models that tell us what exact gender displays portray heterosexual correctness.

Fashion designers and media stars are quite important. They become the cultural trend setters for the young. No one who has observed the fashion impact of Britney Spears, Lindsay Lohan, and other teen idols can deny with a straight face (as it were) that popular culture creates gender norms. And, I should add, it is not just children or teens who use movie stars and band members as guides to sexual correctness: the Academy Awards telecast is watched by millions of avid viewers with one of the central agendas of the entire evening being the observation of who wears what, who appears with whom, and how all of this translates into sexiness. Just about every sitcom and drama is a commentary on who is a man's man, who is a man's woman, and how do characters carry off their evocation of male and female sexual power. Even as we note characters as caricatures, they serve as sexual ideals. The fan magazines exist and prosper because millions of Americans want to follow the stars' lives, copy their wedding dress, gossip about their love affairs, and resemble them as much as possible. This goes way beyond casual ogling; stars are the new royals and their lifestyle choices—such as turning to plastic surgery—begin national trends, in this case creating a new acceptance of plastic surgery so that standards of attractiveness in middle-aged women are changing (helped, of course, by television shows making the process as well as the product fascinating. *The Swan* and several other programs actually show operations or stages of recovery, touting the self-determination of the patient while minimizing the pain and possibility of complications. Of course, in the very act of setting standards based on stars, gender roles become more problematic, since it is hard to measure up against the fantasy embodiment of masculinity and femininity). It is fair to assume that for many who mimic the style and look of a sex god or goddess, the gap between their idol and themselves serves to erode the individual's confidence in competent heterosexual performance. Who can ever be as "male" and macho as

Bruce Willis, wisecracking as he incinerates a building full of bad guys, saves his buddy, and beds the astoundingly beautiful women who populate action films? Who can be as charming as Cameron Diaz—perfectly proportioned and the object of everyone's desire? Who can be as winsome and pure of heart as Julia Roberts, a woman leggier than most runway models, in the storybook romances in which she stars? In drama after drama, she offers the eternal portrayal of female heterosexuality: seeking Prince Charming, losing Prince Charming, regaining Prince Charming. The themes of romantic acquisition and loss may be recast within the frame of a professional woman's life, but this reframing pales next to the strong outline of normative female heterosexuality: that is, for a woman, the central and most important theme in her life will be love. Love is the question, love is the answer, and whatever it takes to get it, keep it, maintain it, and cherish it is what the movie is really about.

We venerate and create fantasy masculinity and femininity—often, ironically enough, portrayed through the exquisite acting of gay or lesbian actors—but the truth really doesn't matter. The James Bonds, the lone wolves, and the cynical detectives and cops tell us what male sexuality in America is supposed to look like. The young lovelies and studmuffins of the movies and TV sitcoms tell us what adequate heterosexuality is supposed to look like. The unspoken sub-clause is that the rest of us who could not fit well in the ensemble casts of *Friends*, *CSI*, or *Grey's Anatomy* have a sexuality that is unfinished, inadequate, and somehow unworthy. This is a disastrous recognition for those who have already experienced self-doubt about their masculinity or femininity within their peer group. Most young girls and women are insecure about whether they are attractive, articulate or desirable. Even without comparison to mythic media icons, they struggle mightily to feel sexually worthy. Women turn themselves into wraiths trying to be thin enough, and put themselves in physical jeopardy by paying surgeons to sculpt their bodies so that they can have thighs, abdomens, and breasts that fit the sexual profile of what they believe men want. Women, and increasingly men, spend thousands of scarce discretionary dollars to change their faces and physiques to fit prevailing standards of beauty so that they will be able to compete in the heterosexual mating market or retain spouses who might otherwise stray to better models of masculinity and femininity.

One can't help but reflect on this: while noblemen of the eighteenth century might have had to work at being dandies, twenty-first-century men are spared these indignities. Just being male used to be enough to be granted provisional heterosexual status. However, increasingly, in some sort of cosmic justice, men seem to be following suit: commercial interests have finally realized that having both sexes terminally insecure is better for business than just having one sex feel inadequate, so now men are in the mix of creating better bodies, more hair (on their head; now many men feel required to get electrolysis for the stuff on their back!), and stiffer erections to make sure that they look and act like the cultural cut-outs they believe will ensure their sexual selection by women. The medical establishment is only too happy to oblige these neuroses.

The past decade has seen the collusion of pharmaceutical research with the medical establishment to create a cultural crisis about potency. The new standard of genital adequacy is to have penises that could compete with the fantasy penises in purple passages in X-rated books and movies. Now "rock hard penises" and "hot throbbing members" will actually exist in life as they do on porn stars. The vision of what a penis ought to look and act like can come true by using Viagra, Levitra, or Cialis, even if few men naturally match the size or performance of these porno-penises unaided by a drug. Viagra, so the media and doctors on lease from Pfizer have said, can give you the erection you've always dreamed of, and as a result, a new baseline standard of erections and performance gets created. Penis performance, always a potential problem for men, now invokes new fears: readiness throughout the lifestyle becomes standard. The natural aging of the organ becomes deviant as we try to create genitals that conform to standards created by chemists rather than nature. Male heterosexuality requires a stiff erection unto death. In order to make male heterosexuality unambiguous, we create a new version of what constitutes achievement of competent sexuality.

There is, of course, a female equivalent. Far before Viagra became a global brand, women's and fashion magazines created yearly standards for the year's "look," which often meant a new kind of body. The mass media would launch cover stories announcing "breasts are back" (I'm not kidding—this was a real cover in 2005) or "the six secrets to making him go crazy all night." Women's magazines, and increasingly men's magazines, do not have stories on sex—the magazines are almost *entirely* about mating and dating—and even the products are advertised to help live the good life of a popular sexual being. If we stand back for a moment, it becomes clear that the entire message of advertising is that heterosexuality is *not* natural: it is not easy—and, indeed, it will take everything they can sell you for you to even hope to sustain a decent sexual presentation and the possibility of creating a successful seduction, engagement, and marriage. Being successful—as a body—as an actor—as a heterosexual—is certainly not seen as a fact of nature. No—*it is seen as an act of will.*

10

Which leads us to the obvious conclusion that, far from being normal, heterosexual identity is fragile. Very fragile. Easily polluted. Given all the possible paths leading to failure of sexual competence, we are warned that we must be very careful in our construction of it.

This ability to fail publicly brings us to our second proposition: that our performance of heterosexuality is supposed to be accepted and applauded by others. All of this dressing up and strutting out is not just to attract the opposite sex—it is supposed to fend off criticism and attribution as a homosexual. Homosexuality and heterosexuality are like twins: no matter how different they become, they are part of the same piece, the same drama. Homosexuality exists in its own right—but if it did not, it would be invented to enforce compliance to proper gender enactment.

Straight men dress in ways to announce their sexuality, much the way the homosexual men often mimic it to announce their own: exaggerating the costumes of masculinity into mating signals for men with men. The two sexualities, considered so polar, actually butt up next to each other, trying to accomplish different things with the same cultural and physical equipment.

But that is the point, is it not? Heterosexual men and homosexual 15 men have the same socialization, as do heterosexual women and homosexual women, so it takes some work to distinguish our sexual presentation from one another. No wonder then that we have "fey" gay men and "butch" lesbians. Gay men and women need to work hard to create territory that is unambiguously in revolt against heterosexuality because heterosexuality itself is much more subtle and problematic than we pretend it to be. Hence, exaggerated performances exist among both heterosexuals and homosexuals as each group tries to demonstrate who they are to like others and elicit appropriate reactions. Still, no matter how broad a sexual display is, the audience may not react to even the most counternormative gender role if sexuality is not seen as problematic in that area. For example, there are some locales where people seem almost naïvely unconscious. One sees, for example, environments where women present themselves as "butch" and may even have the build and demeanor of a man, and men who are as fey as anyone who ever cross-dressed in a San Francisco gay rights parade are benignly unconscious of the thin line they walk in the gender role enactment wars. Part of this innocence is one of place: residents of small towns that cannot imagine that anyone in their town could be gay and so integrate their friend's and neighbor's generally non-normative gender display into some other social construct ("weird," "eccentric," "not vain," etc.) rather than gayness. Even though the butch farmer's wife may be secretly hankering after the farmer's wife next door, "audiences" may attribute the non-normative gender or sexual display to asexuality rather than homosexuality. As long as the person in question does not claim an alternate sexuality, they may be spared approbation. On the other hand, this is not always the case. The young who resemble disapproved-of, nonheterosexual attributes can justly quake in school halls, worrying that they will be attacked emotionally or physically—or just disdained.

This brings up a third specification: we are supposed to have certain kinds of bodies that reveal our heterosexuality. For all the jokes about "Pat" on *Saturday Night Live* (the person we could not figure out as male or female, who would confuse us by tempting us with a clue as to her "real" gender and then add another clue that would cancel out the first lead), the truth is that the real joke on us was how much anxiety it caused the viewer to watch a character without a gender and/or sexual identity we could identify. In general, we *hate* the idea that someone is not firmly assigned to a body type and look that telegraphs both gender and sexuality. In fact, it occurs to me that this intolerance of gender ambiguity may be one of the reasons our society hates fat people. Fat pads out physical differences between the sexes; the roundness we associate with women covers both men and women who are fat: breasts and chests look alike, genitals shrink in reference to the greater bulk of the body, and facial contours become more similar. It is another kind of androgyny, and most people are extremely uncomfortable with it when it is so extreme that they cannot distinguish biological sex. Extreme androgyny like Pat is seen as sexual failure—and therefore sexual identity may be imputed as homosexual even though homosexuality really has nothing to do with body type. Still, all kinds of gender ambiguity or cross-referencing the other gender (especially using the other gender's costumes or customs) has been historically grounds for severe punishment (including death, in some countries and during certain periods of history) or humiliation (open season as a target for humor or bullying). Interestingly, temporary trespass of gender/sexual confabulation is allowable for certain kinds of ritual celebrations such as fraternity costume parties, English music hall performances or Halloween. Anyone who wants to continue the joke too long, however, is quickly labeled deviant, and—to show how strong our feelings are—subjected to violence or contempt. Our culture does not want to lose the hard edges of gender, precisely because people depend on the standards of gender enactment to help them delineate heterosexuality from homosexuality. Imprecise as that may be, it is the tool most people use for a quick assessment of sexual identity.

This brings me to a fourth point about heterosexuality, which has to do not with the body, but the psyche: In order to be considered heterosexual, individuals are presumed to be singularly and unproblematically aroused [by] the opposite sex and the opposite sex only.

Within sexual identity, the heterosexual package includes the idea that heterosexuality is unitary—all or nothing. We are not supposed to have to learn heterosexuality; it is supposed to come with our genitals and gender behavior. Any indication of flexibility (a continuum of arousal and attraction that may be greatest toward people of the opposite sex but has some arousal to same-sex persons) is, even among the most sophisticated of people, seen as discrediting heterosexuality. In some American Indian cultures, bisexuality is acknowledged as having a place in the sexual pantheon and can be seen as a gift; heterosexuality can co-exist with homosexuality in the same person without putting either into question. In most Western societies, however, and in many non-Western societies, same-sex arousal immediately incurs identity reassignment; we do not want to think of our sexuality as polymorphous. Indeed, the Freudian phrase would be "polymorphous perverse": a disordered drive rather than merely a lusty or extensive one. In our society, sexual identity as a heterosexual allows for no trespass of this central vision of unadulterated heterosexuality.

Interestingly, though, we have developed a pragmatic out for some people who can satisfy the gender norms of heterosexuality so satisfactorily that if they choose the right explanation for same-sex behavior we will not discredit them. While, in most cases, we disallow any behavior but heterosexual conduct, we do have a vision of male and female sexuality that allows a "loophole"—if you will, an apt phrase for the conundrum. Indeed, there are men who so satisfy the norms of masculinity that they can get away with nonheterosexual behavior, at least for a time, and not be reassigned a gay identity. These are the men who are so hypermasculine we believe their accounts of a sexuality so brutish that, when they say any hole will do, we believe them! Rock stars who are outrageous in every other respect are often allowed to have both male and female partners and continue to maintain their dominant sexual status as heterosexual. Another common example are men in prisons, men who have a scarcity of females, or men from cultures where maleness is considered so sexually powerful that they can just enforce their definition of the situation on anything as long as they take in certain cultural scripts that protect heterosexual identity. As an example, I once interviewed a Greek man named Spiro who was sexually adept with both men and women. He seemed to have no trouble having both male and female partners without having either leave him because of his bisexual activity. When I asked him how he could have sex with both men and women without being labeled as gay, he replied, "It is no problem. You see we have four types of men in Greece: men who fuck men, men who fuck men and women, men who fuck women, and queers." I was somewhat flummoxed since I knew he had sex with both men and women and would not consider himself "queer." So I asked him, "Who are the people you consider 'queer'?" "Oh," he said. "The queers are the ones who *get* fucked." Or, put another way, Spiro had a culture that created a vision of men as voracious sexual creatures who naturally will have what they can—as long as they are not degraded by taking the female role, a humiliation from which, apparently, one is denied reentry into the club of heterosexual men. If you are a man who wants to have sex with men in Greece, yet do not want to be thought of as homosexual, you can accomplish this goal, as long as you do not blunder into the "female" sexual role. How this translates intrapsychically may be more difficult, except if you are, like Spiro, from a culture where sexually available women are scarce and sex, any way you can get it, is approved of by your friends.

The allowances for women are different, though not entirely. There are some women whose heterosexual credentials are so impeccable that they evoke increased erotic interest in men rather than relabeling when they take on a same-sex lover. Madonna, for example, gave a well-publicized passionate kiss on the lips to Britney Spears, which, while it got headlines, did not hurt Madonna's draw as a performer or her perception by fans as an outrageous heterosexual woman. In some parts of the United States there are those who would give erotic points to women who have sex with women even if they are not superstars . . . as long as the sexual encounter is done for the pleasure of men. Women can have sex with women as performers—or as the hors d'oeuvre in a meal that will be consummated in heterosexual intercourse. Simply put, in our contemporary urban culture, situational bisexuality is sexy, but real lesbianism is an affront.

One exemption from that reaction is lesbianism as a heterosexual porno fantasy. Women who look like *Playboy* bunnies, who are voracious sexual creatures—wild enough to do anything—are asked to do the inevitable porno three-way, and doing so does not endanger their heterosexual status. As long as female performers in porno eventually show that they are sexually available to men, their homosexual sex is seen as kinky rather than as deviant. These women never take on a lesbian identity; their job is to be warm-up artists, create sexual titillation, and make sure that the male viewer simply sees them as an erotic surrogate until he "finishes" the "job." The women in porno movies who make love to one another create a drama of female ecstasy that excites the male viewer rather than threatens him. These actresses do not leave the folds of heterosexuality even in fantasy (although, in reality, many of them are stalwartly lesbian). For our purposes, however, what is interesting is that there are these temporary havens for homosexuality—but sexual identity is preserved because of the belief that beautiful, sexy women will be steadfastly immune to female charms when men are available. Furthermore, if the women who have had sex with each other follow convention and don't try to also take on male prerogatives (such as male dress or demeanor), same-sex appetite is seen as an erotic augmentation rather than a substitution. It is an odd erotic peccadillo of male sexuality that almost all female sexual behavior is catalogued as a dress rehearsal for male sexual enjoyment. Only when the male is truly convinced that the woman has absolutely no desire for the male voyeur does the wrath of homophobia come to rest at lesbian destinations. Lesbians to most men are bisexuals, and bisexuals are heterosexuals-in-waiting; however, this fluid assignment is often not so gently experienced by the women who must decide if there is a sexual central self that is not really performing for men, but instead seeks a way to justify erotic and/or emotional desire for other women.

This relates to the fifth point: that heterosexual arousal is supposed to be strong and unambiguous. This is a very interesting requirement, and it flies in the face of almost every fact we know about sexual performance. More correctly, sexual arousal is always problematic some of the time: there when you don't want it, absent when you are hoping it will overwhelm you. Arousal is highly sensitive to other emotions—fear of rejection, tension, performance anxieties, distraction, and fatigue; in other words, numerous states of mind and body. Additionally, we are affected by subtle cues in the environment or in the other person's behavior that may consciously or unconsciously affect our behavior: the wrong words, the wrong look and suddenly we are deflated; a serious performance problem for men, especially if it happens often and becomes habitual. Many men, reflecting back on their boyhood, have talked about how disorienting it was not to have an erection under conditions one was supposed to (or to have it when one was not supposed to) and the doubts and fears and dysfunction that followed. Because an erection is supposed to be "natural"—both a perk and prerequisite of heterosexuality—its absence, or the presence of ambivalence, is supposed to be instructive of malfunction, or, in the eyes of society, potential deviance. In other words, your status as a heterosexual goes up or down with your penis.

Women have a variation of this theme, albeit not such a publicly noticeable one. For example, in a sexual interaction, women may be quite worried about the presence or absence of lubrication. Some women's vaginas lubricate quite copiously when aroused; other women remain quite dry no matter how aroused they are, or become less lubricated as they age and approach perimenopause or menopause. Women, like men, vary in the way their body reacts to stimulation. However, in the Book of Heterosexuality, aroused women are supposed to lubricate, and the lack thereof has been known to cause women—and their partners—some worry that the body is the truer source of information than the mind, and that not lubricating indicates lesser sexual interest or excitement. Lubrication, while easily fixable by modern water-based or silicone products, is perceived to be telling the woman (and her partner) something elemental. A standard of competent heterosexuality is unmet. Women have been let off this hook somewhat by being defined as having a mostly reactive sexuality (i.e., "you do not have to be the first to be sexually aroused," "as a woman you are entitled to be only mildly interested until you are aggressively aroused by a man"). In this scenario, if you are *not* aroused, it is not that you are not heterosexual, it is just that this is the wrong person, you are not in love enough, or that your lover is not man enough to arouse you. In general, however, women's heterosexuality is perceived to be awakened by love. Love is supposed to be the motor of women's sexual emotions. In fact, female sexuality is supposed to be so relational that even inappropriate (i.e., homosexual) arousal can sometimes happen without necessarily impacting heterosexual identity. In this perspective, women are turned on because they are in love, and love is the motivating sexual force. Same-sex behavior, rather than exhibiting an essential part of a woman's true nature, is merely another act of true womanhood—female sexuality created by the power of love. Many women who have had extended lesbian relationships in their biography but do not wish to identify as a lesbian may, post hoc, define their same-sex love affair as primarily a love relationship with a sexual component that could only last for the length of that relationship. This vision of self-limiting sexuality (over when the love relationship is over) is not sustained by our culture when it concerns men. One moment of adult non-heterosexual arousal—no matter how passing the moment—is likely to be seen as definitive evidence of a core homosexual set of desires.

Sixth: the appropriate [sex]—that is to say, the opposite sex—is supposed to be attracted to us. Sexual identity can be so shaky that it can also be changed by other people's attention to us rather than our own feelings about ourselves. In the movie *In and Out*, actor Kevin Kline

is woefully out of touch with his sexual psyche. He is in his early for-
ties and has gone with his girlfriend for years and years without any
genital contact. When one of his famous students assumes he is gay—
because of inappropriate gender behavior (including, if you will, that
he is neat!) and "outs" him, it is the first time he is forced to confront
himself. The gay news reporter who is sent to cover the story immediately sees the Kline character as a "closet case." Not one really sexual moment happens that shows Kline demonstrating sexual desire
for another man, but the beginning of his uncloseting is not proved
by whom he is attracted to (or not attracted to, as the case may be) but
also by how others see him and by *who* wants him.

Thus, every heterosexual who is not claimed by the opposite sex as   25
a heartthrob in their youth has doubts—and not only because of being ignored or feeling invisible, but also because of sexual aspirations
lofted his or her way by other people with insecure sexual identities.
Teenagers, young men and women, and women and men with sexually mixed biographies are all unsure of who they are and who they
want, and so they all are more likely to project their own lack of ease
onto another person.

Straw Dogs, a subtly homophobic film released several decades ago,
insinuates that the central figure Dustin Hoffman is emasculated
because he cannot control his flirtatious, wayward wife. This does not
mean an immediate homosexual label, but it does mean that his character is not adequately heterosexual because he isn't macho enough
to make the men fear him when they ogle and sexually harass her.
Written to be a "ball buster" by nature, she is humiliated when the men
verbally insult her and he does nothing. In turn, the "virile" workmen
have nothing but contempt for a man who will not get physically aggressive when other men decline to respect his woman and ogle her
without retribution. The local men hate him for his effeteness and
his social class (he has been pilloried by the working-class men fixing his house as being a "poof") and it becomes a war to the death
when the working men get more and more contemptuous of him
and turn into sexually salivating males who plan to lay claim to the
wife. They study Hoffman and decide that he is a putz because they
can see his wife is running around on him, and they are pretty sure
he knows that she is. Whether or not he knows or does not know, in
their minds he *should* know, and do something about it. They decide
to do with her as they will since he is obviously not a manly man who
deserves to have his female property respected. In the end, however,
in order to protect his home, woman, and life, Hoffman "gets it" and
resorts to primordial battle to retrieve his wife and his self-respect.
They attack him and he triumphs over them, but in order to do so, it

is necessary for him to kill every one of these men. At the end of the film, in the eyes of his wife, himself and the director, the Hoffman character becomes a true man in the deepest sense of heterosexual glory.

For women, the archetypal story is the transformation story—that of a woman not sufficiently self-discovered enough to take on the accoutrements of femininity and win her man. Pure evocations of this theme can be found in the musical *Annie Get Your Gun* when the Annie Oakley character cleans up to try to get her man, or when the Rancher's Daughter in *Rodeo* puts on a dress to go to the dance. The high point of claiming heterosexuality is claiming one's birthright of loveliness and recognizing one's longing for a man. Women do not necessarily get assigned a lesbian identity if they do not put men in as the obvious center of their life, but they may be seen as desexed if they are not adequately heterosexually active.

Being desexed is not an easy place to be sent to, however. Let a woman tell you what it feels like to be invisible—that is, not sexually attractive enough to be noticed as they walk by, enter a room, or try to engage in interactions with men. Women see other women drawing male attention but feel too old, too heavy, too short, too tall, too awkward, too bright—too *something* to get some of that attention themselves. When a woman feels this way, her sexuality is irrelevant and therefore denied her. If she is not desired, she does not exist. Many teenage as well as older women feel consigned to this purgatory where nature or nurture has somehow failed to give them the talents they need to feel fully sexual.

Given how hard all of this is to accomplish, my seventh point is both ironic and laughable: once our sexuality is enacted, it is supposed to be stable and unconflicted. Heterosexuality is supposed to be a rock. Once established, it is not supposed to turn into anything else, which is a comfort to young men and women who may feel that once heterosexuality is initially established, they can relax *if* they become satisfied with the way they look, turn on to people, get turned on to, match the norms of the present gender culture, and so on.

My own research tells me that that reassessment of one's sexual self can occur, and when it does, it is most likely to come through relationships—that indeed our sexuality *is* relational, especially (but not only) for women. The annals of research on sexual identity are full of stories of women who had never had even a same-sex fantasy who unexpectedly became besotted with a specific person and found their sexuality bending towards the bright light of that love. For example, I have interviewed a woman who was having an affair with another woman while her husband, dreadfully ill, was incapacitated for half a year. They met at work and it was love at first sight. They stayed together for years without the husband finding out and the revelation to one of the partners of the extent of her sexual interest was deeply unsettling to her. She could not deny the fact of her love and attraction—and she was 60 years old when she received this new information about herself! Whether the revision of self-identity occurs because of a special partnership or because one is just totally furious with men because of a series of bad intentions or behaviors, it is shocking to most people to realize they have a flexible sexual self. I have interviewed many women who became homosexual not through lust, but through disgust with the men who had disappointed and abused them. Heterosexual identity may not always unravel when a person shuts down because of a disastrous relationship or a love affair that seems to transcend gender, but most people would not be surprised that it had to change.

The fact is that change is shocking to participants. Heterosexual identity—all sexual identity—is considered immutable by most lay people, except insofar as someone's "true" sexuality may be repressed, suppressed, or denied. The cultural prejudice and presumption is that the presence of any homosexual feeling is a dead giveaway of one's sexual essence because homosexual behavior is somehow more a truth of the body than heterosexuality. (The reasoning seems to be that any homosexual behavior demonstrates a true core sexual predilection, since no person would take on the stigma of homosexuality if it were not compulsively necessary.) Both homosexuals and heterosexuals have displayed incredulity and downright rejection of an applicant for a new sexual identity or claim when the claim is from a heretofore homosexual male who is now in love with a woman and believes that his sexuality is oriented in a new way. Our culture doesn't even want to believe such a male really feels what he says he feels. Heterosexuality, in this instance, is so weak that it is easily eclipsed and overpowered by homosexuality. In cases of homosexual exploration, even minimal acts are coded maximally, but in cases of heterosexual exploration by gay men, new sexual experience with women is considered trivial and even psychologically distressed. Despite this reaction, from the lay and scientific community alike, there is still some scientific evidence and certainly adequate anecdotal evidence that both men and women can regroup sexual identity in adulthood when a single important emotional relationship refocuses their sexual energy.

Finally, my eighth and last point about heterosexuality is that intercourse is the heterosexual lingua franca and all else is tangential embroidery. Men and women are not just catalogued because of the gender eroticized but how we eroticize our partner of any gender. Our acts define us, not just our psychology. Key among these acts is the central act of heterosexuality, intercourse. Competent and complete heterosexuals are supposed to prefer intercourse to all other acts. Heterosexuals should have intercourse more frequently than other acts; it should be the main location for our ejaculations and orgasms; and, in general, it should be played as the main event in lovemaking, even if there is a very full program of other kinds of sexual behaviors. Indeed, we seem to need to check in with various kinds of studies, to be checked against the facts and figures of normalcy. While the famous Kinsey studies tried to make it clear that, in their opinion, one pattern of "outlets" was as good as another, those famous studies showed means and medians for sexual acts that made the mean not only average but prescriptive.

This presumption continues in modern texts on human sexuality. Questionnaires, which get at only a rough estimate of sexual habits, are given credence way beyond what their crafters ever believed in, and these ballpark figures now not only define heterosexuality, they define "healthy" or "inhibited" heterosexuality, thereby giving heterosexuals new ways to feel insufficient or suspect. A gigantic field of sexual therapy has arisen since the late 1960s (when Masters and Johnson first published their books on actual sexual behavior), and the public has become quite aware of all the ways there are to fail sexual "competency."

In sum, while heterosexuality is seen as natural, naturally organized around intercourse, strongly held, invariant once achieved, and wholly captivating by those who own it, we know, inside our hearts, and in the light of evidence, that none of these suppositions are entirely true. The question I would pose now is, does this obvious social construction of heterosexuality really matter? Does it matter if heterosexuality is much less unitary, stable or scripted than we thought it was?

That's Not Clear . . .

We are far more a work in progress—a tender rather than solid   35
template—than most of us are comfortable with. However, our intolerance of ambiguity makes it likely that we wish to overdefine our sexual identity, to not code our homosexual attractions or fantasies if at all possible, and to try like hell to accomplish heterosexuality as best we can. Except for the bravest and culturally independent among us, we want sexual categories, not open-ended choices or a continuum of desire and identity. Because heterosexuality is so hard to achieve

and so fragile to sustain, we seem to need to continue to ignore the gradations of sexual reality and construct a sexual persona that gives us peace of mind in the present, if not necessarily for the future.

As for we social scientists, we continue to ignore such discordant data about sexual identification, desire, or fantasy, or believe it only defines a small number of heterosexually functioning men and women. We know that many heterosexuals have occasional same-sex fantasies or dreams of same-sex behavior, but we do not include it to reshape our definition of heterosexuality and its potential plasticity.

This is why the Kinsey scale has remained an academic rather than a popular concept. The scale, which goes from 0 to 6, with 0 being totally heterosexual, 6 being totally homosexual, and 3 being you don't care what comes through the door, was revolutionary in the late 1940s and early 50s, when the study was initially done, but arguably could be just as revolutionary today. If we believe, as we might, that heterosexuality is a continuum of sexual desire rather than a bipolar construction, heterosexuality would be more truly described as often co-existing with homosexual desire, fantasy, love, or attraction. But we have intense resistance to trying to know how heterosexuality is actually practiced rather than socially constructed, and this has rather grave costs for everyone:

First, the stereotypes of invariant heterosexuality help us all fail being heterosexual enough, and this causes among many people low self-esteem, miscategorization of their sexuality, and fear of being "deviant." If our sexuality were less prescribed as a central identity and more as a behavior—one open to a multitude of expressions—we would be less immobilized by fear if we thought or did something less common. Indeed, in today's society, there is movement toward a less static vision of heterosexuality. The young, perhaps more with bravado than anything else, are more comfortable with various combinations of ambisexuality and more often than not, unapologetic for their choices.

Second, this same fear encourages some people in our society to discourage extending civil liberties to gays because we are fearful of compromising our heterosexuality. This school wants all the rewards in society to bolster heterosexuality, thereby keeping us more protected from, I guess, ourselves. There are movements to keep gay people from having legal marriage. Could it be that restrictions of same-sex couples originate because we are so unsure about the steadiness of our heterosexuality that we feel extending heterosexual institutions to same-sex couples will endanger heterosexuality itself? This casts heterosexuality as a strangely unpowerful identity, one so weak that if its institutions are shared that marriage will unravel—but there is really no evidence at all that this will happen.

The third and maybe most important response to the perspective   40
I have offered about our present vision of heterosexuality is that of
the intrapsychic costs—of the present exaggerated naturalness of
heterosexuality. The unannounced and unspoken contradictions of
a pure heterosexuality cause great emotional difficulty to many
people—especially at tender ages when self-confidence is low. With
little reality to lean on, men and women experience extreme discomfort as they must face their fantasies or discordant early behavior. Surely much of our sexual dysfunction, insecurity, and panic
comes from these early years of contradictions and high expectations.

My fourth and final point: even if many individuals concretize
their heterosexual identity without much suffering or feelings of in-
sufficiency, do we not incur sexual or psychic costs because we see
heterosexuality as incongruent with certain kinds of acts or fantasies? For example, can a heterosexual man enjoy (without guilt or fears
of sexual deviance) the experience of anal sex or have sex, happily,
without intromission? Can a heterosexual woman enjoy a man who is
less than traditionally masculine or prefer sexuality without intercourse as the centerpiece of her heterosexual life without feeling that
she has betrayed "normal" heterosexuality? Intercourse itself is so central to the proof of heterosexuality that men and women who might
enjoy oral sex more might never feel free to downgrade intercourse
as the way they generally have the most pleasure. Why shouldn't
sexuality be more varied if it is about pleasure and not demonstration
of heterosexual membership?

In conclusion, I think it is clear that if heterosexuality were indelible, easy to achieve, and easy to keep, we wouldn't make all this fuss
over it. The liberation of all sexualities is the liberation of each one.
While political activism may be organized around the integration of
homosexuality and homosexuals into the mainstream, it is not clear
that there is a mainstream to be integrated into. Rather, there are
many people trying to find a sexual identity that integrates their desires, experiences, and fantasies, however diverse they may be. Opening up the definition of heterosexuality will not endanger our welfare.
We need to be able to do life as it evolves, creating sexualities that are
unique rather than scripted from the one-size-fits-no-one-very-well
tradition.

Understanding the Text

1. Schwartz explains that heterosexuality is normative and is articulated through a set of presumptions and social scripts. Try to explain this concept in your own words so that you fully understand what "normative" means and how our society articulates these expectations.

2. Choose one of the examples Schwartz offers as evidence of her argument and offer an additional example of how that script is enacted in contemporary culture.

3. Schwartz says that even today, heterosexual dress codes, mannerisms, and body language are strictly mandated. Provide some examples. Can you think of exceptions to this claim?

Reflection and Response

4. Think about whether you have experienced any of these social scripts, and then write a paragraph or two on how normative heterosexuality has or has not affected your life. If you believe these scripts have not affected your life, speculate about why that is the case.

5. Choose one popular male celebrity or an iconic fictional male character who demonstrates the epitome of male sexuality. How does this person demonstrate his sexuality? Does his sexuality seem central to his popularity, or is it just part of his overall image?

6. Schwartz argues that "far from being normal, heterosexual identity is fragile" (p. 189). What does she mean by this? What motivates people to maintain a fragile identity if it would be so easy to let it fail?

Making Connections

7. Schwartz argues that because heterosexuality is not natural we have to learn to be heterosexual. Choose two other readings in *Composing Gender* and use them to argue for or against Schwartz's thesis. What evidence exists in those readings that either demonstrates or refutes her point?

8. How do Halloween costumes or other kinds of performative rituals where we dress up as someone other than ourselves affect what Schwartz is arguing? Do you find evidence in these costumes and rituals that normative heterosexuality is allowed to be disrupted, or do these rituals support normative heterosexuality? Refer to one of the other articles in *Composing Gender*, such as Rosenbloom about costumes (p. 164) or Best about the prom (p. 128).

9. Toward the end of the article, Schwartz indicates that there are many costs associated with this ongoing performance of heterosexuality. Choose one of those "costs" and expand it. Explain how that cost has effects that are visible in today's society, and discuss whether or not you think this cost is worth trying to create changes in the normative expectations we have for a person's sexuality. Do some library research to prove your point or to offer a possible solution to this problem.

On Judith Butler

Sandra Bem

Sandra Bem is a professor emerita of psychology at Cornell University whose work focuses largely on the social construction of gender and sexuality. She created the Bem Sex Role Inventory (BSRI), which allows individuals to rate themselves on a series of questions to determine their relationship to femininity and masculinity. She has won a number of awards for her work, including the American Psychological Association Distinguished Scientific Award for an Early Career Contribution to Psychology and the Distinguished Publication Award from the Association for Women in Psychology. This selection was originally published in the *Journal of Sex Research* in 1995.

Judith Butler is a philosopher, and the book of hers that I know best is entitled *Gender Trouble: Feminism and the Subversion of Identity*, published in 1990. The question Butler set out to answer in this book was how best to make gender trouble, i.e., how best to "trouble the gender categories that support gender hierarchy and compulsory heterosexuality" (p. viii). Her answer was to challenge the conceptual foundations of the sex/gender/desire system. In her words, this means a "genealogical" critique, which is not a search for "origins" or "inner truth" but an investigation of "the political stakes in designating as an *origin* and *cause* those identity categories that are in fact the *effects* of institutions, practices, discourses with multiple and diffuse points of origin" (pp. viii–ix). More simply, her answer was to "trace the way in which gender fables establish and circulate the misnomer of natural facts" (p. xi).

Even in this one-paragraph introduction to Butler's work, we can already see one of its distinguishing hallmarks. Butler is a master of nifty little reversals, three of which I am now going to show you.

The traditional view in both Western culture and Western science is that there are two and only two sexes that are naturally both different from [one] another and attracted to one another. This division of all human beings into two bipolar categories of sex/gender/desire (the one category being male/masculine/attracted to women and the other category being female/feminine/attracted to men) may be differently elaborated in different cultures but, proponents of the traditional system say, it is also the biological foundation upon which culture is built.

Butler's first reversal is as follows. Rather than these two bipolar groups being the cause of exclusive and compulsory heterosexuality, they are instead the effect of exclusive and compulsory heterosexuality. In other words, for there to be a system of exclusive and compulsory heterosexuality, two such bipolar groups had to come into existence and so, voilà, the system produces them. That very cultural and historical production is then hidden, according to Butler, by an extraordinarily clever sleight of hand that casts the historical and cultural construction of the two-and-only-two into the realm of the pre-social, the pre-cultural, the pre-discursive. Thus it comes to pass that the two-and-only-two are accepted as a taken-for-granted and natural given of existence.

Another traditional view in Western culture, especially in certain branches of psychoanalysis, is that homosexuality is a pathetic imitation of heterosexuality, which is itself the natural or original form of sexuality. The same assumption holds for both drag and butch/femme roles, at least as enacted by gay men and lesbians.

Butler's second reversal goes like this. First, she argued, *all gender is drag*. In other words, all gender is an imitation of some phantasmagorical vision of what a man or a woman is supposed to be like. Hence there is nothing more natural, original, or unconstructed about a female dressing up like a woman than a male dressing up like a woman. That, of course, was the subtext of the movie *The Crying Game*. That, of course, is also why all the many dressed-up, made-up, and coiffed-up women walking along New York's Madison Avenue always look, to my eyes at least, not like women, but like people of whatever sex trying to look the way they think women are supposed to look.

> *All gender is drag.* In other words, all gender is an imitation of some phantasmagorical vision of what a man or a woman is supposed to be like.

Not only, according to Butler, is all gender drag, including that performed by the most conventional of masculine men and feminine women. In addition, heterosexuality can be said to require homosexuality as a foundation at least as much as homosexuality has been said to require heterosexuality. Put somewhat differently, heterosexuality can be seen as having needed to construct an allegedly perverse, unnatural, and imitative homosexuality as the counterpoint against which to define itself as normal, natural, and original.

The same point can be expressed in another way. It is the traditional Western view that people who do not have the so-called normal clustering of sex/gender/desire have something wrong with them. They are anomalies, pathologies, developmental failures; hence they need, in some way, to be corrected, cured, healed, or fixed.

Butler's third reversal is that these so-called anomalies are defined as anomalous not because they really are anomalous but because the system of compulsory heterosexuality requires that they be defined this way. In other words, compulsory heterosexuality requires that there exists only a very narrow range of all possible sex/gender/desire configurations. Hence it excludes all other configurations from the "matrix of intelligibility" (p. 17) and then uses these so-called perverse others as the counterpoint to establish the two-and-only-two that are allowed to exist within the framework of the system. The two-and-only-two is thus created by a historical process in which everything else is either excluded or demonized, and the border between the normal and the perverse is carefully patrolled.

Another way to say all this is that the demonized are as necessary   10
to the system of compulsory heterosexuality as the privileged. This is so because the contrast with the so-called abnormal or perverse is what defines—and thereby brings into conceptual and empirical existence—the so-called normal.

Reference
Butler, J. (1990). *Gender trouble: Feminism and the subversion of identity.* New York: Routledge.

Understanding the Text

1. Bem summarizes an important book in gender studies by Judith Butler titled *Gender Trouble: Feminism and the Subversion of Identity.* She starts by explaining that Butler is trying to "trouble" (p. 202) the categories of gender that we generally accept as natural and normal. What does the word "trouble" mean in this context? Why do you think this word is the one that Butler chose for her purpose?

2. Bem says that Butler is a "master of nifty little reversals" (p. 202). Choose one of these reversals and explain it in your own words. Make sure you explain what makes it a "reversal."

3. One of the most interesting of the three reversals Butler makes is to say that "all gender is drag" (p. 203). What does this mean? How are women walking down Madison Avenue in "drag," exactly?

4. Throughout this short selection, Bem uses the term "compulsory heterosexuality." What does this phrase mean to Bem? How does the system of compulsory heterosexuality become privileged in Bem's and Butler's estimation? How is compulsory heterosexuality a system?

Reflection and Response

5. If Butler is correct that all gender is drag, think about or write about several examples where gender seems most like drag to you. What makes these examples fit Butler's theory about gender and performance? Also, try to think of situations in which gender seems unlike drag or where you think gender

seems more genuine. Can you find a situation that might prove Butler's theory wrong or faulty?

6. Compulsory heterosexuality is something that we often cannot see or recognize until it is pointed out to us, as it is briefly in Bem's summary of Butler. Why do you think it is so difficult to see the system of compulsory heterosexuality?

7. How do representations of actual drag or cross-dressing fit into Bem's description of Butler's argument? If all gender is drag, would it follow that men who dress as women and women who dress as men are somehow challenging traditional gender representations, even if they're trying hard to accurately look like the gender they're dressing up as? Could we consider dressing in drag a political act, or is it just another version of gender performance? In your answer to each question, provide one or two hypothetical or real-life examples to support your position.

Making Connections

8. Bem notes that the system of compulsory heterosexuality is "carefully patrolled" (p. 204). What other readings in this chapter or throughout *Composing Gender* support the idea that there is patrolling and enforcing of sex and gender stereotypes? What readings most support the argument that compulsory heterosexuality is not natural but has to be rigidly and carefully enforced in order to exist? Do you see patrolling and enforcing in Kimmel's "Guy Code" (p. 142) or Geller's wedding planner (p. 155), for instance?

9. How have you seen sex and gender anomalies or pathologies "corrected, cured, healed, or fixed," as Bem describes toward the end of the selection? Think about examples from *Composing Gender* or from your own research in which people who fall outside the sex/gender norm are required to fit into categories of sex and gender that are considered normal or natural.

10. Compare Butler's theory of sex and gender to some of the arguments we read in Chapter 1 on gender and dualism. Does Butler seem to be extending the arguments of Lorber (p. 19), Devor (p. 35), Hubbard (p. 46), and Doan (p. 53), or does she seem to be making a different argument, a more theoretical argument, than their arguments about dualism? If the latter (that Butler is more theoretical than those earlier readings), think about the value of theory. What does a complicated theory like Butler's offer that more straightforward theories about dualisms in gender cannot? Or, conversely, what are the limitations to Butler's theory as described by Bem; what trouble does Butler's theory pose to readers like us, even when filtered through Bem's summary of it?

Dude, You're a Fag: Adolescent Male Homophobia

C. J. Pascoe

Professor C. J. Pascoe is a sociologist at Colorado College whose work focuses on gender, sexuality, inequality, and youth culture. Her book *Dude, You're a Fag: Masculinity and Sexuality in High School*, from which this selection is drawn, was published in 2011 and received wide acclaim, including an Outstanding Book Award from the American Education Research Association. Her recent scholarship focuses on love relationships in contemporary youth cultures, and her most recent article was published in a book titled *Hanging Out and Messing Around: Living and Learning with New Media*. She also blogs about her work at *Social (in) Queery* (socialinqueery.com).

The sun shone bright and clear over River High's annual Creative and Performing Arts Happening, or CAPA. During CAPA the school's various art programs displayed students' work in a fairlike atmosphere. The front quad sported student-generated computer programs. Colorful and ornate chalk art covered the cement sidewalks. Tables lined with student-crafted pottery were set up on the grass. Tall displays of students' paintings divided the rear quad. To the left of the paintings a television blared student-directed music videos. At the rear of the back quad, a square, roped-off area of cement served as a makeshift stage for drama, choir, and dance performances. Teachers released students from class to wander around the quads, watch performances, and look at the art. This freedom from class time lent the day an air of excitement because students were rarely allowed to roam the campus without a hall pass, an office summons, or a parent/ faculty escort. In honor of CAPA, the school district bussed in elementary school students from the surrounding grammar schools to participate in the day's festivities.

Running through the rear quad, Brian, a senior, yelled to a group of boys visiting from the elementary schools, "There's a faggot over there! There's a faggot over there! Come look!" Following Brian, the ten-year-olds dashed down a hallway. At the end of the hallway Brian's friend Dan pursed his lips and began sashaying toward the little boys. As he minced, he swung his hips exaggeratedly and wildly waved his arms. To the boys Brian yelled, "Look at the faggot! Watch out! He'll get you!" In response, the ten-year-olds raced back down the hallway screaming in terror. Brian and Dan repeated this drama throughout the following half hour, each time with a new group of young boys.

Making jokes like these about faggots was central to social life at River High. Indeed, boys learned long before adolescence that faggots were simultaneously predatory and passive and that they were, at all costs, to be avoided. Older boys repeatedly impressed upon younger ones through these types of homophobic rituals that whatever they did, whatever they became, however they talked, they had to avoid becoming a faggot.

Feminist scholars of masculinity have documented the centrality of homophobic insults and attitudes to masculinity (Kimmel 2001; Lehne 1998), especially in school settings (Burn 2000; Kimmel 2003; Plummer 2001; G. Smith 1998; Wood 1984). They argue that homophobic teasing often characterizes masculinity in adolescence and early adulthood and that antigay slurs tend to be directed primarily at gay boys. This [selection] both expands on and challenges these accounts of relationships between homophobia and masculinity. Homophobia is indeed a central mechanism in the making of contemporary American adolescent masculinity. A close analysis of the way boys at River High invoke the faggot as a disciplinary mechanism makes clear that something more than simple homophobia is at play in adolescent masculinity. The use of the word *fag* by boys at River High points to the limits of an argument that focuses centrally on homophobia. Fag is not only an identity linked to homosexual boys but an identity that can temporarily adhere to heterosexual boys as well. The fag trope is also a racialized disciplinary mechanism.

Homophobia is too facile a term with which to describe the deployment of *fag* as an epithet. By calling the use of the word *fag* homophobia—and letting the argument stop there—previous research has obscured the gendered nature of sexualized insults (Plummer 2001). Invoking homophobia to describe the ways boys aggressively tease each other overlooks the powerful relationship between masculinity and this sort of insult. Instead, it seems incidental, in this conventional line of argument, that girls do not harass each other and are not harassed in this same manner. This framing naturalizes the relationship between masculinity and homophobia, thus obscuring that such harassment is central to the formation of a gendered identity for boys in a way that it is not for girls.

Fag is not necessarily a static identity attached to a particular (homosexual) boy. Fag talk and fag imitations serve as a discourse with which boys discipline themselves and each other through joking relationships. Any boy can temporarily become a fag in a given social space or interaction. This does not mean that boys who identify as or are perceived to be homosexual aren't subject to intense harassment.

5

Many are. But becoming a fag has as much to do with failing at the masculine tasks of competence, heterosexual prowess, and strength or in any way revealing weakness or femininity as it does with a sexual identity. This fluidity of the fag identity is what makes the specter of the fag such a powerful disciplinary mechanism. It is fluid enough that boys police their behaviors out of fear of having the fag identity permanently adhere and definitive enough so that boys recognize a fag behavior and strive to avoid it.

> Becoming a fag has as much to do with failing at the masculine tasks of competence, heterosexual prowess, and strength or in any way revealing weakness or femininity as it does with a sexual identity.

An analysis of the fag discourse also indicates ways in which gendered power works through racialized selves. The fag discourse is invoked differently by and in relation to white boys' bodies than it is by and in relation to African American boys' bodies. While certain behaviors put all boys at risk for becoming temporarily a fag, some behaviors can be enacted by African American boys without putting them at risk of receiving the label. The racialized meanings of the fag discourse suggest that something more than simple homophobia is involved in these sorts of interactions. It is not that gendered homophobia does not exist in African American communities. Indeed, making fun of "negro faggotry seems to be a rite of passage among contemporary black male rappers and filmmakers" (Riggs 1991, 253). However, the fact that "white women and men, gay and straight, have more or less colonized cultural debates about sexual representation" (Julien and Mercer 1991, 167) obscures varied systems of sexualized meanings among different racialized ethnic groups (Almaguer 1991). Thus far male homophobia has primarily been written about as a racially neutral phenomenon. However, as D. L. King's (2004) recent work on African American men and same-sex desire pointed out, homophobia is characterized by racial identities as well as sexual and gendered ones.

What Is a Fag? Gendered Meanings

"Since you were little boys you've been told, 'Hey, don't be a little faggot,'" explained Darnell, a football player of mixed African American and white heritage, as we sat on a bench next to the athletic field. Indeed, both the boys and girls I interviewed told me that *fag* was the worst epithet one guy could direct at another. Jeff, a slight white sophomore, explained to me that boys call each other fag because "gay people aren't really liked over here and stuff." Jeremy, a Latino junior, told me that this insult literally reduced a boy to nothing: "To call someone *gay* or *fag* is like the lowest thing you can call someone. Because that's like saying that you're nothing."

Most guys explained their or others' dislike of fags by claiming that homophobia was synonymous with being a guy. For instance, Keith, a white soccer-playing senior, explained, "I think guys are just homophobic." However, boys were not equal-opportunity homophobes. Several students told me that these homophobic insults applied only to boys and not to girls. For example, while Jake, a handsome white senior, told me that he didn't like gay people, he quickly added, "Lesbians, okay, that's *good*." Similarly Cathy, a popular white cheerleader, told me, "Being a lesbian is accepted because guys think, 'Oh that's cool.'" Darnell, after telling me that boys were warned about becoming faggots, said, "They [guys] are fine with girls. I think it's the guy part that they're like ewwww." In this sense it was not strictly homophobia but a gendered homophobia that constituted adolescent masculinity in the culture of River High. It is clear, according to these comments, that lesbians were "good" because of their place in heterosexual male fantasy, not necessarily because of some enlightened approach to same-sex relationships. A popular trope in heterosexual pornography depicts two women engaging in sexual acts for the purpose of male titillation. The boys at River High are not unique in making this distinction; adolescent boys in general dislike gay men more than they dislike lesbians (Baker and Fishbein 1998). The fetishizing of sex acts between women indicates that using only the term *homophobia* to describe boys' repeated use of the word *fag* might be a bit simplistic and misleading.

Girls at River High rarely deployed the word *fag* and were never called fags. I recorded girls uttering *fag* only three times during my research. In one instance, Angela, a Latina cheerleader, teased Jeremy, a well-liked white senior involved in student government, for not ditching school with her: "You wouldn't 'cause you're a faggot." However, girls did not use this word as part of their regular lexicon. The sort of gendered homophobia that constituted adolescent masculinity did not constitute adolescent femininity. Girls were not called dykes or lesbians in any sort of regular or systematic way. Students did tell me that *slut* was the worst thing a girl could be called. However, my field notes indicate that the word *slut* (or its synonym *ho*) appeared one time for every eight times the word *fag* appeared.

Highlighting the difference between the deployment of *gay* and *fag* as insults brings the gendered nature of this homophobia into focus. For boys and girls at River High *gay* was a fairly common synonym for "stupid." While this word shared the sexual origins of *fag*, it didn't *consistently* have the skew of gender-loaded meaning. Girls and boys often used *gay* as an adjective referring to inanimate objects and male or female people, whereas they used *fag* as a noun that denoted only unmasculine males. Students used *gay* to describe anything from someone's clothes to a new school rule that they didn't like. For instance, one day in auto shop, Arnie pulled out a large older version of a black laptop computer and placed it on his desk. Behind him Nick cried, "That's a gay laptop! It's five inches thick!" The rest of the boys in the class laughed at Arnie's outdated laptop. A laptop can be gay, a movie can be gay, or a group of people can be gay. Boys used *gay* and *fag* interchangeably when they referred to other boys, but *fag* didn't have the gender-neutral attributes that *gay* frequently invoked.

Surprisingly, some boys took pains to say that the term *fag* did not imply sexuality. Darnell told me, "It doesn't even have anything to do with being gay." Similarly, J. L., a white sophomore at Hillside High (River High's cross-town rival), asserted, "*Fag*, seriously, it has nothing to do with sexual preference at all. You could just be calling somebody an idiot, you know?" I asked Ben, a quiet, white sophomore who wore heavy-metal T-shirts to auto shop each day, "What kind of things do guys get called a fag for?" Ben answered, "Anything . . . literally, anything. Like you were trying to turn a wrench the wrong way, 'Dude, you're a fag.' Even if a piece of meat drops out of your sandwich, 'You fag!'" Each time Ben said, "You fag," his voice deepened as if he were imitating a more masculine boy. While Ben might rightly *feel* that a guy could be called a fag for "anything . . . literally, anything," there were actually specific behaviors that, when enacted by most boys, could render them more vulnerable to a *fag* epithet. In this instance Ben's comment highlights the use of *fag* as a generic insult for incompetence, which in the world of River High was central to a masculine identity. A boy could get called a fag for exhibiting any sort of behavior defined as unmasculine (although not necessarily behaviors aligned with femininity): being stupid or incompetent, dancing, caring too much about clothing, being too emotional, or expressing interest (sexual or platonic) in other guys. However, given the extent of its deployment and the laundry list of behaviors that could get a boy in trouble, it is no wonder that Ben felt a boy could be called fag for "anything." These nonsexual meanings didn't replace sexual meanings but rather existed alongside them.

One-third (thirteen) of the boys I interviewed told me that, while they might liberally insult each other with the term, they would not direct it at a homosexual peer. Jabes, a Filipino senior, told me, "I actually say it *[fag]* quite a lot, except for when I'm in the company of an actual homosexual person. Then I try not to say it at all. But when I'm just hanging out with my friends I'll be like, 'Shut up, I don't want to hear you anymore, you stupid fag.'" Similarly J. L. compared homosexuality to a disability, saying there was "no way" he'd call an actually gay guy a fag because "there's people who are the retarded people who nobody wants to associate with. I'll be so nice to those guys, and I hate it when people make fun of them. It's like, 'Bro do you realize that they can't help that?' And then there's gay people. They were born that way." According to this group of boys, gay was a legitimate, or at least biological, identity.

There was a possibility, however slight, that a boy could be gay and masculine (Connell 1995). David, a handsome white senior dressed

This image captures one of the many gestures popular among boys and young men that function as nonverbal insults.

smartly in khaki pants and a white button-down shirt, told me, "Being gay is just a lifestyle. It's someone you choose to sleep with. You can still throw around a football and be gay." It was as if David was justifying the use of the word *fag* by arguing that gay men could be men if they tried but that if they failed at it (i.e., if they couldn't throw a football) then they deserved to be called a fag. In other words, to be a fag was, by definition, the opposite of masculine, whether the word was deployed with sexualized or nonsexualized meanings. In explaining this to me, Jamaal, an African American junior, cited the explanation of the popular rap artist Eminem: "Although I don't like Eminem, he had a good definition of it. It's like taking away your title. In an interview they were like, 'You're always capping on gays, but then you sing with Elton John.' He was like 'I don't mean gay as in gay.'" This is what Riki Wilchins (2003) calls the "Eminem Exception. Eminem explains that he doesn't call people 'faggot' because of their sexual orientation but because they're weak and unmanly" (72). This is precisely the way boys at River High used the term *faggot*. While it was not necessarily acceptable to be gay, at least a man who was gay could do other things that would render him acceptably masculine. A fag, by the very definition of the word, could not be masculine.

This distinction between fag as an unmasculine and problematic   15
identity and gay as a possibly masculine, although marginalized, sexual identity is not limited to a teenage lexicon; it is reflected in both psychological discourses and gay and lesbian activism. Eve Sedgwick (1995) argues that in contemporary psychological literature homosexuality is no longer a problem for men so long as the homosexual man is of the right age and gender orientation. In this literature a homosexual male must be an adult and must be masculine. Male homosexuality is not pathologized, but gay male *effeminacy* is. The lack of masculinity is the problem, not the sexual practice or orientation. Indeed, the edition of the *Diagnostic and Statistical Manual of Mental Disorders* (a key document in the mental health field) that erased homosexuality as a diagnosis in the 1970s added a new diagnosis in its wake: Gender Identity Disorder. According to Sedgwick, the criteria for diagnosis are different for girls and boys. A girl has to actually assert that she is a boy, indicating a psychotic disconnection with reality, whereas a boy need only display a preoccupation with female activities. The policing of boys' gender orientation and of a strict masculine identity for gay men is also reflected in gay culture itself. The war against fags as the specter of unmasculine manhood appears in gay male personal ads in which men look for "straight-appearing, straight-acting men." This concern with both straight and gay men's masculinity not only reflects teenage boys' obsession with

hypermasculinity but also points to the conflict at the heart of the contemporary "crisis of masculinity" being played out in popular, scientific, and educational arenas.

Becoming a Fag: Fag Fluidity

"The ubiquity of the word *faggot* speaks to the reach of its discrediting capacity" (Corbett 2001, 4). It's almost as if boys cannot help shouting it out on a regular basis—in the hallway, in class, or across campus as a greeting. In my fieldwork I was amazed by the way the word seemed to pop uncontrollably out of boys' mouths in all kinds of situations. To quote just one of many instances from my field notes: two boys walked out of the PE locker room, and one yelled, "Fucking faggot!" at no one in particular. None of the other students paid them any mind, since this sort of thing happened so frequently. Similar spontaneous yelling of some variation of the word *fag*, seemingly apropos of nothing, happened repeatedly among boys throughout the school. This and repeated imitations of fags constitute what I refer to as a "fag discourse."

Fag discourse is central to boys' joking relationships. Joking cements relationships among boys (Lyman 1998) and helps to manage anxiety and discomfort (Freud 1905). Boys both connect with one another and manage the anxiety around this sort of relationship through joking about fags. Boys invoked the specter of the fag in two ways: through humorous imitation and through lobbing the epithet at one another. Boys at River High imitated the fag by acting out an exaggerated "femininity" and/or by pretending to sexually desire other boys. As indicated by the introductory vignette in which an older boy imitated a predatory fag to threaten little boys, male students at River High linked these performative scenarios with a fag identity. They also lobbed the *fag* epithet at each other in a verbal game of hot potato, each careful to deflect the insult quickly by hurling it toward someone else. These games and imitations made up a fag discourse that highlighted the fag not as a static but rather as a fluid identity that boys constantly struggled to avoid.

In imitative performances the fag discourse functioned as a constant reiteration of the fag's existence, affirming that the fag was out there; boys reminded themselves and each other that at any moment they could become fags if they were not sufficiently masculine. At the same time these performances demonstrated that the boy who was invoking the fag was *not* a fag. Emir, a tall, thin African American boy, frequently imitated fags to draw laughs from other students in his introductory drama class. One day Mr. McNally, the drama teacher, disturbed by the noise outside the classroom, turned to the open door, saying, "We'll shut this unless anyone really wants to watch sweaty boys playing basketball." Emir lisped, "I wanna watch the boys play!" The rest of the class cracked up at his imitation. No one in the class actually thought Emir was gay, as he purposefully mocked both same-sex sexual desire (through pretending to admire the boys playing basketball) and an effeminate gender identity (through speaking with a lisp and in a high-pitched voice). Had he said this in all seriousness, the class most likely would have responded in stunned silence. Instead, Emir reminded them he was masculine by immediately dropping the fag act. After imitating a fag, boys assure others that they are not a fag by instantly becoming masculine again after the performance. They mock their own performed femininity and/or same-sex desire, assuring themselves and others that such an identity deserves derisive laughter.

Boys consistently tried to force others into the fag position by lobbing the *fag* epithet at each other. One day in auto shop, Jay was rummaging through a junk-filled car in the parking lot. He poked his head out of the trunk and asked, "Where are Craig and Brian?" Neil responded with "I think they're over there," pointing, then thrusting his hips and pulling his arms back and forth to indicate that Craig and Brian might be having sex. The boys in auto shop laughed. This sort of joke temporarily labeled both Craig and Brian as faggots. Because the fag discourse was so familiar, the other boys immediately understood that Neil was indicating that Craig and Brian were having sex. However, these were not necessarily identities that stuck. Nobody actually thought Craig and Brian were homosexuals. Rather, the fag identity was fluid—certainly an identity that no boy wanted but that most boys could escape, usually by engaging in some sort of discursive contest to turn another boy into a fag.

In this way the fag became a hot potato that no boy wanted to be left holding. One of the best ways to move out of the fag position was to thrust another boy into that position. For instance, soon after Neil made the joke about Brian having sex with Craig, Brian lobbed the *fag* epithet at someone else, deflecting it from himself by initiating a round of a favorite game in auto shop, the "cock game." Brian said quietly, looking at Josh, "Josh loves the cock," then slightly louder, "Josh loves the cock." He continued saying this until he was yelling, "JOSH LOVES THE COCK!" The rest of the boys laughed hysterically as Josh slunk away, saying, "I have a bigger dick than all you motherfuckers!" These two instances show how the fag could be mapped, for a moment, onto one boy's body and how he, in turn, could attach it to another boy, thus deflecting it from himself. In the first instance Neil made fun of Craig and Brian for simply hanging out together. In the

20

second instance Brian went from being a fag to making Josh into a fag through the "cock game." Through joking interactions boys moved in and out of the fag identity by discursively creating another as a fag.

Given the pervasiveness of fag jokes and the fluidity of the fag identity, it is difficult for boys to consistently avoid the brand. As Ben stated, it almost seemed that a boy could get called a fag for "anything." But most readily acknowledged that there were spaces, behaviors, and bodily comportments that made one more likely to be subject to the fag discourse, such as bodily practices involving clothing and dancing.

According to boys at River, fags cared about the style of their clothes, wore tighter clothes, and cared about cleanliness. Nils explained to me that he could tell that a guy was a fag by the way he dressed: "Most guys wear loose-fitting clothing, just kind of baggy. They [fags] wear more tight clothes. More fashionable, I guess." Similarly, nonfags were not supposed to care about dirtying their clothes. Auto shop was a telling example of this. Given that the boys spent two hours working with greasy car parts, they frequently ended up smudged and rumpled by the end of class. While in the front of the classroom there was a room boys could change in, most of them opted not to change out of their school clothes, with a few modifying their outfits by taking their shirts off and walking around in their "beaters." These tank tops were banned at River High because of their association with gang membership. Auto shop was the one place on campus where boys could wear them with impunity. Like most of the boys in auto shop, Ben never changed out of his jeans or heavy-metal T-shirts. After working on a particularly oily engine he walked into the classroom with grease stains covering his pants. He looked down at them, made a face, and walked toward me laughing, waving his hands around with limp wrists, and lisping in a high-pitched sing-song voice, "I got my good panths all dirty!" Ben's imitation indicated that only a fag would actually care about getting his clothes dirty. "Real" guys didn't care about their appearance; thus it didn't matter if they were covered in grease stains. Of course, to not care about one's clothes, or to make fun of those who care about their clothes, ironically, is to also care about one's appearance. In this sense, masculinity became the carefully crafted appearance of not caring about appearance.

Indeed, the boys' approach to clothing and cleanliness mirrored trends in larger society and the ascendance of the "metrosexual." *Metrosexual* is the recently coined label for straight men who care about their appearance, meticulously piecing together outfits, using product in their hair, and even making manicure appointments (for clear polish, of course). Because these sorts of grooming practices are associated with gay men, straight men developed a new moniker to differentiate themselves from other straight men and from gay men.

Dancing was another practice that put a boy at risk of being labeled a fag. Often boys would jokingly dance together to defuse the sexualized and feminized meanings embedded in dancing. At dances white boys frequently held their female dates tightly, locking their hips together. The boys never danced with one another unless they were joking or trying to embarrass one another. The examples of boys jokingly dancing together are too numerous to discuss, but the following example was particularly memorable. Lindy danced behind her date, Chris. Chris's friend Matt walked up and nudged Lindy aside, imitating her dance moves behind Chris. As Matt rubbed his hands up and down Chris's back, Chris turned around and jumped back, startled to see Matt there instead of Lindy. Matt cracked up as Chris turned red and swore at his friend.

A similar thing happened at CAPA as two of the boys from the band   25
listened to another band play swing music. These two boys walked toward each other and began to ballroom-dance. Within a second or two they keeled over in laughter, hitting each other and moving away. This ritualized dance, moving closer and then apart, happened again and again when music played at River High. Boys participated in this ritualized exchange to emphasize that indeed they weren't fags.

When boys were forced to dance with one another, as in classroom activities, this sort of joking escalated. In the drama class Mr. McNally walked the students through an exercise that required them to stand so close to each other that most parts of their bodies touched. He instructed the students to stand in two circles on the stage, with each person on the outer circle directly behind someone in the inner circle. He began to play a haunting instrumental song with no vocals. As the song continued Mr. McNally told the students in the inner circle to close their eyes and let their bodies go limp, while still standing. He instructed the students in the outer circle to move the person in front through an interpretive dance, following his lead as he moved the student in front of him. As the music continued, most of the students in the outer circle watched Mr. McNally's movements intently, trying their best to mirror his actions. The result was an intimate and beautiful puppet-and-puppeteer-like dance with the student in back moving the student in front through slow, fluid poses. Instead of following Mr. McNally's movements like the rest of the class, one pair of white sophomores, Liam and Jacob, barely touched. Jacob stood in back of Liam and, instead of gently holding Liam's wrist with their full arms touching as the other students did, picked up Liam's wrist with two fingers as if picking up something repulsive and flung Liam's hand to its destination. He made jokes with Liam's arm, repeatedly flinging it up against Liam's chest in a movement that indicated Liam was "retarded." The jokes continued as the students switched places, so that the inner circle became the outer circle, with Liam now "in control" of Jacob. Liam placed Jacob's hand against his forehead as if saluting, made his arms flap like birds, and used Jacob's finger to poke at his eyes, all the while, unlike the other students, never letting the majority of his body touch Jacob's. At the end of the exercise Mr. McNally asked for the students' feedback. One of the girls said, a little embarrassed, "I hate to say it, but it was almost sexual." To which Mr. McNally responded, "Yeah, it's full physical contact," at which point Liam and Jacob took two steps apart from one another. Even though the entire class was assigned to touch one another simultaneously, Jacob and Liam had a hard time following the instructions because it was so dangerous to actually "dance" together like this. Even in a class situation, in the most nonsuspect of interactions, the fag discourse ran deep, forbidding boys to touch one another.

The constant threat of the fag regulated boys' attitudes toward their bodies in terms of clothing, dancing, and touching. Boys constantly engaged in repudiatory rituals to avoid permanently inhabiting the fag position. Boys' interactions were composed of competitive joking through which they interactionally created the constitutive outside and affirmed their positions as subjects.

References

Almaguer, Tomas. 1991. "Chicano Men: A Cartography of Homosexual Identity and Behavior." *Differences* 3, 75–100.

Baker, J. G., & H. D. Fishbein. 1998. "The Development of Prejudice towards Gays and Lesbians by Adolescents." *Journal of Homosexuality* 36, 89–100.

Burn, Shawn M. 2000. "'Heterosexuals' Use of 'Fag' and 'Queer' to Deride One Another: A Contributor to Heterosexism and Stigma." *Journal of Homosexuality* 40, 1–11.

Connell, R. W. 1995. *Masculinities*. Berkeley: University of California Press.

Corbett, Ken. 2001. "Faggot = Loser." *Studies in Gender and Sexuality* 2, 3–28.

Freud, Sigmund. 1905. *The Basic Writings of Sigmund Freud*. Translated and edited by A. A. Brill. New York: The Modern Library.

Julien, Isaac, and Kobena Mercer. 1991. "True Confessions: A Discourse on Kehily, Mary Jane and Nayak, Anoop (1997) 'Lads and Laughter: Humour and the Production of Heterosexual Masculinities.'" *Gender and Education* 9, 69–87.

Kimmel, Michael. 2001. "Masculinity as Homophobia: Fear, Shame, and Silence in the Construction of Gender Identity." In *The Masculinities Reader*, ed. Stephen Whitehead and Frank Barrett, 266–287. Cambridge: Polity.

——. 2003. "Adolescent Masculinity, Homophobia, and Violence: Random School Shootings, 1982–2001." *American Behavioral Scientist* 46, 1439–1458.

King, D. L. 2004. *Double Lives on the Down Low.* New York: Broadway Books.

Lehne, Gregory. 1998. "Homophobia among Men: Supporting and Defining the Male Role." In *Men's Lives*, ed. Michael Kimmel and Michael Messner, 237–253. Boston, MA: Allyn and Bacon.

Lyman, Peter. 1998. "The Fraternal Bond as a Joking Relationship: A Case Study of the Role of Sexist Jokes in Male Group Bonding." In *Men's Lives*, ed. Michael Kimmel and Michael Messner, 171–193. Boston, MA: Allyn and Bacon.

Plummer, David C. 2001. "The Quest for Modern Manhood: Masculine Stereotypes, Peer Culture and the Social Significance of Homophobia." *Journal of Adolescence* 24, 15–23.

Riggs, Marlon. 1991. "Black Macho Revisited: Reflections of a SNAP! Queen." In *Brother to Brother: New Writings by Black Gay Men*, ed. Essex Hemphill, 153–260. Boston, MA: Alyson Publications.

Sedgwick, Eve K. 1995. "Gosh, Boy George, You Must Be Awfully Secure in Your Masculinity!" In *Constructing Masculinity*, ed. Maurice Berger, Brian Wallis and Simon Watson, 11–20. New York: Routledge.

Smith, George W. 1998. "The Ideology of 'Fag': The School Experience of Gay Students." *The Sociological Quarterly* 39, 309–335.

Wilchins, Riki. 2003. "Do You Believe in Fairies?" *The Advocate*, no. 882, 4 February, p. 72.

Wood, Julian. 1984. "Groping toward Sexism: Boy's Sex Talk." In *Gender and Generation*, ed. Angela McRobbie and Mica Nava, 54–84. London: Macmillan.

Understanding the Text

1. Pascoe sees the use of the term "faggot" as more than just a sign of homophobia. Rather, it is a term that polices the borders of adolescent male sexuality. Explain how Pascoe makes this argument. Why isn't "fag" just a term that indicates homophobia? How does Pascoe use River High as an example to illustrate his point?

2. Why is it that girls rarely use the word "fag" at River High? What explains the fact that it's a term almost exclusively used by boys and directed at other boys?

3. What is the difference between "fag" and "gay," according to Pascoe? Why is "fag" a term that boys pay more attention to than "gay"?

4. Pascoe says that jokes help manage anxiety and discomfort in adolescent boy culture. How do jokes serve this purpose? What is it about joking that allows boys to accept the label of "faggot" temporarily, even if they might dislike or disagree with this label in a nonjoking context?

Reflection and Response

5. Think about other slurs or negative terms you've heard used among adolescent boys that are similar to "fag." Are they used in similar ways or are they less harsh or dangerous? What commonalities exist between the terms you can think of and the word "fag"?

6. Why do you think the word "gay" is not used as a slur against girls? Do you agree that the worst word used for girls is "slut"? Why is "slut" among the worst words one can use to refer to a girl? Is there a similar word used to describe male sex practices? How are the words construed differently?

7. Why do you think that words about sexuality are so commonly used as slurs among adolescents?

Making Connections

8. Do a little bit of field research about the terms "fag" and "gay" by interviewing friends or classmates about how they've heard these terms used in recent years. Have the people you've interviewed found these terms to be problematic, or are they seen as acceptable terms? After reading Pascoe, do you find yourself bothered by these terms when you hear them used negatively (if you do hear them used negatively)?

9. Consider other readings in *Composing Gender* about definitions of heterosexual and homosexual, such as those in Kimmel (p. 140) and Schwartz (p. 184). How does River High demonstrate that these definitions are socially constructed?

10. Consider the ways the terms or the representations of "gays" and "fags" in movies or on television help construct contemporary attitudes toward homosexuality. Also, consider in general how sexual practices for men and women are presented differently on television and in movies.

Hegemonic Masculinity and Black Gender Ideology

Patricia Hill Collins

Patricia Hill Collins is a distinguished university professor of sociology at the University of Maryland, and her work focuses on issues of social class, sexuality, and nationality. She has published several important books in feminist theory, including *Black Feminist Thought: Knowledge, Consciousness and the Politics of Empowerment* (1990) and *From Black Power to Hip Hop: Racism, Nationalism, and Feminism* (2005). This selection is from her 2004 book *Black Sexual Politics*.

Since the 1912 publication of *Tarzan of the Apes*, the first Tarzan novel, the Tarzan myth has not only been immensely popular but it has been a central feature in disseminating ideas about White masculinity. Twenty-four Tarzan novels in all were published, primarily from the 1910s through the 1930s. Over fifty Tarzan films appeared after the first Tarzan movie was released in 1917. As late as 1963, one out of every thirty paperbacks sold was a Tarzan novel.[1] With one infamous yell, Tarzan subdued all the beasts of the jungle and ruled fictional natives who, unlike actual colonized Africans, appeared to welcome colonialism with a smile on their faces. Although Tarzan was a fictional character, his image helps frame ideas about masculinity: "Tarzan has defined himself as a 'man' by his difference from the apes, from blacks, and from females. . . . He needs now to preserve his 'manliness,' his aloneness, figuratively if not literally. He does this through establishing power hierarchies in which all others— and especially blacks and women—are subordinate to him."[2]

Tarzan constitutes one well-known example of how mass media shapes White masculinity within U.S. society. The construction of White masculinity is not confined to fictional images. Whether the composition of the U.S. Senate or executives of global corporations or an American literary canon that glorifies the exploits of pioneers and patriots, elite White men run America. It doesn't matter that, to paraphrase the title of a Hollywood film of the same name, "White men can't jump," because they can make others jump for them. Moreover, because this group so dominates positions of power and authority,

---

[1] Torgovnick 1990, 42.
[2] Torgovnick 1990, 55.

the view of masculinity patterned on Tarzan, U.S. senators, corporate executives, and cowboys is well known and is often taken as normal, natural, and ideal. It becomes hegemonic in that the vast majority of the population accepts ideas about gender complementarity that privilege the masculinity of propertied, heterosexual White men as natural, normal, and beyond reproach.[3] In this fashion, elite White men control the very definitions of masculinity, and they use these standards to evaluate their own masculine identities and those of all other men, including African American men.

Hegemonic masculinity is fundamentally a dynamic, relational construct.[4] Because it is constantly tested by the behaviors of others,

---

[3] Hegemony is a mode of social organization that relies on ideology to make oppressive power relations seem natural and normal. One goal of hegemonic ideologies is to absorb the dissent of oppressed groups, thereby dissipating its political effects. For example, if African Americans come to believe the dominant Black gender ideology circulated within the mass media, then Black political dissent about gender and sexuality becomes weakened. Hegemonic ideologies may seem invincible. But ideologies of all sorts are never static but instead are always internally inconsistent and are resisted (Magubane 2001).

[4] Emerging in conjunction with a men's movement, and influenced by Western feminism (although this debt is not typically acknowledged) as well as the constructionist turn in the American academy in the 1990s, gender scholarship rejected the apolitical and nonhistorical framework of traditional sex role theory. New analyses of masculinity approached it as a system of gender power. "To understand a system of inequality, we must examine its dominant group—the study of men is as vital for gender analysis as the study of ruling classes and elites is for class analysis," argued R. W. Connell (Connell 1992, 736). Within this framework, the term "hegemonic masculinity" came to refer to the dominant form of masculinity in any given society and created the space to view representations of White masculinity and Black masculinity not as descriptions of nature but as social constructions rooted in American power relations.

Rejecting the term "patriarchy" as overly simplistic, at any given moment a range of masculinities exists in any social order, including masculinities that are hegemonic, marginalized, and subordinated. Some key features characterize hegemonic masculinity. First, hegemonic masculinity is defined in relation to the subordination of women *and* in relation to other subordinated and marginalized masculinities (Messner 1990, 205). Second, hegemonic masculinity does not refer to a personality type or an actual male character. Rather, it describes a set of prescriptive social norms, symbolically represented, that operate as a crucial part of daily, routine activities (Wetherell and Edley 1999, 336). Third, the constellation of ideas and social practices that constitute hegemonic masculinity are accepted, rejected, and performed by men from diverse social class groupings, racial/ethnic groups, ages, and religions. Whereas men are not equal in their ability to control the very definitions of masculinity itself, the vast majority of men are, in some fashion, complicit in upholding hegemonic masculinity (Connell 1995). Finally, the power relations that construct these relational masculinities enable the erasure of whiteness, class privilege, and assumptions of heterosexuality, in short, the workings of hegemonic masculinity itself. As a result, hegemonic discourses of American masculinity operate as unquestioned truths. Ironically, despite the ubiquity of gender, race, class, and sexuality in constructing American masculinity, masculinity can be discussed without referencing these systems at all.

such masculinity must always be achieved. These relations are not merely interconnected; they reflect the hierarchal power relations of a racialized system of sexism that frames the multiple expressions of masculinity and femininity available to African American men and women, as well as all other groups. In the American context, hegemonic masculinity becomes defined through its difference from and opposition to women, boys, poor and working class men of all races and ethnicities, gay men, and Black men.[5] In other words, hegemonic masculinity is a concept that is shaped by ideologies of gender, age, class, sexuality, and race. Ideas about groups formed within these ideologies, for example, women or LGBT people, constitute an important benchmark for defining a hegemonic masculinity that must constantly construct itself. Without these groups as ideological markers, hegemonic masculinity becomes meaningless.

In the United States, hegemonic masculinity is installed at the top of a hierarchical array of masculinities. All other masculinities, including those of African American men, are evaluated by how closely they approximate dominant social norms. Masculinity itself becomes organized as a three-tiered structure: those closest to hegemonic masculinity, predominantly wealthy White men, but not exclusively so, retain the most power at the top; those men who are situated just below have greater access to White male power, yet remain marginalized (for example, working-class White men and Latino, Asian, and White immigrant men); and those males who are subordinated by both of these groups occupy the bottom (for example, Black men and men from indigenous groups). Moreover, hegemonic masculinity *requires* these marginalized and subordinated masculinities.

Men from varying races, classes, and sexualities jockey for position within this hierarchy of masculinities. For example, like African American men, the vast majority of Latino and Asian American men are excluded from the category of hegemonic masculinity. Instead, they are assigned social scripts of marginalized masculinities, the

5

Over time, this literature on masculinities devoted increasing attention to the socially constructed nature of hegemonic masculinities in relation to a variety of other constructed masculinities across differences of class, race, ethnicity, and sexuality. Masculinity itself was seen as highly heterogeneous and relational, with masculinities constructed in relation to one another emerging as an important area of study (Connell 1992, 1995). One important idea now possible with the emergence of this literature is that, from the perspectives of subordinated groups, all masculinities are in some sense hegemonic—a situation in which, for example, White men encounter a hegemonic White masculinity of what a White man should be and do, and Black men encounter equally hegemonic ideas about what Black men should be and do. In a sense, there are levels of hegemonic masculinity, all designed to control.

[5] Kimmel 2001.

former because of dedication to family and the latter due to representations of hard work and being a "model minority." Those Latino and Asian American men who falter can be demoted to the subordinated masculinity reserved for African American men. Those who manage to approximate the norms of hegemonic masculinity may enter the inner circle, often as "honorary" elite White men. Not surprisingly, this hierarchy of successful and failed manhood matches up to the White normality/Black deviancy framework that accompanies racism; the heterosexual/homosexual binary that supports heterosexism; structures of age that grant seniority to older males over younger ones; and a class system that grants propertied individuals more power and status than those who lack it.

It is important to stress that *all* women occupy the category of devalued Other that gives meaning to *all* masculinities. Yet, just as masculinities are simultaneously constructed in relation to one another and hierarchically related, femininities demonstrate a similar pattern. Within these crosscutting relationships, Latina, Asian, and Black women routinely inherit social scripts of marginalized and/or subordinated femininities. For example, one study of representations of Latina and Black women in fiction and of Latinas and Blacks who had careers in Hollywood films finds similarities in treatment that illuminate how marginalized and subordinated femininities are constructed.[6] Latinas are routinely presented as members of a conquered people whereas Black women appear as slaves. In this regard, both groups of women symbolize subordinated femininities and share the status of sexual outlaws: "the Latina of conquest fiction is portrayed as the half-breed harlot whose purpose is to pique the male sexual appetite and whose mixed blood elicits similar behavior to that of her Black counterpart, the mulatto."[7] Thus, within hierarchies of femininity, social categories of race, age, and sexual orientation also intersect to produce comparable categories of hegemonic, marginalized, and subordinated femininities.

Black femininity is constructed in relation to the tenets of hegemonic masculinity that subordinates all femininities to masculinity. At the same time, the social power granted to race and class in the United States means that sexism is not an either/or endeavor in which all men dominate all women. Rather, gender norms that privilege men typically play out *within* racial/ethnic and/or social class groups as well as *between* such groups. For example, working-class Latino men may

---

[6] Freydberg 1995, 2257.
[7] Freydberg 1995, 2257.

expect obedience from working-class Latinas, yet when both arrive at their jobs, they may be deferential to White employers, male and female. In one sense, Black femininity is the ultimate "other" juxtaposed to hegemonic White masculinity, with poor, young Black lesbians such as fifteen-year-old murder victim Sakia Gunn saddled with an intensified version of costs attached to Black femininity.[8] In contrast, George W. Bush can be a "C" student at Yale University, have a drinking problem, and get elected president of the United States in 2000. He benefits from an intensified version of the privileges of hegemonic masculinity, namely the privileges of Whiteness, family ties, heterosexuality, and the power that money can buy. Varying combinations of race, class, sexuality, and gender create intermediate positions between these two poles for working-class Black men, middle-class Latinas, poor gay White men, Haitian immigrants, and other groups. As a group, Black men fall between these two poles and many of the contradictions that affect Black manhood reflect this intermediate location. It is important to keep this overarching frame in mind because everyday lived experience is not this neat. Selected individual African American women such as Oprah Winfrey and Condoleezza Rice may wield considerable power and, as individuals, are definitely not oppressed. But for Black women as a class, the concept of a subordinated Black femininity holds sway. Despite the massive media attention given to African American men and women who seem to be exceptions to the rules, Black masculinity and Black femininity thus are both constructed in relation to hegemonic masculinity, a situation that also shapes their relation to one another.

Keeping It "Real": African American Men and Hegemonic Masculinity

Hegemonic masculinity in the United States has several benchmarks. For one, "real" men are primarily defined as *not* being like women. Real men are expected to be forceful, analytical, responsible, and willing to exert authority, all qualities that women seemingly lack. The use of women in the construction of masculinity is so widespread that this dimension of hegemonic masculinity seems hidden in plain sight. For example, boys on American sports teams are routinely ridiculed for "playing like girls." Boys are discouraged from crying "like girls." A major insult hurled at men is that they are "soft" like women.

---

[8] "Skeleton in Newark's Closet: Laquetta Nelson Is Forcing Homophobia Out into the Open" 2003.

Within this ideological framework, simply being unlike women is not enough. For this version of masculinity to be plausible, men require female validation as constant reminders of male superiority. Otherwise, how would men know that they are not like women if only in the company of men? The irony is that, whereas dependency is typically seen as a female attribute, femininity does not *depend* on males staying in their place. In contrast, men who accept this dimension of dominant gender ideology require control over women (which takes many forms) in order to know that they are "real" men.

Within this logic, men who seem too closely aligned with women, who lack authority with the women of their racial ethnic group and/or social class, or, worst yet, who seem to be dominated by women suffer a loss of manhood. In other words, male dominance occurs within racial/ethnic categories and is one marker of male power. The legacy of seeing women as property or "booty," the spoils of warfare, establishes this theme of needing to exert male authority over at least one woman, typically a girlfriend, wife, or daughter. Representations of Black masculinity within mass media that depict working-class Black men as aggressive thugs or as promiscuous hustlers seem designed to refute accusations that Black men are "weak" because they cannot control Black women. If "real" men are those who can control women, then these representations suggest that Black men can shake the stigma of weakness by dominating unnaturally strong Black women. Being strong enough to "bring a bitch to her knees" becomes a marker of Black masculinity. Moreover, trying to exert male dominance over women places African American men and women in an adversarial relationship. Women who do not let men be men become blamed for Black male behavior. Abusive men routinely blame their partners for their own violent behavior—if she had been more of a woman (submissive), she would have let him be more of a man.[9]

Another dimension of hegemonic masculinity is that "real" men 10 exercise control not just over women but also over their own emotions, in leadership positions, and over all forms of violence. In other words, exercising male authority is a vital component of masculinity. Yet men's access to the apparatuses of authority and violence differs depending on their social location within race and social class hierarchies. White men exercise violence within a wide array

---

[9] This fear of feminization may help explain why many Black men reject feminism: "it is the idea of feminism connected to a perverse notion of the feminine that in the historical memory of Black men conjures up images of feminization, castration, and ultimately death" (Lemons 1997, 45). In everyday life, such men are viewed as being emasculated or, in Black vernacular, "pussy whipped."

of social settings and possess legitimate authority over the mechanisms of violence. For example, elite White men run military and police forces—they have the authority to set policies concerning the legitimate use of force while erasing their own culpability for wars and other violent outcomes. Propertied White males also control the forums of symbolic violence within U.S. society, for example, sports and mass media (television, film, and music).[10] From the Revolutionary War to the 2003 War in Iraq, poor and working-class White men have joined or been drafted into military service. These men may carry the guns, but they also enforce policies that often were made without their input.

In contrast, because so many African American men lack access to the forms of political and economic power that are available to elite White men, the use of their bodies, physicality, and a form of masculine aggressiveness become more important. Black men experience violence, often at the hands of other Black men. Working-class and poor Black men have access to street weapons and their own bodies as weapons. Rather than expressing masculine authority by running corporations or holding high-level government positions, Black men search for respect from marginal social locations. Sociologist Elijah Anderson suggests that in economically depressed neighborhoods affected by drugs and crime, interpersonal violence among young African American men reflects a desperate search for respect. Possession of respect—an indicator of male authority and manhood—is highly valued. As Anderson points out, "the code of the street emerges where the influence of the police ends and personal responsibility for one's safety is felt to begin, resulting in a kind of 'people's law,' based on 'street justice.' . . . In service to this ethic, repeated displays of 'nerve' and 'heart' build or reinforce a credible reputation for vengeance that works to deter aggression and disrespect, which are sources of great anxiety on the inner-city street."[11] In the context of the closing door of opportunity of the post–civil rights era, the often-explosive interactions among African American men on the street become more comprehensible.

---

[10] Initially, sports operated as a White, middle- and upper-class male-created homosocial cultural space that provided elite men a psychological separation from the perceived "feminization" of society while providing symbolic proof of male superiority. As Messner observes, "it is not simply the bonding among men and the separation from women, but the physicality of the activity which gives sports its saliency in gender relations" (Messner 1990, 204). Over time, as this space became dominated by working-class White men, by Black men, and most recently by women, sport delivers less of this "symbolic proof of White male superiority."

[11] Anderson 1999, 9–10.

Boys constitute yet another benchmark used to construct hegemonic masculinity. "Real" men do not resemble or behave like immature, irresponsible males (boys) who have not yet been properly socialized into the responsibilities and benefits of adult masculinity. Physical appearance distinguishes men from boys. Men are muscular and have facial and body hair. In contrast, boys are still hairless and physically weaker. Boys are quasi women. Moreover, unlike men who have had sexual intercourse with adult women, primarily by genital penetration, boys remain sexual virgins. Sexual intercourse with a woman initiates them into manhood. Boys are also financially dependent on others—they do not hold jobs and are not expected to support any dependents. Moreover, just as less powerful men are pressured to submit to dominant ones (e.g., criminals to cops and factory workers to managers), boys are expected to submit to adult male authority, most notably their fathers. Within this age-stratified male drama, boys become men by submitting to adult male authority and by trying to become like their fathers. Conversely, men who lack fathers or access to male authority organized through patriarchy suffer a distinct disadvantage in hierarchies of masculinity.

Viewing people of African descent as being like children has a long history within Western culture, and, within the United States, treating African American men as boys constitutes a gender-specific manifestation of it. The use of the term *boy* in the segregated South to humiliate and demean adult Black men gave voice to this portion of hegemonic masculinity that needed Black boys to give it meaning. Western colonialism and slavery contain numerous examples of efforts to infantilize men of African descent. The Tarzan novels and movies provide one of the most visible and enduring examples of how ideologies of hegemonic masculinity needed and were constructed on the backs of men of African descent conceptualized as "boys" or "boy servants." From images of Uncle Tom and Uncle Ben to the sidekicks within contemporary popular culture, Black men have been depicted as immature men, if not actual boys.

Recognizing this history, African American men have responded with various strategies, with varying degrees of success. Black men's visibility within basketball, rap, and hip-hop culture has provided a new and highly visible cultural arena for reasserting an adult Black masculinity and rejecting the traditional "boy" status reserved for Black men. The "bad boys" of basketball are so "bad" that they can self-define as "boys" with little fear of being mistaken for them. The media spectacles of Latrell Sprewell choking his coach, Charles Barkley refusing to be a role model, Mike Tyson biting off part of an opponent's ear, and legions of crotch-grabbing young rappers who glare angrily at the camera, proclaiming their manhood, seemingly reject any efforts to treat them like children. They reject the discourse of Black sidekicks and sissies as the route for White acceptance and as a path to adult masculinity and claim media space to argue that there is another way to be Black, male, and adult.

Possessing property and the power that it commands operates as yet another benchmark of hegemonic masculinity. There are definite social class dimensions to hegemonic masculinity—"real" men are not financially dependent on others, but instead support others. They take responsibility for their families by getting married and financially supporting their wives and children. They are neither sexual renegades running from one woman to another nor pimps and hustlers who expect women to support them. Historically, working-class men lobbied for an adequate "family wage" that would enable them to support their wives and children.[12] Unemployed and underemployed working-class and poor men who fail to meet these criteria of masculinity are depicted as irresponsible, and the number of children they father with their unmarried partners provides evidence for their sexual irresponsibility and refusal to grow up. Talk shows operate as contemporary morality plays to showcase and censure poor and working-class men, many of whom are Black, who refuse to assume their financial obligations. At the same time, shows like *The Cosby Show* mask how difficult it actually is for a Black man (or woman) to become a doctor and to make enough money to purchase a New York City brownstone and support a wife and five children in style.

Being heterosexual constitutes another important benchmark of hegemonic masculinity—"real" men are also *not* gay or homosexual. In this construction of hegemonic masculinity, gay men mark the contradictions that plague male heterosexuality itself: "heterosexual men must deny desire except for the gendered Other, while making a hated Other of the men who desire them."[13] Gay men are belittled because they are seen as being like women, the stereotypical view of gay men as being "sissies," "faggots," or effeminate men. This relation between heterosexual and homosexual men carries heavy symbolic weight in the context of contemporary Western masculinity. To many

15

---

[12] The concept of a "family wage" also leads to pay discrimination against women. It argues that men should be paid more than women because men have the responsibility of financially supporting their wives and children. In contrast, women are more likely to have babies and leave the labor market to care for them.

[13] Connell 1992, 748.

people, because "homosexuality is a negation of masculinity . . . homosexual men must be effeminate."[14]

Heterosexual African American men are extremely protective of this dimension of their manhood, often resorting to violence if they feel threatened. Stereotyping Black gay men as effeminate and weak, even though the majority of Black gay men do not fit this profile, becomes an important factor in constantly asserting Black male heterosexuality. In essence, Black gay men become the ultimate weak men under the "weak men/strong women" thesis.[15] Their visibility symbolizes the Black community's collective weakness.

Finally, race itself plays an important part as a benchmark in constructing the hegemonic masculinity that defines "real" men in the United States. Black men, *by definition*, cannot be real men, *because they are Black*. The fact of Blackness excludes Black men from participating fully in hegemonic masculinity because, if they do so, they decenter the assumed Whiteness of those installed in the center of the definition itself. Within the father-son family drama of American masculinity, White fathers cannot or will not claim their Black sons. This interracial relationship violates the basic taboo of racial purity that has long characterized American society. The best that Black men can do is to achieve an "honorary" membership within hegemonic masculinity by achieving great wealth, marrying the most desirable women (White), expressing aggression in socially sanctioned arenas (primarily as athletes, through the military, or law enforcement), and avoiding suggestions of homosexual bonding.

Work That Body: African American Women and Hegemonic Femininity

As a group, women are subordinated to men, yet a pecking order among women also produces hegemonic, marginalized, and subordinated femininities. This ideology proscribes behavior for *all* women based on these assumptions, and then holds all women, including African American women, to standards that only *some* women (including many White ones) may be able to achieve. All women engage an ideology that deems middle-class, heterosexual, White femininity as normative. In this context, Black femininity as a subordinated gender identity becomes constructed not just in relation to White

---

[14] Connell 1992, 736.
[15] Dalton 1999, 333.

As a group, women are subordinated to men, yet a pecking order among women also produces hegemonic, marginalized, and subordinated femininities. women, but also in relation to multiple others, namely all men, sexual outlaws (prostitutes and lesbians), unmarried women, and girls. These benchmarks construct a discourse of a hegemonic (White) femininity that becomes a normative yardstick for all femininities in which Black women typically are relegated to the bottom of the gender hierarchy.

One benchmark of hegemonic femininity is that women *not* be like men. Maintaining an appropriately feminine demeanor invokes two standards, one physical and the other behavioral. Because women in Western societies are judged by their physical appearance more so than men, women should not resemble men. The appearance of women's bodies is subject to sustained scrutiny, and the way that women work their bodies (adorn them, carry them, use them sexually, use them to produce children, or alter them through cosmetic surgery) constitutes an important criterion for evaluating femininity. On a basic biological level, the presence of breasts, hips, a round booty, and the absence of muscles and facial hair become important indicators of womanhood that distinguish women from men, boys, and girls. Women need not actively earn femininity to the degree required of masculinity, for example, having sex with a woman, bringing home a paycheck, or demonstrating athletic prowess. Instead, women wait passively, depend on physical maturation, and hope that the adult female bodies they receive will meet social approval.[16]

Because femininity is so focused on women's bodies, the value placed on various attributes of female bodies means that evaluations of femininity are fairly clear-cut. Within standards of feminine beauty that correlate closely with race and age women are pretty or they are not. Historically, in the American context, young women with milky White skin, long blond hair, and slim figures were deemed to be the most beautiful and therefore the most feminine women. Within this interpretive context, skin color, body type, hair texture, and facial features become important dimensions of femininity. This reliance on these standards of beauty automatically render the majority of African American women at best as less beautiful, and at worst, ugly. Moreover,

20

---

[16] This theme of body politics has a prominent place in feminist theory. For discussions of women's biology and human nature, see Bordo 1993. For an alternative analysis of the meaning of the body within Western societies, see Oyĕwùmí 1997.

these standards of female beauty have no meaning without the visible presence of Black women and others who fail to measure up. Under these feminine norms, African American women can never be as beautiful as White women because they never become White.

In this context of the new color-blind racism, the significance attached to skin color, especially for women, is changing. In response to the growing visibility of biracial, multiracial, Latino, Asian, and racially ambiguous Americans, skin color no longer serves as a definitive mark of racial categorization. Rejecting historical rules whereby an individual with "one drop" of "black blood" was seen as Black, the new multiracial America uses more fluid racial categories. For many Black women, Blackness can be "worked" in various ways. For example, light-skinned Halle Berry is biracial and projects a certain kind of beauty that is not purely Black. She self-identifies as an African American woman but her film career suggests that she can work her body in various ways. Berry played many Black women before her Oscar-winning performance in *Monster's Ball*. For example, in *Losing Isaiah* (1995), she plays a Black mother on crack, and in *Bulworth* (1998) she plays a streetwise confidant to a White politician. In contrast, in *X-men* (2000) and *Swordfish* (2001) Berry plays characters in which White or Latino actresses could just as easily have been cast. In contrast to Halle Berry, who can work her biracial appearance in many ways, darker-skinned actresses such as Alfre Woodard and Angela Bassett have far fewer options.

Hair texture, a female feature that is far more malleable, also matters greatly in re-creating femininity in the context of the new color-blind racism. Because a good deal of women's beauty is associated with their hair, this aspect of women's physical appearance takes on added importance in the process of constructing hierarchies of femininity. As Banks suggests, "the 'good hair' and 'bad hair' distinction is probably the most indelible construction of hair that occupies the psyche of African Americans."[17] Some authors claim that hair texture has long been more important than skin color in racial politics. For example, in his exhaustive cross-cultural analysis of slavery, Orlando Patterson contends that dominant groups usually perform elaborate rituals on their subordinates. Shearing of hair is a key part of rituals of domination cross-culturally. Patterson points out, "it was not so much color differences as differences in hair type that become critical as a mark of servility in the Americas."[18] To explain this pattern,

---

[17] Banks 2000, 28.
[18] Patterson 1982, 61.

Patterson contends that hair provides a clearer and more powerful badge of status than skin color. Differences between Whites and Blacks were sharper in hair quality than in color and persisted much longer with miscegenation. Patterson notes, "Hair type rapidly became the real symbolic badge of slavery, although like many powerful symbols, it was disguised . . . by the linguistic device of using the term 'black,' which nominally threw the emphasis to color."[19] Raine, one of the participants in Banks's study, agrees with this position, and explains how ideas about "good hair" and "bad hair" articulate with ideas about skin color:

Blacks are judged on their hair. I think basically the long, straight hair people are more favorable. The shorter, kinkier, nappier [the] hair, the less favoritism is shown. I've lived that, coming through school as a young girl I was dark, but I had long hair. I was put in with the little light [skin] long-haired kids. But the ones who had the short, measly, nappy hair, no matter what they looked like, they were always last, in the back.[20]

Hair increases in importance in a society where biracial, multiracial, and racially ambiguous individuals become more visible within a racially heterogeneous society. Moreover, because hair is seen as a badge of beauty for women, this physical feature becomes more central in constructing hierarchies of femininity than is the case for men.

Maintaining an appropriately feminine demeanor constitutes another dimension of trying *not* to be like men. Women can also avoid the stigma of being judged too masculine by avoiding so-called male characteristics. Women are expected to defer to men, and those women who project a submissive demeanor allegedly receive better treatment than those who do not. This theme of female submissiveness permeates the public sphere of labor market practices and government office-holding in which nurses defer to doctors, teachers to principals, and secretaries to managers. Despite a new legal structure that provides equal opportunities to girls and boys, job categories remain gender segregated. The theme of female submissiveness also shapes private, domestic sphere activities of family and community. Well-functioning families adhere to this allegedly natural authority structure that fosters female submissiveness. Women with the appropriate demeanor should remain safely sequestered in private homes and community endeavors, thus allowing men to engage in appro-

25

---

[19] Patterson 1982, 61.
[20] Banks 2000, 29.

priately masculine behaviors of work and leadership in the public sphere.[21]

As was the case for hegemonic masculinity, there are numerous mass media examples of White women who model the art of submissiveness. The women need not have submissive personalities; they only need to recognize the boundaries of White male authority. For example, the depiction of White women in Tarzan novels and films illustrates how White women are depicted as needing (to submit to) male protection. As Tarzan's helpmate, the fictional character of Jane is an adventuresome, energetic White woman. Jane has spunk—she lives in Africa among wild animals and African natives. Jane's formal education ties her more closely to European civilization than Tarzan, and because she is a woman, she represents the civilizing influence of femininity both in the home and in the jungle itself. In the context of wild, uncivilized space, Jane keeps home and hearth functioning. She also needs White male protection. The treatment of White women like Jane in the Tarzan novels demonstrates female dependency. White women are repeatedly abducted in the Tarzan novels, on average three times per woman per novel. When the triple abduction occurs, the first abductor is usually a renegade European, the second either an Arab or an African, and the third an ape.[22]

Black women have long struggled with the behavioral dimensions of femininity whereby the very characteristics of femininity were neither possible nor desirable. African American writer Gloria Naylor encapsulates the contradictions that accompany Black women's inability to be submissive and the effects that this had on family and relationships:

---

[21] Girls constitute a related benchmark used to construct hegemonic femininity. Girls are allegedly pure, innocent, and sexual virgins. They should be unspoiled. Interestingly, representations of young women/girls within contemporary popular culture contain the contradictions currently plaguing views of young White womanhood. On the one hand, women are expected to aspire to a body type that approximates that of adolescent girls. The inordinate pressure placed on thinness within U.S. society advances a social norm that values youth. At the same time, these same inordinately thin adolescent girls are dressed as highly sexualized women within high fashion. Black women as sexualized, full-figured women become juxtaposed to the thin, young, fragile and increasingly ornamental and sexualized young White girls.

[22] Torgovnick 1990, 53. This theme of White female submissiveness also appears in other major icons of Western popular culture. For example, the various remakes of *King Kong* take this need to rescue White womanhood from sexual predators to an entirely new level. With King Kong theorized to be symbolic of Black men as animals or "apes" run amuck, just as Jane needed saving from the predators in the jungle, the White woman in Manhattan needed saving from a lustful Kong now transplanted to an urban jungle (Dines 1998).

We need to speak of submissiveness. That was never in the cards for us. . . . Whether in the cotton fields of the South or the factories of the North, Black women worked side by side with men to contribute to the welfare of the family. This did not mean that men were demeaned and unloved, but it did mean that women had a voice about the destiny of their families. That independence and resiliency were admired because they aided in the collective survival when society made it difficult for Black men to find work. But when we began to internalize Euro-American values, then Black women were no longer "real" women—and of course only a real woman would love or be loved by a man.[23]

As controlling images of Black femininity, the bitch and bad Black mother both present the unassimilated, working-class Black woman as unacceptable, primarily because she lacks appropriate female qualities of submissiveness. Mass media ideologies hold out solutions to this seeming problem of working-class Black female assertiveness— either become more like the middle-class modern mammies (assertive in defense of White authority while remaining submissive to it) or aspire to become Black ladies.

Being appropriately heterosexual constitutes another important benchmark of hegemonic femininity. In a context of male dominance, heterosexual men's access to women's bodies as sexual partners constitutes an important component of hegemonic femininity. Appropriately feminine women should be married to heterosexual male partners and dedicated to sexually pleasing them. Women's actual sexual behavior within the sanctity of heterosexual marriage is less important than adhering to male-defined norms about who controls women's sexuality. Sex workers, women who control their own sexuality and who take money for sexual favors, and lesbians, women who reject heterosexual male partners, are judged as being less feminine women. When it comes to the male prerogative of access to women's bodies and sexuality, sex workers and lesbians both behave like men because they (and not men) control their own sexuality.

African American women have been stigmatized with both dimensions of seemingly deviant sexuality. Historically, Black women have been constructed as sexually immoral women, with the recurring image of the Black prostitute and, more recently, that of the Black lesbian serving as anchors for a deviant Black female sexuality that defeminizes Black women. Take, for example, how Black women

30

---

[23] Naylor 1988, 28.

are routinely typecast as prostitutes in contemporary mass media. From network television to feature films, when prostitutes are depicted, typically one or more are African American. By depicting Black lesbians as "mannish," mass media representations also show lesbians as being less feminine Black women. Queen Latifah's portrayal of Cleo in the film *Set It Off* exemplifies the "mannish" Black lesbian who exudes qualities of dominance. In the film, Cleo is big, muscular, dominates her female partner, and is physically threatening. This depiction of the "mannish" lesbian flows into perceptions of dark-skinned, big-boned Black women as being less feminine and more "mannish."[24]

Another marker of hegemonic femininity concerns the significance of work and marriage in accessing income and wealth. The higher the status of a woman, the less likely she is to work, and the more likely she is to be married and have access to income generating property. Her job is to run the family. Moreover, the behavioral norm of female submissiveness counsels married women to become mothers. Motherhood within family and male authority not only becomes another behavioral marker of whether a woman is appropriately submissive to male authority, it becomes essential to the economic survival of the heterosexual, nuclear family. Women may not earn salaries, but they produce legitimate heirs for the intergenerational transmission of property. There are definite class dimensions of hegemonic femininity—women should seek out good marriages that will provide them with economic security. Therefore, women's true femininity remains contingent on their legally sanctioned relationship to men.

Black women have had great difficulty "catching" wealthy men to marry, sharing their marital assets, and passing on marital property to their children.[25] Because the family structure of African Americans has diverged from social norms, achieving this benchmark of hegemonic femininity has been virtually impossible. The financial necessity that sent Black women to work outside the home since emancipation enabled various patterns of female authority and sub-

---

[24] Gomez 1999, 174. Gomez observes that Black lesbians are rarely represented on film or in print and that, if they are, the fully developed characters presented by Audre Lorde or Alice Walker are missing. Instead, Black lesbians are typically presented as tragic (television adaptation of *The Women of Brewster Place*), as peripheral to the main story, or as caricature (Cleo played by Queen Latifah). Given this history, the character of Kima on the HBO series *The Wire* constitutes a breakthrough character.

[25] Collins 2000.

ordination to emerge within African American families. In essence, Black women were not financially subordinated within African American families and communities and, as a result, were deemed to be less feminine because they had to work. African American women's behavior as workers violated the assumptions of hegemonic femininity. For one, Black women did hard labor as agricultural workers or as domestic workers. The type of work that they did made it difficult to see them as fragile, ornamental, or beautiful. Because they were employed outside the home and brought home their own independent income, they seemingly usurped Black male authority within Black families. Their incomes were not supplemental—their income was essential to family survival. Black women also became mothers without benefit of marriage, and they maintained families on their own when men left.[26]

Finally, race itself plays an important part as a benchmark in constructing hegemonic femininity. Black women, by definition, cannot achieve the idealized feminine ideal because the fact of Blackness excludes them. Dominant gender ideology provides a social script for Black women whereby everyone else needs Black women to be on the bottom for everything else to make sense. Just as hegemonic White masculinity occupies the most desired social script, an equally hegemonic Black femininity organized via images of bitches, bad mothers, mammies, and Black ladies coalesces to mark the least desirable form of femininity.

References

Anderson, Elijah. 1999. *Code of the Street: Decency, Violence and the Moral Life of the Inner City.* New York: W. W. Norton.

Banks, Ingrid. 2000. *Hair Matters: Beauty, Power, and Black Women's Consciousness.* New York: New York University Press.

Bordo, Susan. 1993. *Unbearable Weight.* Berkeley: University of California Press.

Collins, Patricia Hill. 2000. "Gender, Black Feminism, and Black Political Economy." *Annals of the American Academy of Political & Social Science* 568 (March): 41–53.

Connell, R. W. 1992. "A Very Straight Gay: Masculinity, Homosexual Experience, and the Dynamics of Gender." *American Sociological Review* 57 (December): 735–751.

——. 1995. *Masculinities.* Cambridge: Polity Press.

Dalton, Harlon L. 1999. "AIDS in Blackface." *Black Men on Race, Gender, and Sexuality.* Ed. Devon W. Carbado, 324–337. New York: New York University Press.

Dines, Gail. 1998. "King Kong and the White Woman: *Hustler* Magazine and the Demonization of Black Masculinity." *Violence against Women* 4, no. 3 (June): 291–307.

---

[26] For general discussions of Black women, family, and work, see Giddings 1984; Jones 1985.

Freydberg, Elizabeth Hadley. 1995. "Sapphires, Spitfires, Sluts, and Superbitches: Aframericans and Latinos in Contemporary American Film." *Black Women in America.* Ed. Kim Vaz, 222–243. Thousand Oaks, Calif.: Sage.

Giddings, Paula. 1984. *When and Where I Enter: The Impact of Black Women on Race and Sex in America.* New York: William Morrow.

Gomez, Jewelle. 1999. "Black Lesbians: Passing, Stereotypes and Transformation." *Dangerous Liaisons: Blacks, Gays, and the Struggle for Equality.* Ed. Eric Brandt, 161–177. New York: New Press.

Gomez, Jewelle, and Barbara Smith. 1994. "Taking the Home Out of Homophobia: Black Lesbian Health." *The Black Women's Health Book: Speaking for Ourselves.* Ed. Evelyn C. White, 198–213. Seattle: Seal Press.

Guy-Sheftall, Beverly, ed. 1995. *Words of Fire: An Anthology of African-American Feminist Thought.* New York: New Press.

Jones, Jacqueline. 1985. *Labor of Love, Labor of Sorrow: Black Women, Work, and the Family from Slavery to the Present.* New York: Basic Books.

Kimmel, Michael S. 2001. "Masculinity as Homophobia: Fear, Shame, and Silence in the Construction of Gender Identity." *Men and Masculinity: A Text Reader.* Ed. Theodore F. Cohen, 29–41. Belmont, Calif.: Wadsworth Press.

Lemons, Gary L. 1997. "To Be Black, Male, and 'Feminist'—Making Womanist Space for Black Men." *International Journal of Sociology and Social Policy* 1, no. 2: 35–61.

Lorde, Audre. 1982. *Zami, A New Spelling of My Name.* Freedom, Calif.: Crossing Press.

Magubane, Zine. 2001. "Which Bodies Matter? Feminism, Poststructuralism, Race, and the Curious Theoretical Odyssey of the 'Hottentot Venus.'" *Gender and Society* 15, no. 6: 816–834.

Messner, Michael A. 1990. "When Bodies Are Weapons: Masculinity and Violence in Sport." *International Review of the Sociology of Sport* 25: 203–217.

Mohanty, Chandra Talpade. 1997. "Women Workers and Capitalist Scripts: Ideologies of Domination, Common Interests, and the Politics of Solidarity." *Feminist Genealogies, Colonial Legacies, Democratic Futures.* Ed. M. Jacqui Alexander and Chandra Talpade Mohanty, 3–29. New York: Routledge.

Naylor, Gloria. 1988. "Love and Sex in the Afro-American Novel." *The Yale Review* 78, no. 1: 19–31.

Oyěwùmí, Oyèrónké. 1997. *The Invention of Women: Making an African Sense of Western Gender Discourses.* Minneapolis: University of Minnesota Press.

Patterson, Orlando. 1982. *Slavery and Social Death: A Comparative Study.* Cambridge, Mass.: Harvard University Press.

"Skeleton in Newark's Closet: Laquetta Nelson Is Forcing Homophobia Out into the Open." Web page [accessed July 30, 2003]. Available at http://www.thegully.com /essays/gaymundo/030619_race_gays_newark.html.

Torgovnick, Marianna. 1990. *Gone Primitive: Savage Intellects, Modern Lives.* Chicago: University of Chicago Press.

Wetherell, Margaret, and Nigel Edley. 1999. "Negotiating Hegemonic Masculinity: Imaginary Positions and Psycho-Discursive Practices." *Feminism & Psychology* 9, no. 3: 335–356.

Understanding the Text

1. Collins argues that the performance of masculinity is particularly physical for African American men. Why is this so? Cite at least one of her most useful examples in your explanation.

2. Similarly, Collins suggests that there are physical characteristics for African American women that mark them as feminine or "normal." Explain what these physical characteristics are and cite at least one of her most useful examples in your explanation.

3. What is Collins's overall point about how race and masculinity/femininity interact? What role does race play in defining masculinity and femininity, and why is it important to Collins that we consider the interaction between race and gender?

4. Collins suggests that African Americans and other men of color are assigned to social scripts about "marginalized masculinities." What does this mean? Why can they not access the kinds of masculinity that are assigned to white men?

Reflection and Response

5. How accurate do Collins's descriptions of African American masculinity and femininity seem to you? Do her examples ring true or are they dated? If they're dated, can you come up with more modern examples that would help prove her point more accurately?

6. What do you associate with "real men" and "real women"? Why are people so drawn to these kinds of terms about "realness"?

Making Connections

7. Consider Gail Dines's argument about the hypersexualization of young women in the media (p. 250). Is there a difference in the hypersexualization of young black women as compared to young women of other races and ethnicities? Are young black men hypersexualized in a way that young white men are not, and if so, why? Support your answers with specific examples from contemporary culture.

8. Do some research about an African American celebrity. How does that celebrity fit into Collins's descriptions of marginalized masculinities or femininities? Do you think that it would be possible for a celebrity to get out of these marginalized identities? If so, how might he or she go about doing so?

5 | How Do the Media Shape Gender?

Every day, we are inundated with mass media images of men and women, together and apart, in all conceivable forms of interaction. The "media"—this term that seems to hold almost all available forms of representation—are both a reflection and a central producer of our cultural lives. If we even briefly consider the range and extent of mass media's impact on our perceptions of reality, we can quickly conclude—as researchers long have—that television, film, magazines, commercial and print advertisements, video games, and many more outlets of visual culture are throughout our lives an almost inescapable facet of our everyday experiences. It is thus inevitable that the images, idealizations, and social scripts we see portrayed in these forms will have some impact on our sensibility about what is real, right, natural, normal, and expected of us in our social interactions. Gender, even when it is not the focus of a given representation, is always a dimension of this intimate, socially constructive relationship we have with mass media.

The readings in this chapter address only a portion of the possible implications mass media representations have on our beliefs and behaviors, particularly those having to do with the power of mass media to structure our collective perceptions of gendered and sexualized bodies. The most personal relationship we have—the relationship with ourselves, our own self-conception— is impacted by the messages we receive through media. The relationships we conduct with others—our romantic dating and mating scripts—are also frequently based on the norms we see constructed through media. The media's enormous power not only to establish our sense of reality but also to produce alluring fantasies that affect our imaginative lives is well worth considering.

The first reading in the chapter, Susie Orbach's "Losing Bodies," looks briefly at the effects of media idealizations of beauty to assess the ways individuals evaluate, develop, and alter their bodies in accordance with mass dissemi-nated (and relatively homogenous) images of male and female beauty. The pressures and anxieties people feel about their bodies in response to the seemingly endless array of media messages about "improving" the body lie at the heart of Orbach's critique. In "Visible or Invisible: Growing Up Female in

Porn Culture," Gail Dines, an outspoken critic of pornography, examines the popularization of pornography in mainstream public culture. Once more or less underground as a media form, pornography in the digital age not only has become more ubiquitous and more accepted as mainstream entertainment but at the same time has become more dramatically degrading and violent toward women. How these changes have affected both men's and women's ideas of sex, sexuality, and sexual scripts is the subject of Dines's analysis. Jia-Rui Chong extends this analysis in a brief survey of "whitening" trends among Asian Americans in "Beauty and the Bleach."

The last three articles focus on a contemporary problem having to do with the "sexualization" of children in American culture. The American Psychological Association summary report on the psychological effects on young girls of media messages about female sexuality details the ways girls in particular are encouraged through media to envision themselves primarily as sexual beings, if not sexual objects, to the exclusion of other character traits. Amy Adler's "To Catch a Predator" uses the popular NBC/MSNBC series to theorize mass culture's complicity in the sexualization of children at the very same time the taboo of childhood sexuality has seemed to reach a critical point.

Losing Bodies

Susie Orbach

Susie Orbach is a British psycho-therapist whose work entails both a private clinical practice and an academic career in which she has been a visiting scholar at institutions including the New School for Social Research in New York and the London School of Economics. Her first book, *Fat Is a Feminist Issue* (1978), was a best seller, and it argued that Western women should give up dieting and focus instead on recognizing hunger and appetite, not "body hatred." She has also been a consultant for the Dove Campaign for Real Beauty. Her other books include *The Impossibility of Sex* (2000), *On Eating* (2002), and *Bodies* (2009). This selection was published in 2011 in the journal *Social Research*.

It could be said that media has a great deal to answer for when it comes to how we understand our bodies today. Information, disinformation, commercial practices, and crazes arrive through the media. It is the medium that stimulates public conversation and trends. It is the means by which the individual finds out things and is impacted by them. Even those of us who feel ourselves to be outside of or perhaps critical of the impact of media are rarely unaffected.

Think of the food we eat now and how it is prepared and presented compared to 25 years ago. How did that update occur? Think of the furniture in our homes and the ways in which we have wanted to refresh or renovate the look of our abodes. Think of going into a restaurant and there being an A-list movie star at the next table. She or he becomes compelling not because of his or her art per se but because visual culture and the publicity machine create the notion of a star, which then works on us.

Something outside of us—film, print, photo, magazine, newspaper, TV—magnifies the object. It is hard to escape. It enters us, and then our interest in that object becomes part of who we are, entwined with our sense of self and community, an aspect of our identity as crucial as church iconography was several centuries ago.

We don't like to think of ourselves as beguiled by this beast called the media. We like to think of ourselves as agents with the force to act and make an impact. And of course we do. We can see this energy very clearly through social media, which has quasi-democratized the possibility of having a voice. But there is no straightforward relationship between "us" and the media, no clear divide that has an uncontaminated "us." The us that we are is not created in isolation. The us that we are and the way we perceive of our bodies are the outcome of the intimate relationship that we make with the world around us.

When we try to tease apart the outside and the inside it becomes quite difficult. The thoughts and pictures we carry inside of us express this complexity. Take for example the compelling desire of many young Western women to have labiaplasty. It doesn't help the young woman to say: what you see projected in the media as a labia is not *the* labia. Your labia is meant to look the way it does. Or rather it doesn't help much. She doesn't feel that to be so. She feels ashamed of the way the folds of skin come together. She's been having a Brazilian wax since she first got pubic hair. For her that was an entry point into grown-up femininity and it pleased her and confirmed her membership in that identity. But not quite.

The Brazilian wax has been a prelude to the disgust and plan to reshape her labia, her breasts, and her buttocks. These are now the procedures she will undergo to find some body peace.

We could just call it body hatred. We could call it fashion. We could call it psychopathology. We could call it opportunistic medical greed. If we compare female genital surgery (FGS) to a practice we find unethical, female genital mutilation (FGM), and link these first world practices to those we condemn elsewhere, we take pause. We ask whether the way in which a neoliberal agenda has designated the female body, either purposefully or unintentionally, as the site for transformation, control, and profit is being delivered to us through the media's exhortation for us to reshape our bodies? We ask, how have consumption and the notion of choice, two exhortations of late capitalism, combined with the imperative to reconstruct and perfect the body through visual media?

In 1995, a television channel started broadcasting in Fiji. It showed imported U.S. shows, such as *Friends*. By 1998, a mere three years later, 11.9 percent of Fijian adolescent girls were over the toilet bowl with bulimia, where previously none existed.

These young women had identified modernity with the Westernized body shape of the last few decades and they had embraced it. In their attempt to find a place in global culture, they understood that the reshaping of their body was crucial. The idea—reshape the body— was an outside one but it insinuated itself into their own longings and desires. They didn't experience themselves as having been done over by the media and—this is an important point—they didn't feel themselves the passive recipients of a rapacious and controlling media. They felt themselves rather to be in dialogue with what was being presented (Becker 1995). Like women in so many locations in the world, they felt excited and interested. They perceived the way they were to be radically out of date and in need of upgrade. *The site of modernity for them became the reconstruction of their bodies.*

In Shanghai, a fashionable operation is to break the thigh and ex- 10 tend the leg by 10 centimeters. In Singapore, the latest craze is for the Western nose. In Eastern Europe, thin has become a requisite for the young wishing to enter global culture. In South Korea, 50 percent of teenage girls have the double eyelid slit operation to Westernize the look of the eyelid. Cosmetic surgery, whether on visible body parts or the more intimate genital area, has become a serious growth industry.[1] The Singapore government has funded a center to attract cosmetic surgery tourism. In Argentina, those with health insurance have the right to a cosmetic procedure annually or biannually. Those without health care coverage can buy their new breasts and have them inserted in the public hospital. So deep and so pervasive is the sense that our bodies are not okay as they are that private organizations see profitable opportunities while state organizations see obligations toward their citizenry. This is shown most dramatically in the West as government bodies regulate and measure children and adults on the basis of a spurious statistical whim, the Body Mass Index (BMI) (Oliver 2005). Those of us over 40 did not grow up with this measure but with weight charts divided into small-, medium-, and large-framed. Today, health economics has been captivated and captured by a measure of weight and height that, despite being contested by the National Institutes of Health, has come to hold sway among health professionals. They decree what is an acceptable body and they then provide contracts to diet companies to regulate the unacceptable. The diet industry, already highly successful through a combination of factors around size acceptability, fear of food, societal panic about "obesity," and the industry's high recidivism and subsequent repeat customers (Orbach 1978), is now being bloated by government funds.

The populace is instructed on how to manage media-generated cues on eating that are propagated by a food distribution industry in search of greater numbers of products with longer shelf life that can lure customers by another section of the food industry: the diet companies. An unvirtuous circle pertains. Heinz owns Weight Watchers, Unilever owns Slimfast, Nestlé owns Lean Cuisine. Questions that relate to internal body prompts such as hunger and satiety are virtually invisible. Those cues do not generate excess profits. They may even create contented bodies. But this latter experience is rapidly

---

[1] The seriousness of the situation has been recognized by the Vienna city government, which has produced guidelines on female genital surgery. See www.frauengesundheit-wein.at.

becoming foreign as the parents of 6- and 7-year-olds are warned about the implications of their child's BMI.

What kind of conception do we have of the body? Can we speak in any sense of a normal body or is it more accurate to say that what is at stake today, especially for the young—young women and young men—is the acquisition of a body "normalized" by visual dictate: a body whose dimensions, whose look, is not simply stylized but homogenized; a body created by the style industries (the beauty, cosmetic, fashion, media, celebrity industries) that is then reshaped by the cosmetic surgeons, the gym instructors, and diet industries.

> Can we speak in any sense of a normal body or is it more accurate to say that what is at stake today . . . is the acquisition of a body "normalized" by visual dictate: a body whose dimensions, whose look, is not simply stylized but homogenized. . . .

You may protest bodies were always shaped, normalized by cultural forces. There is no such thing as a body not marked or shaped by culture. To be unmarked, as in uncircumcised, for example, is to be unclaimed and unclaimable. The body is marked by gender, by class, by nationality, ethnicity, by custom. The body as natural, as unmediated, is a bucolic, naïve Rousseauian fiction. Romantic notions efface the impact of contemporary culture without being able to erase culture at all, for this is an impossibility.

We look at the history of the world as we understand it through the costumes, clothing, and physical stance of its people—from the ancient Babylonian togas to the Masai warrior markings to the Victorian crinolines. Even the Wild Child of Aveyron grew in a context—it wasn't a human context—so his body was formed in proximity to the animals and he developed the sensibilities suitable for his environment. His body temperature self-regulated to cope with snow or sunshine without the clothing we find so necessary. He moved in ways similar to the animals he grew up with. And so on. Every body requires a context. There is no such thing as "a body." There is only a body as an outcome of relationship. And that relationship is always culturally situated (Orbach 1986, 2009).

Our bodies are given to us by our mothers (Orbach 1978). They do 15 this in two ways: by the bodies they themselves inhabit and represent to us, and also through how they perceive our own bodies' capacities; introduce us to our bodies' wonders; constrict, enable or shape our bodies in ways relevant to the cultural context, with nary a conscious thought for doing so. A Jewish or Muslim boy is circumcised; a girl, too, in certain Muslim traditions. Deep in the Amazonian forest in Brazil, the Kaiapo Indian children absorb their way of kissing, which, to our way of interpreting physical gesture, is a bite. The behaviors are enacted as part of the ordinary social matrix of relating. There is some specific instruction, such as when I was a girl, which related to sitting with my legs together or being told not to whistle because it wasn't ladylike, but there was nothing particularly forced about such instructions; they were the medium in which femininity in the United Kingdom from my class background was formed. There was a specificity to that body that meant that when another encountered it, it could be read as the body of a girl from or aspiring to a particular milieu.

What is markedly different today is that mothers' bodies are under assault. There is no stable body for a woman. There is no milieu that has constancy. The body is being reshaped by visual culture in literally thousands of presentations weekly we receive through television, magazines, newspapers, digital media, and advertising. No one can count the images accurately. The advertising agencies, whose income depended upon knowing such things, said 5,000 a week, but that was before the Internet and social media took off and images were propagated on screens continually.

What is remarkable is the homogeneity of the images broadcast internationally. At the Hayward Gallery six years ago, a photographer took pictures of individual models and melded them one to another. The morphed image could have been any one of them. They were—they are—all super-slim and tall with features that can be painted out so that new ones can be painted on. As models and celebrity culture infuse public space, indeed become a form of discourse, so the images of femininity (and it is happening with masculinity, too) become ever more reduced and uniform.

Pascal Dangin, the artistic retoucher, routinely remakes pictures. In the March 2008 issue of U.S. *Vogue*, for example, he changed 144 images (Collins 2008). Meanwhile, some obstetricians have been prepared to allow women to follow the example of movie stars and celebrities who proclaim the virtue of caesarean sections at eight months for the spurious cosmetic purpose [of] regaining their pre-pregnancy bodies by six weeks postpartum. The notion of a full-term pregnancy, with women learning their baby's rhythm and their own, is becoming endangered, with grave consequences for their bodily sense of self and their internal, body-based knowledge of appetite and satisfaction. One day they will have a chance to be the maids of honor who are offered cosmetic surgery a year before the wedding to complement the bride they are serving. Body insecurity will have ensured a lack of corporeal confidence, and the imperative to shape up, to reconstruct—not only to aspire to but to physically enact bodily alteration—will speak to them.

What does all this mean?

One thing it means is that the body of the mother as experienced 20 by the baby may well be one marked by anxiety (Orbach 1995). Another thing it means is that the anxiety the baby absorbs prepares her or him for a sense that a body does not exist as a place to live from but as something one needs to be ever watchful of and tending to. As a toddler, the little girl sees this explicitly. She hears her mother sigh at her own body in front of the mirror or hears her berate herself for "indulging" in foods. The child may not know what any of this means but it is the medium in which her own relationship to her body develops. The mother may Photoshop the baby's or toddler's photos, inserting a dimple or a cute gap between the teeth, in a facsimile of what a baby, toddler, child is to look like. Neither the body of the mother nor the body of the child is deemed good enough as they are. Panasonic's 2011 camera, the Luminex FX77, can whiten teeth, magnify eyes, and add makeup. The bodies and faces of mothers and babies are both being "perfected." The child is being unwittingly prepared for the combined blandishments of the beauty, style, food, and diet industries, whose greed knows no bounds and in whose wake the cultural diversity of bodies all over the world are eaten up. The person grows up thinking/believing that bodies are inevitably unstable and always in need of attention and transformation.

The individual body is the outcome of that most intimate of relationships between the mothering person and her child as she personally enacts the cultural dictates vis-à-vis the body. At this moment in history, those personal enactments include the reshaping of the body, with the most unfortunate consequence of creating body distress and body hatred.

Indeed, one of the West's hidden exports to the developing world is body reshaping and its concomitant rejection of the local body. We are losing bodies faster than we are losing languages. Women from all over the world shed their local body as they enter modernity, whether from Nigeria, Ladak, or Kosovo. The formerly plump tradition for beauty queens in Nigeria has been superseded by a Westernized thin shape. The first slim Miss Nigeria (chosen by eyes dominated by Western cultural imagery) was initially assumed to have HIV/AIDS, but rapidly her body spurned a Nigerian diet industry. The female body, reshaped as thin and preferably long, has become the insignia of belonging. It is not the clothes that brand the body but the honed body as brand itself; the sign that one has shed one's indigenous culture and taken up the world body.

We are losing bodies as we are losing mother tongues. Commercial pressures disseminated through the media are restructuring bodies, supplanting diversity with sameness and offering membership in global culture through having a body that fits. These bodies become the calling card of identity and belonging, while supplying gargantuan profits to the industries that breed body hatred. Globalization as a modern form of imperialism reshapes not just the architecture, industry, and agriculture of the external world, but the private, corporeal space we endeavor to inhabit. Corporeal colonialism is a hidden glue that links in with colonial histories of the past.

References

Becker, Anne E. *The Body, Self and Society: The View from Fiji.* Philadelphia: University of Pennsylvania Press, 1995.

Collins, Lisa. "Pixel Perfect." *The New Yorker,* May 12, 2008.

Oliver, J. E. *Fat Politics: The Real Story Behind America's Obesity Epidemic.* New York: Oxford University Press, 2005.

Orbach, S. *Fat Is a Feminist Issue.* London and New York: Paddington Press, 1978.

——. *Hunger Strike: A Metaphor for Our Age.* London: Faber, 1986.

——. "Countertransference and the False Body." *Winnicott Studies* 10 (1995).

——. *Bodies.* London: Profile Books, 2009.

Understanding the Text

1. One of Orbach's main points is that "every body requires a context" (p. 245). What does this mean? What kind of context does Orbach want us to consider in relation to our bodies and the bodies of other people (both historical and contemporary)?

2. Briefly explain what Orbach means when she says that "mothers' bodies are under assault" (p. 246). Who is assaulting them and what are their means of attack? What impact does Orbach diagnose for new generations of women?

3. What does Orbach mean by the phrase "losing bodies" (p. 247)?

Reflection and Response

4. In this article, Orbach cites numerous statistics and examples in building her case. What were the most and least effective statistics or examples in your opinion? In each case, why did you find them to be especially effective or ineffective?

5. Orbach notes that women around the world are starting to conform to the Western thin body featured in movies and advertisements, in part because to

be Western is to be part of the modern world. Do you agree that achieving a more or less standard global ideal of beauty is part of modernity? Or are other forces at work? Support your position with examples from the reading or from contemporary culture.

6. Many women experience beauty and body practices, such as wearing makeup and "dressing attractively," as pleasurable and empowering. What is the paradox about "choosing" or even enjoying these activities that Orbach sees as a form of coercion by mass media?

Making Connections

7. Orbach states that children today are growing up with the idea that their bodies are "always in need of attention and transformation" (p. 247). What evidence can you find that this is true (either in other readings from *Composing Gender* or in your research)? What are the likely implications of a generation raised to feel inadequate? What institutions and industries have a stake in encouraging people to strive for bodily improvements?

8. If every body requires a context, it might be valuable to trace your own body's context. How has that context evolved, and what are the pressures through which it has been shaped?

9. Revisit some of the readings from Chapter 2 of *Composing Gender* and consider how the discourses of gender in childhood end up playing out in adult body contexts. For example, do the gender stereotypes described by Renzetti and Curran (p. 76) seem similar to those described by Orbach, and if so, why are these stereotypes so persistent? If not, in what ways do you see these stereotypes as different and are these differences significant?

Visible or Invisible: Growing Up Female in Porn Culture

Gail Dines

Gail Dines is a professor of sociology and women's studies at Wheelock College in Boston, Massachusetts. Her work focuses on images of sexuality in mainstream pop culture, and she is a founding member of Stop Porn Culture, an educational and activist group concerned with the hypersexualization of the media. She has also coedited a best-selling textbook, *Gender, Race, and Class in Media* (2011). This selection is excerpted from her most recent book, *Pornland* (2010).

. . . The Stepford Wife image, which drove previous generations of women crazy with its insistence on sparkling floors and perfectly orchestrated meals, has all but disappeared, and in its place we now have the Stepford Slut: a hypersexualized, young, thin, toned, hairless, and, in many cases, surgically enhanced woman with a come-hither look on her face. Harriet Nelson and June Cleaver have morphed into Britney, Rihanna, Beyoncé, Paris, Lindsay, and so on. They represent images of contemporary idealized femininity—in a word, hot—that are held up for women, especially young women, to emulate. Women today are still held captive by images that ultimately tell lies about women. The biggest lie is that conforming to this hypersexualized image will give women real power in the world, since in a porn culture, our power rests, we are told, not in our ability to shape the institutions that determine our life chances but in having a hot body that men desire and women envy.

In today's image-based culture, there is no escaping the image and no respite from its power when it is relentless in its visibility. If you think that I am exaggerating, then flip through a magazine at the supermarket checkout, channel surf, take a drive to look at billboards, or watch TV ads. Many of these images are of celebrities—women who have fast become the role models of today. With their wealth, designer clothes, expensive homes, and flashy lifestyles, these women do seem enviable to girls and young women since they appear to embody a type of power that demands attention and visibility.

For us noncelebrities who can't afford a personal stylist, the magazines dissect the "look," giving us tips on how to craft the image at a fraction of the price. They instruct us on what clothes to buy, what shoes to wear, how to do our hair and makeup, and what behavior to adopt to look as hot as our favorite celebrity. The low-slung jeans, the short skirt that rides up our legs as we sit down, the thong, the tattoo on the lower back, the pierced belly button, the low-cut top that shows cleavage, the high heels that contort our calves, and the pouting glossed lips all conspire to make us look like a bargain-basement version of the real thing. To get anywhere close to achieving the "look," we, of course, need to spend money—lots of it—as today femininity comes in the form of consumer products that reshape the body and face. The magazines that instruct us in the latest "must-have" fashions have no shortage of ads that depict, in excruciating detail, what it means to be feminine in today's porn culture.

While the fashion industry has always pushed clothes that sexualize women's bodies, the difference today is that the "look" is, in part, inspired by the sex industry. We are now expected to wear this attire everywhere: in school, on the street, and at work. Teachers, including elementary school teachers, often complain that their female students look more like they are going to a party than coming to school. It is as if we females now have to carry the marker of sex on us all the time, lest we forget (or men forget) what our real role is in this society. . . .

> While the fashion industry has always pushed clothes that sexualize women's bodies, the difference today is that the "look" is, in part, inspired by the sex industry.

People not immersed in pop culture tend to assume that what we see today is just more of the same stuff that previous generations grew up on. After all, every generation has had its hot and sultry stars who led expensive and wild lives compared to the rest of us. But what is different about today is not only the hypersexualization of mass-produced images but also the degree to which such images have overwhelmed and crowded out any alternative images of being female. Today's tidal wave of soft-core porn images has normalized the porn star look in everyday culture to such a degree that anything less looks dowdy, prim, and downright boring. Today, a girl or young woman looking for an alternative to the Britney, Paris, Lindsay look will soon come to the grim realization that the only alternative to looking fuckable is to be invisible.

One show that popularized porn culture was *Sex and the City*, a show that supposedly celebrated female independence from men. At first glance this series was a bit different from others in its representation of female friendships and the power of women to form bonds that sustain them in their everyday lives. It also seemed to provide a space for women to talk about their own sexual desires, desires that were depicted as edgy, rebellious, and fun. However, these women claimed a sexuality that was ultimately traditional rather than resistant. Getting a man and keeping him were central to the narrative, and week after week we heard about the trials and tribulations of four white, privileged heterosexual women who seemed to find men who take their sexual cues from porn.

Porn-type sex is a fixture on the show, which regularly featured plotlines about men who like to watch porn as they have sex, men who are aroused by female urination, men who want group sex, men who can get aroused only by masturbating to porn, men who are into S&M, men who want anal sex, and men who are willing to have only hookup sex and not a relationship. In one episode, called "Models and Mortals," Carrie (Sarah Jessica Parker) finds out that a male friend of hers is secretly taping his girlfriends as they have sex. Rather than being appalled at this invasion of privacy, Carrie is immediately interested and sits down with him to watch the tapes. Later in the show, Samantha (Kim Cattrall) shows some interest in the man, and when she finds out that he tapes his girlfriends, she becomes even more determined to have hookup sex with him. Another one of the story lines of the show was Charlotte's (Kristin Davis) first husband's inability to sustain an erection during sex. One night Charlotte hears noises coming from the bathroom and, thinking that her husband is crying, she walks in, only to see him masturbating to porn. Shocked at first, Charlotte later glues pictures of herself in the magazines.

These examples show how the *Sex and the City* women capitulated to the pornography that invades their sex lives. In their desire to get a man and keep him, they were willing to do anything, even if they felt uncomfortable. In the episode about urination, for example, Carrie is clearly uncomfortable with the idea, but eventually offers to either pour warm liquid on her partner or urinate with the door open so he can hear her. The idea that these women are independent is undermined by their dependency on men and male approval. At the end of the final season, Carrie is living with an emotionally unavailable artist in Paris and is saved by the equally emotionally unavailable Mr. Big. In the movie released in the summer of 2008, Mr. Big leaves her standing at the altar, but in typical *Sex and the City* style, Carrie eventually forgives him and marries him.

What critics have noted about the show and the movie is the role that consuming products plays in the lives of the women. Media scholar Angela McRobbie notes that the "show functions as a televisual magazine and shop window for the successful launching of shoes, accessories and fashion lines well beyond the means of average female viewers."[1] The *Sex and the City* women are described as being independent not because they refuse to submit to men's power but because they can afford to buy their own high-end goods. Through the endless buying of goods, the women constructed their femininity, styling and restyling themselves depending on their latest purchase. Their bodies and their clothes spoke to a conventional—albeit upmarket—femininity that was constructed out of the culture's mainstream images. Nowhere did we see a resistance to the fabricated image; rather, their very sexuality was dependent on the products they consumed. These women looked hot because they were perfectly turned out in designer gear. In one episode, in which Carrie has a first date with Mr. Big, she vows not to have sex with him, but the dress she buys for the occasion says otherwise, and the two do have sex—the dress becoming the marker of her sexuality. The problem with this is that women's so-called independence became seamlessly meshed with their ability to consume rather than being about a feminist worldview that insists on equality in heterosexual relationships.

Nowhere is this pseudo-independence more celebrated than in *Cosmopolitan*, a magazine that claims to have "served as an agent for social change, encouraging women everywhere to go after what they want (whether it be in the boardroom or the bedroom)." It is hard to see how *Cosmopolitan* helped women advance in corporate America, given that most of the Cosmo girl's time is taken up with perfecting her body and her sexual technique. But this doesn't stop the magazine from boasting that "we here at *Cosmo* are happy to have played such a significant role in women's history. And we look forward to many more years of empowering chicks everywhere."[2] In porn culture empowering women translates into "chicks" having lots of sex, and no magazine does more than *Cosmopolitan* to teach women how to perform porn sex in a way that is all about male pleasure.

With headlines every month promising "Hot New Sex Tricks," "21 Naughty Sex Tips," "Little Mouth Moves That Make Sex Hotter," "67 New Blow-His-Mind Moves," "8 Sex Positions You Haven't Thought Of," and so on, women seem to experience no authentic sexual pleasure; rather, what she wants and enjoys is what he wants and enjoys. While there might be an odd article here and there on what to wear to climb

[1] Angela McRobbie, "Young Women and Consumer Culture," *Cultural Studies* 22, no. 5 (2008): 543.

[2] Jennifer Benjamin, "How *Cosmo* Changed the World," *Cosmopolitan*, September 2005, http://www.cosmopolitan.com/about/about-us_how-cosmo-changed-the-world (accessed July 7, 2008).

the corporate ladder, the magazine as a whole is all about "him" and "his" needs, wants, desires, tastes, and, most importantly, orgasm. In *Cosmopolitan*, as in much of pop culture, her pleasure is derived not from being a desiring subject but from being a desired object.

Women's magazines that focus on "him" are not new, as earlier generations were also inundated with stories about "him," but then the idea was to stimulate his taste buds rather than his penis. *Cosmopolitan* is the contemporary equivalent of *Ladies' Home Journal* in that it pretends to be about women, but it is in fact all about getting him, pleasing him, and (hopefully) keeping him. For previous generations of women, the secret to a happy relationship lay in being a good cook, cleaner, and mother—for the young women of today, the secret is, well, just being a good lay. If the reader is going to *Cosmopolitan* for tips on how to build a relationship or ways of developing intimacy, she will be disappointed, as conversation only matters in the world of *Cosmo* if it is about talking dirty.

With its manipulative "We are all girls together" tone coupled with the wise older mentor approach that promises to teach young women all they need to know to keep "him coming back for more," *Cosmopolitan*, like most women's magazines, masquerades as a friend and teacher to young women trying to navigate the tricky terrain of developing a sexual identity in a porn culture. *Cosmopolitan*'s power is its promise to be a guide and friend, and it promotes itself as one of the few magazines that really understand what the reader is going through. A promotional ad for *Cosmopolitan* geared toward advertisers boasts that it is "its readers' best friend, cheerleader and shrink."[3]

In *Cosmopolitan*, hypersexualization is normalized by virtue of both the quantity of articles on sex and the degree to which they are explicit. For example, one article instructs the reader, in a somewhat clinical manner, on how to bring a man to orgasm: "While gripping the base of the penis steadily in one hand, place the head between your lips, circling your tongue around the crown. When you sense your guy is incredibly revved up, give his frenulum a few fast tongue licks." For the uninitiated, the magazine explains that the frenulum is "the tiny ridge of flesh on the underside of his manhood, where the head meets the shaft."[4]

Cosmopolitan is quick to suggest using porn as a way to spice up 15
sex. In one article, entitled "7 Bad Girl Bedroom Moves You Must Mas-

---

[3] http://www.assocmags.co.za/images/pdfs/Cosmopolitan%20Rate%20Card.pdf (accessed June 6, 2008).
[4] Ronnie Koenig, "Thrill Every Inch of Him," *Cosmopolitan*, June 2006, 150.

ter," the reader is told to take "the plunge into porn" as it "will add fiery fervor into your real-life bump and grinds." The article quotes a reader who, after watching porn with her boyfriend, evidently ended up "having sex so hot that the porn looked tame in comparison." The article suggests that if the reader feels embarrassed, she should "drive to a store in another neighborhood, shop online, or go to a place that stocks X-rated."[5]

In the world that *Cosmopolitan* constructs for the reader, a world of blow jobs, multiple sexual positions, anonymous porn sex, and screaming orgasms (usually his), saying no to his erection is unthinkable. The options on offer in *Cosmopolitan* always concern the type of sex to have and how often. What is not on offer is the option to refuse his demands since he has (an unspoken and unarticulated) right of access to the female body. Indeed, readers are warned that not having sex on demand might end the "relationship." Psychologist Gail Thoen, for example, informs *Cosmopolitan's* readers that "constant cuddling with no follow-through (i.e., sex) can be frustrating to guys," and what's more, "he is not going to like it if you leave him high and dry all the time."[6] The reader is pulled into a highly sexual world where technique is the key, and intimacy, love, and connection appear only rarely as issues worthy of discussion. The message transmitted loud and clear is that if you want a man, then not only must you have sex with him, you must learn ways to do it better and hotter than his previous girlfriends.

That the magazine teaches women how to have porn sex is clear in an article that ostensibly helps women deal with the etiquette of how to behave in the morning after the first sexual encounter. Women are told: "Don't Stay Too Long." The article warns women that "just because he had sex with you doesn't mean he's ready to be attached at the hip for the day." Actually, the entire day seems like a long shot— "Bo" informs readers that "I was dating this girl who wanted to hang out the next morning, but after only a couple of hours with her, I realized I wasn't ready to be that close." What advice does *Cosmopolitan* have for women in this situation? "Skip out after coffee but before breakfast."[7]

Media targeted to women create a social reality that is so overwhelmingly consistent it is almost a closed system of messages. In this way, it is the sheer ubiquity of the hypersexualized images that gives

---

[5] *Cosmopolitan*, http://www.cosmopolitan.com/sex-love/sex/420935 (accessed July 7, 2008).

[6] "Cuddle Overkill," *Cosmopolitan*, June 2007, 137.

[7] "You Had Sex—Now What?" *Cosmopolitan*, June 2007, 76.

them power since they normalize and publicize a coherent story about women, femininity, and sexuality. Because these messages are everywhere, they take on an aura of such familiarity that we believe them to be our very own personal and individual ways of thinking. They have the power to seep into the core part of our identities to such a degree that we think that we are freely choosing to look and act a certain way because it makes us feel confident, desirable, and happy. But as scholar Rosalind Gill points out, if the look was "the outcome of everyone's individual, idiosyncratic preferences, surely there would be greater diversity, rather than a growing homogeneity organized round a slim, toned, hairless body."[8]

This highly disciplined body has now become the key site where gender is enacted and displayed on a daily basis. To be feminine requires not only the accoutrements of hypersexuality—high heels, tight clothes, and so on—but also a body that adheres to an extremely strict set of standards. We need to look like we spend hours in the gym exhausting ourselves as we work out, but whatever the shape of the body, it is never good enough. Women have so internalized the male gaze that they have now become their own worst critics. When they go shopping for clothes or look in a mirror, they dissect themselves piece by piece. Whatever the problem, and there is always a problem—the breasts are too small, the thighs not toned enough, the butt too flat or too round, the stomach too large—the result is a deep sense of self-disgust and loathing. The body becomes our enemy, threatening to erupt into fatness at any time, so we need to be hypervigilant. What we end up with is what Gill calls a "self-policing narcissistic gaze," a gaze that is so internalized that we no longer need external forces to control the way we think or act.[9]

We cannot talk about the contemporary feminine body without 20 mention of the complicated relationship that most women and girls have to food: we want it, enjoy it, and yet feel guilty for eating it. The need to eat is taken as a sign of weakness, as not measuring up to being a real woman since celebrity women manage to survive on minimal amounts of food. Whenever I am in places where women congregate—the hairdresser, gym, clothes shops—I hear long and involved conversations about dieting. Women recite lengthy lists about what they have eaten, what they intend to eat, and what they need to

---

[8] Rosalind Gill, "Supersexualize Me! Advertising and the Midriff," in *Mainstreaming Sex: The Sexualization of Western Culture*, ed. Feona Attwood (London: I.B. Tauris, 2009), 106.
[9] Ibid., 107.

stop eating. A kind of shame hangs over the conversations as every-one assumes that they are too fat and hence weak willed.

In her excellent book on body image and food, feminist philoso-pher Susan Bordo looks at the ways the culture helps shape women's ideas about what constitutes the perfect body.[10] The bodies of the women we see in magazines and on television are actually very un-usual in their measurements and proportions, with long necks, broad shoulders, and high waists. Yet because these are more or less the only images we see, we take them to be the norm rather than the ex-ception and assume that the problem lies with us and not the fashion and media industries that insist on using a very specific body type. This is what the media do: they take the abnormal body and make it normal by virtue of its visibility, while making the normal bodies of real women look abnormal by virtue of their invisibility. The result is a massive image disorder on the part of society. Since we all de-velop notions of ourselves from cultural messages and images, it would seem that a truly disordered female is one who actually likes her body.

Bordo's discussion of the way culture shapes notions of the body asks us to rethink the idea that women with eating disorders are some-how deviants. Women who starve themselves are actually overcon-forming to the societal message about what constitutes female per-fection. They have taken in the messages and come to what looks like a very reasonable conclusion: thin women are prized in this culture, I want to be prized, and therefore I need to be thin, which means that I can't eat. How can it be any different in a world where anorexic-looking women such as Kate Moss, Victoria Beckham, Mary Kate Ol-sen, and Lindsay Lohan are praised by the celebrity magazines for their "look"? I do not mean to be glib here about the devastating ef-fects of starving one's body. I have seen many students with a long list of health problems due to long-term starvation. But somewhere in this discussion, we need to see the society as pathological rather than the adolescent girl in the hospital ward who is being diagnosed with multiple disorders.

Many of the young women I have spoken to who have been hospi-talized for eating disorders talk about all the new tricks they learned from fellow patients for losing weight even faster. Not many talk about their hospitalizations in terms of recovery. While many of these young women end up hospitalized for complex reasons, the cultural

---

[10] Susan Bordo, *Unbearable Weight: Feminism, Western Culture and the Body* (Berkeley and Los Angeles: University of California Press, 1994).

obsession with female thinness has to figure in somewhere for most of them. Yet these recovery programs do not have classes on media literacy and cultural constructions of gender or rap sessions on resisting sexist imagery. Instead the focus is squarely on the individual female and her assumed psychological problems, which somehow dropped from the sky. . . .

Understanding culture as a socializing agent requires exploring how and why some girls and young women conform and others resist. For all the visual onslaught, not every young woman looks or acts like she takes her cues from *Cosmopolitan* or *Maxim*. One reason for this is that conforming to a dominant image is not an all-or-nothing act but rather a series of acts that place women and girls at different points on the continuum of conformity to nonconformity. Where any individual sits at any given time on this continuum depends on her past and present experiences as well as family relationships, media consumption, peer group affiliations and sexual, racial, and class identify. We are not, after all, blank slates onto which images are projected. . . .

Those girls and young women who resist the wages of sexual objectification have to form an identity that is in opposition to mainstream culture. What I find is that these young women and girls tend to have someone in their life—be it a mother, an older woman mentor, or a coach—who provides some form of immunization to the cultural messages. But often this immunization is short-lived. Every summer I co-teach an institute in media literacy, and many of the participants are parents or teachers. Year after year we hear the same story: they are working hard to provide their daughters or students with ways to resist the culture, and in their early years the girls seem to be internalizing the counter-ideology. However, at some point, usually around puberty but increasingly earlier, the girls begin to adopt more conventional feminine behavior as their peer group becomes the most salient socializing force.[11] This makes sense because adolescence is the developmental stage that is all about fitting in. Indeed, in a strange way, one becomes visible in adolescence by looking like everyone else, and to look and act differently is to be rendered invisible.

What many of these young women and girls need to be able to continue resisting the dominant culture is clearly a peer group of like-minded people as well as an ideology that reveals the fabricated, exploitative, and consumerist nature of contemporary femininity. . . .

25

---

[11] For a fuller discussion of the role of peers in adolescent development, see L. M. Brown and C. Gilligan, *Meeting at the Crossroads: Women's Psychology and Girls' Development* (Cambridge, MA: Harvard University Press, 1992).

Understanding the Text

1. What is Dines's argument about the link between the media-shaped image of women and the sex industry?

2. The women's magazine *Cosmopolitan* is one of Dines's major examples. Describe a few of the things about *Cosmo* that cause Dines to cite it as contributing to the problem.

3. Toward the end of the article, Dines, quoting Rosalind Gill, says that young women are internalizing a "self-policing narcissistic gaze" (p. 256). What does this mean?

Reflection and Response

4. How accurate do you think Dines's claim is that mainstream culture is increasingly imitating the dynamics of "porn culture"? Does this seem like a valid description? Support your answer to these questions with specific examples from the article or from contemporary culture.

5. Toward the end of the article, Dines comments that we should consider society pathological, not the adolescent girl in the hospital ward who is simply complying with society's demands through visual culture. Is this a reasonable assertion? If so, why, and if not, what is problematic about it?

6. Pornography has become increasingly visible in public culture, and porn-stylings according to Dines have infiltrated everyday media. Since pornography is produced largely by and for men, how does this help you understand what Dines means when she claims that women have internalized the "male gaze" (p. 256)?

7. Do you think sexual scripts—the sexual activities everyday people engage in—have been affected by "porn culture" (p. 250)? If so, how? And if not, why not?

8. Dines sees *Cosmopolitan* magazine's stated mission of "empowering chicks" as advocating a form of "pseudo-independence" (p. 253). In what ways do sexual liberation and sexual display constitute "empowerment," and in what ways might they conceivably be a form of "disempowerment"?

Making Connections

9. Dines cites several examples in her article. Consider whether there are others that would add to her case. Find at least three examples of how women's lives are modeled in the media after sex industry ideals and be ready to discuss how they support Dines's argument.

10. Compare Dines's argument with that of Amy Adler, who writes about the TV show *To Catch a Predator* (p. 281). How are Dines and Adler discussing a similar dynamic of sexualization via the media? What do you see as their differences?

11. Think about childhood and the readings from earlier chapters. Does it seem that this trend toward sexualization and porn culture begins before adulthood? Support your answer with specific examples from other readings in *Composing Gender*.

Beauty and the Bleach

Jia-Rui Chong

Jia-Rui Chong is a journalist for the *Los Angeles Times* whose reporting has ranged from medical news to stories about returning U.S. veterans from Iraq and Afghanistan. She received an undergraduate degree from Harvard and a master's degree from Oxford University in English literature. This selection was originally published in the *Los Angeles Times* in 2005.

For many Southern Californians, summer is the season for beaches, chaise longues and the quest for the perfect tan.

Not for Margaret Qiu. She and thousands of other Asian American women are going to great lengths to avoid the sun—fighting to preserve or enhance their pale complexions with expensive creams, masks, gloves, professional face scrubs and medical procedures.

For these women, a porcelain-like white face is the feminine ideal, reflecting a long-held belief that pale skin represents a comfortable life. They also believe it can hide physical imperfections.

"There's a saying, 'If you have white skin, you can cover 1,000 uglinesses,'" said Qiu, a 36-year-old Chinese immigrant who lives in Alhambra.

Qiu goes through a regimen of skin-whitening products twice a 5 day. She is one of many customers who have turned Asian whitening creams and lotions into a multimillion-dollar industry in the United States.

But that's just the beginning.

Take a daylight drive through Asian immigrant enclaves like Monterey Park and Irvine, and you'll see women trying to shield themselves with umbrellas—even for the short dash from a parking lot into a supermarket. While driving, many wear special "UV gloves"—which look like the long gloves worn with ball gowns—to protect their forearms, and don wraparound visors that resemble welders' masks.

At beauty salons, women huddle around cosmetics counters asking about the latest cleansers and lotions that claim to control melanin production in skin cells, often dropping more than $100 for a set. Beauticians do a brisk business with $65 whitening therapies. Women dab faces with fruit acid, which is supposed to remove the old skin cells that dull the skin, and glop on masks with pearl powder or other ingredients that they believe lighten the skin.

There are doctors who, for about $1,000, will use an electrical field to deliver vitamins, moisturizers and bleaching agents to a woman's face in a procedure known as a "mesofacial."

Whitening products have been a mainstay in Asia for decades, but 10 cosmetics industry officials said they have emerged as a hot seller in the United States only in the last four years. Whitening products now rack up $10 million in sales a year, according to the market research firm Euromonitor.

But their popularity has sparked a debate in the Asian American community about the politics of whitening. Qiu and others say the quest for white skin is an Asian tradition. But others—younger, American-born Asians—question whether the obsession with an ivory complexion has more to do with blending into white American culture, or even a subtle prejudice against those with darker skin.

The market research firm says cosmetics companies have taken note of the sensitivity, saying their Asian skin products in America are intended not for "whitening" but for "brightening."

"It's not a politically correct term because it seems to imply that looking Caucasian via a white complexion is the desired beauty goal," said Virginia Lee, a Euromonitor analyst.

• • •

Qiu, a 36-year-old native of Xi'an, China, thinks there is nothing politically incorrect about using products that whiten the skin, which are known in Mandarin as *mei bai*, or "beauty white."

Qiu, who sells herbal supplements, has used whitening creams for 15 five years and went to Vitativ, a cosmetics store in Monterey Park, one recent morning for a refill.

As she paid for a set of Shiseido "UV White" lotions, Qiu said she was surprised when she first arrived in the U.S. and saw so many young women flaunting their tans.

She came to realize that Eastern and Western ideas of beauty were different. Here, she said, "When you see darker, you think they are very rich. They have a boat. They have enough time to go to the beach."

It's OK for American women to be darker, said her husband, Lei Sun, a 36-year-old sushi chef. "It's part of the sports thing."

But Lei Sun prefers lighter-skinned Asian women, saying that they embody the traditional ideal known as *si si wen wen.* He looked to his wife to explain the concept.

"That means when a lady stands there with white skin and is very 20 polite, and when she laughs, she doesn't make a big noise," Qiu said.

Women with pale skin are more delicate, more feminine and show that they don't have to toil outdoors, Qiu explained.

"Whiter skin also means high class," she said.

> Women with pale skin are more delicate, more feminine and show that they don't have to toil outdoors, Qiu explained.

Every morning and every night, Qiu spends a few minutes applying whitening lotions.

"I never buy the very cheap one," she said one morning as she dabbed her face with whitening moisturizer in the white bathroom of her Alhambra house. "Sometimes with those, your neck and your face are different colors, and people can see that it's not your real color."

Some of the cheaper products can be dangerous, she said.   25

In 2002, newspapers reported that women in Hong Kong were hospitalized for mercury poisoning caused by three brands of whitening cream.

In California, officials at the state's Department of Health Services and the Department of Consumer Affairs said they have received no complaints and have not issued any warnings about whitening cosmetics or treatments.

The products sold in the United States and Asia include ingredients such as licorice extract and green tea, which purportedly control the skin's production of melanin.

For Qiu and others, it's important to find just the right shade of white. Most of the products don't claim to turn a woman's skin the color of white bond paper, but something just a shade paler and more delicate—say, the inside of a woman's upper arm.

Any whiter, Qiu said, and you look sickly.   30

"Then they look like Michael Jackson," she said. "He looks terrible."

• • •

Irvine resident Sarah Mar doesn't use whitening cosmetics, but she has devised a host of other strategies to keep her face pale, such as wearing a large visor when driving. Last Christmas season, she asked her family to forget the scarves and get her a present she would use every day: prescription-strength sunscreen.

"The kids are doing that—burning themselves—but I don't do that," Mar said, saying that her aversion to direct sunlight keeps her face pale and protects her against skin cancer.

Mar, who grew up in Taiwan and oversaw the Chinese-American

Debutante Guild in Irvine for a few years, said she tries her best to stay indoors between 10 a.m. and 3 p.m. So do her friends, with whom she often goes on morning walks.

At outdoor activities like picnics, Mar said, it's never hard to find her girlfriends: They are huddled under a tree or have pitched a big umbrella.

Mar's daughter Catherine never shared her mother's quest for white skin and spent most of her teenage years with a golden tan. But she made her mother and other relatives smile a few years ago when she returned for Christmas break from Boston University. Separated for a full semester from the Southern California sun, she had a perfect white complexion.

"Her cousin was going to Stanford and was very dark," Mar said. "At Christmastime, the grandparents said, 'Look, look! The one from the East looks better because her face is whiter.'"

• • •

For Theresa Lin-Cheng, 50, avoiding the sun and applying creams at night weren't enough. Lin-Cheng, who hosts a cooking show on Chinese-language radio and cable television, moved to Chino Hills nine years ago from Taiwan and soon noticed that the Southern California sun was making her skin darker and drier.

Her friends told her about Dr. George Sun of Arcadia, who offers a procedure called a "fotofacial RF," which uses intense pulses of light and radio frequency to interfere with melanin production in the skin.

When Dr. Sun—who chuckles about the irony of his last name but says it means "descendant" in Chinese—introduced the mesofacial about eight months ago, she started getting that treatment too. Lin-Cheng says she spends a few hundred dollars a month on skin procedures at Sun's office.

Lin-Cheng, whose skin now resembles a pink-white peony, said she gets compliments from her friends on her appearance.

"I know I cannot get there, but always, Nicole Kidman is my idol," she said.

Lin-Cheng religiously reapplies baby sunblock every hour and takes the tinted visor that she calls her "welder's helmet" everywhere. She purchased the helmet on a recent trip to Taiwan and brought extras for "friends who want to be beautiful." She outfitted her daughter Jessica with one of the helmets, and the 22-year-old wore it daily on her walk from her apartment in Westwood to UCLA.

Sun, a plastic surgeon, started treating women for "pigmentation issues" in 1996 after clients asked him how they could lighten their skin and get rid of sun spots and dark patches. Sun said he now treats about 30 women a week.

"It's like Botox," he said. "Do you think people in the past were in- 45 terested in wrinkle improvement? Yes. Could they do something about it, though? [Women's] concerns and their wish for improvement can finally be met in the hands of specialists."

But the idea of Asian women obsessing over white skin troubles Glen Mimura, a 37-year-old assistant professor of Asian American studies at UC Irvine.

"It seems tied primarily to colonial history, a fascination with whiteness," he said. "Dark skin gets associated with manual labor, agrarian communities, being less cosmopolitan."

The pursuit of white skin is all the more troubling because it appears to reinforce long-held prejudices in East Asia against fellow Asians with darker skin, Mimura said. Given the cost of whitening regimens, he added, maintaining that perfect milky glow seems reserved for women who can afford it.

"I think these women see skin-whitening very much along the lines of buying a Louis Vuitton bag," he said.

Anna Park, an associate editor at *Audrey*, an Asian American wom- 50 en's lifestyle and beauty magazine based in Gardena, isn't so sure the whitening boom is about embracing European ideals of beauty.

"If you look at old pictures, old paintings of what is considered to be beautiful in Korea or Japan, all their faces are really pale," said Park, 35.

To understand how much of a phenomenon whitening has become in Asian American communities, step inside Rick Armstrong's tanning salon, Casa del Sol, in Irvine.

Armstrong has installed a sleek apparatus featuring a horseshoe-shaped mask that fits over a person's face. Instead of using light to brown skin, as other machines in his salon do, it uses light to smooth out wrinkles and lighten age spots.

"Over in Japan, they have salons with facial units in them and you put whitening gel on," Armstrong said. "You sit there and have a session."

He's betting the device will become popular with Asians as well as 55 other customers who want to keep their faces smooth. "Nobody's face is perfect."

Understanding the Text

1. Chong cites several examples of women who take advantage of beauty treatments aimed at lightening their skin. What reasons do these women cite for using these treatments?

2. One of the women Chong interviews makes a distinction between "whitening" and "lightening." What is that distinction, and why does she insist one is different from the other?

Reflection and Response

3. What attitudes toward skin color do you think are particularly pervasive in contemporary American culture? How do the women interviewed in Chong's article represent the sentiments about skin color that you find in your region or city?

4. Because Chong is a newspaper reporter, she does not comment on the trend toward skin lightening that she is reporting. If you were writing an editorial or analytical article, what conclusions might you draw from the interviews and information contained in Chong's article? What other information would you want to research to construct a fuller analysis of this trend?

Making Connections

5. The women described in Chong's article are choosing to lighten their skin. In what ways do these choices compare to the choices described earlier in this chapter by Susie Orbach in "Losing Bodies" (p. 244)? Does Orbach's argument, that the West is exporting a globally homogenized "ideal" body, fit with the information presented in Chong's article? If so, provide an example to support your position. If not, explain the differences between Orbach's argument and the information Chong is presenting in her article.

6. The people interviewed in "Beauty and the Bleach" seem to think that they are making an individual choice that is not harmful or dangerous to anyone other than themselves (if they buy an inexpensive and toxic brand, for instance). But is it true that such choices are individual, or is there a cultural cost to an individual's beauty choice? In answering this question, cite evidence from the other readings in *Composing Gender* or from your own research about the potential costs of beauty treatments to support your position.

Report of the Task Force on the Sexualization of Young Girls

American Psychological Association

The American Psychological Association (APA) is the world's largest association of psychologists and as stated on their website (www.apa.org), exists to "advance psychology as a science, a profession and as a means of promoting health, education and human welfare." Its activities include hosting international conferences to share and disseminate knowledge about psychology, establishing professional standards, and broadly encouraging the development of the field of psychology. This selection is an excerpt from a report an APA task force issued in 2007 and is part of a long-standing effort by the APA to investigate the impact of media content on children. Other similar reports include one on the effects of advertising on children from 2004 and another on the impact of violence in video games and interactive media on children published in 2005.

Executive Summary

Journalists, child advocacy organizations, parents, and psychologists have argued that the sexualization of girls is a broad and increasing problem and is harmful to girls. The APA Task Force on the Sexualization of Girls was formed in response to these expressions of public concern.

APA has long been involved in issues related to the impact of media content on children. In 1994, APA adopted a policy resolution on Violence in Mass Media, which updated and expanded an earlier resolution on televised violence. In 2004, the APA Task Force on Advertising and Children produced a report examining broad issues related to advertising to children. That report provided recommendations to restrict advertising that is primarily directed at young children and to include developmentally appropriate disclaimers in advertising, as well as recommendations regarding research, applied psychology, industry practices, media literacy, advertising, and schools. In 2005, APA adopted the policy resolution on Violence in Video Games and Interactive Media, which documented the negative impact of exposure to violent interactive media on children and youth and called for the reduction of violence in these media. These resolutions and reports addressed how violent media and advertising affect children and youth, but they did not address sexualization.

The APA Task Force on the Sexualization of Girls was tasked with examining the psychological theory, research, and clinical experience addressing the sexualization of girls via media and other cultural messages, including the prevalence of these messages and their impact on girls and the role and impact of race/ethnicity and socioeconomic status. The task force was charged with producing a report, including recommendations for research, practice, education and training, policy, and public awareness.

This report examines and summarizes psychological theory, research, and clinical experience addressing the sexualization of girls. The report (a) defines sexualization; (b) examines the prevalence and provides examples of sexualization in society and in cultural institutions, as well as interpersonally and intrapsychically; (c) evaluates the evidence suggesting that sexualization has negative consequences for girls and for the rest of society; and (d) describes positive alternatives that may help counteract the influence of sexualization.

There are several components to sexualization, and these set it 5 apart from healthy sexuality. Sexualization occurs when

- a person's value comes only from his or her sexual appeal or behavior, to the exclusion of other characteristics;
- a person is held to a standard that equates physical attractiveness (narrowly defined) with being sexy;
- a person is sexually objectified—that is, made into a thing for others' sexual use, rather than seen as a person with the capacity for independent action and decision making; and/or
- sexuality is inappropriately imposed upon a person.

All four conditions need not be present; any one is an indication of sexualization. The fourth condition (the inappropriate imposition of sexuality) is especially relevant to children. Anyone (girls, boys, men, women) can be sexualized. But when children are imbued with adult sexuality, it is often imposed upon them rather than chosen by them. Self-motivated sexual exploration, on the other hand, is not sexualization by our definition, nor is age-appropriate exposure to information about sexuality.

Evidence for the Sexualization of Girls

Virtually every media form studied provides ample evidence of the sexualization of women, including television, music videos, music lyrics, movies, magazines, sports media, video games, the Internet, and advertising (e.g., Gow, 1996; Grauerholz & King, 1997; Krassas, Blauwkamp, & Wesselink, 2001, 2003; Lin, 1997; Plous & Neptune, 1997; Vincent, 1989; Ward, 1995). Some studies have examined forms of media that are especially popular with children and adolescents, such as video games and teen-focused magazines. In study after study, findings have indicated that women more often than men are portrayed in a sexual manner (e.g., dressed in revealing clothing, with bodily postures or facial expressions that imply sexual readiness) and are objectified (e.g., used as a decorative object, or as body parts rather than a whole person). In addition, a narrow (and unrealistic) standard of physical beauty is heavily emphasized. These are the models of femininity presented for young girls to study and emulate.

In some studies, the focus was on the sexualization of female characters across all ages, but most focused specifically on young adult women. Although few studies examined the prevalence of sexualized portrayals of girls in particular, those that have been conducted found that such sexualization does occur and may be increasingly common. For example, O'Donohue, Gold, and McKay (1997) coded advertisements over a 40-year period in five magazines targeted to men, women, or a general adult readership. Although relatively few (1.5%) of the ads portrayed children in a sexualized manner, of those that did, 85% sexualized girls rather than boys. Furthermore, the percentage of sexualizing ads increased over time.

Although extensive analyses documenting the sexualization of girls, in particular, have yet to be conducted, individual examples can easily be found. These include advertisements (e.g., the Skechers "naughty and nice" ad that featured Christina Aguilera dressed as a schoolgirl in pigtails, with her shirt unbuttoned, licking a lollipop), dolls (e.g., Bratz dolls dressed in sexualized clothing such as miniskirts, fishnet stockings, and feather boas), clothing (thongs sized for 7- to 10-year-olds, some printed with slogans such as "wink wink"), and television programs (e.g., a televised fashion show in which adult models in lingerie were presented as young girls). Research documenting the pervasiveness and influence of such products and portrayals is sorely needed.

Societal messages that contribute to the sexualization of girls come 10 not only from media and merchandise but also through girls' interpersonal relationships (e.g., with parents, teachers, and peers; Brown & Gilligan, 1992). Parents may contribute to sexualization in a number of ways. For example, parents may convey the message that maintaining an attractive physical appearance is the most important goal for girls. Some may allow or encourage plastic surgery to help girls meet that goal. Research shows that teachers sometimes encourage girls to play at being sexualized adult women (Martin, 1998) or hold beliefs that girls of color are "hypersexual" and thus unlikely to achieve academic success (Rolón-Dow, 2004). Both male and female peers have been found to contribute to the sexualization of girls—girls by policing each other to ensure conformance with standards of thinness and sexiness (Eder, 1995; Nichter, 2000) and boys by sexually objectifying and harassing girls. Finally, at the extreme end, parents, teachers, and peers, as well as others (e.g., other family members, coaches, or strangers) sometimes sexually abuse, assault, prostitute, or traffic girls, a most destructive form of sexualization.

If girls purchase (or ask their parents to purchase) products and clothes designed to make them look physically appealing and sexy, and if they style their identities after the sexy celebrities who populate their cultural landscape, they are, in effect, sexualizing themselves. Girls also sexualize themselves when they think of themselves in objectified terms. Psychological researchers have identified *self-objectification* as a key process whereby girls learn to think of and treat their own bodies as objects of others' desires (Fredrickson & Roberts, 1997; McKinley & Hyde, 1996). In self-objectification, girls internalize an observer's perspective on their physical selves and learn to treat themselves as objects to be looked at and evaluated for their appearance. Numerous studies have documented the presence of self-objectification in women more than in men. Several studies have also documented this phenomenon in adolescent and preadolescent girls (McConnell, 2001; Slater & Tiggemann, 2002).

> Psychological researchers have identified *self-objectification* as a key process whereby girls learn to think of and treat their own bodies as objects of others' desires.

Consequences of the Sexualization of Girls

Psychology offers several theories to explain how the sexualization of girls and women could influence girls' well-being. Ample evidence testing these theories indicates that sexualization has negative effects in a variety of domains, including cognitive functioning, physical and mental health, sexuality, and attitudes and beliefs. Although most of these studies have been conducted on women in late adolescence (i.e., college age), findings are likely to generalize to younger adolescents and to girls, who may be even more strongly affected because their sense of self is still being formed.

Cognitive and Emotional Consequences

Cognitively, self-objectification has been repeatedly shown to detract from the ability to concentrate and focus one's attention, thus leading to impaired performance on mental activities such as mathematical computations or logical reasoning (Fredrickson, Roberts, Noll, Quinn, & Twenge, 1998; Gapinski, Brownell, & LaFrance, 2003; Hebl, King, & Lin, 2004). One study demonstrated this fragmenting quite vividly (Fredrickson et al., 1998). While alone in a dressing room, college students were asked to try on and evaluate either a swimsuit or a sweater. While they waited for 10 minutes wearing the garment, they completed a math test. The results revealed that young women in swimsuits performed significantly worse on the math problems than did those wearing sweaters. No differences were found for young men. In other words, thinking about the body and comparing it to sexualized cultural ideals disrupted mental capacity. In the emotional domain, sexualization and objectification undermine confidence in and comfort with one's own body, leading to a host of negative emotional consequences, such as shame, anxiety, and even self-disgust. The association between self-objectification and anxiety about appearance and feelings of shame has been found in adolescent girls (12–13-year-olds) (Slater & Tiggemann, 2002) as well as in adult women.

Mental and Physical Health

Research links sexualization with three of the most common mental health problems of girls and women: eating disorders, low self-esteem, and depression or depressed mood (Abramson & Valene, 1991; Durkin & Paxton, 2002; Harrison, 2000; Hofschire & Greenberg, 2001; Mills, Polivy, Herman, & Tiggemann, 2002; Stice, Schupak-Neuberg, Shaw, & Stein, 1994; Thomsen, Weber, & Brown, 2002; Ward, 2004). Several studies (on both teenage and adult women) have found associations between exposure to narrow representations of female beauty (e.g., the "thin ideal") and disordered eating attitudes and symptoms. Research also links exposure to sexualized female ideals with lower self-esteem, negative mood, and depressive symptoms among adolescent girls and women. In addition to mental health consequences of sexualization, research suggests that girls' and women's physical health may also be negatively affected, albeit indirectly.

Sexuality

Sexual well-being is an important part of healthy development and overall well-being, yet evidence suggests that the sexualization of girls has negative consequences in terms of girls' ability to develop healthy sexuality. Self-objectification has been linked directly with diminished sexual health among adolescent girls (e.g., as measured by decreased condom use and diminished sexual assertiveness; Im- 15 pett, Schooler, & Tolman, 2006). Frequent exposure to narrow ideals of attractiveness is associated with unrealistic and/or negative expectations concerning sexuality. Negative effects (e.g., shame) that emerge during adolescence may lead to sexual problems in adulthood (Brotto, Heiman, & Tolman, in press).

Attitudes and Beliefs

Frequent exposure to media images that sexualize girls and women affects how girls conceptualize femininity and sexuality. Girls and young women who more frequently consume or engage with mainstream media content offer stronger endorsement of sexual stereotypes that depict women as sexual objects (Ward, 2002; Ward & Rivadeneyra, 1999; Zurbriggen & Morgan, 2006). They also place appearance and physical attractiveness at the center of women's value.

Impact on Others and on Society

The sexualization of girls can also have a negative impact on other groups (i.e., boys, men, and adult women) and on society more broadly. Exposure to narrow ideals of female sexual attractiveness may make it difficult for some men to find an "acceptable" partner or to fully enjoy intimacy with a female partner (e.g., Schooler & Ward, 2006). Adult women may suffer by trying to conform to a younger and younger standard of ideal female beauty. More general societal effects may include an increase in sexism; fewer girls pursuing careers in science, technology, engineering, and mathematics (STEM); increased rates of sexual harassment and sexual violence; and an increased demand for child pornography.

Positive Alternatives to the Sexualization of Girls

Some girls and their supporters, now and in the past, have resisted mainstream characterizations of girls as sexual objects. A variety of promising approaches exist to reduce the amount of sexualization that occurs and to ameliorate its effects.

Because the media are important sources of sexualizing images, the development and implementation of school-based media literacy training programs could be key in combating the influence of sexualization. There is an urgent need to teach critical skills in viewing and consuming media, focusing specifically on the sexualization of women and girls. Other school-based approaches include increased access to athletic and other extracurricular programs for girls and the development and presentation of comprehensive sexuality education programs.

Strategies for parents and other caregivers include learning about the impact of sexualization on girls and co-viewing media with their children in order to influence the way in which media messages are interpreted. Action by parents and families has been effective in confronting sources of sexualized images of girls. Organized religious and other ethical instruction can offer girls important practical and psychological alternatives to the values conveyed by popular culture.

Girls and girls' groups can also work toward change. Alternative media such as "zines" (Web-based magazines), "blogs" (Web logs), and feminist magazines, books, and Web sites encourage girls to become activists who speak out and develop their own alternatives. Girl empowerment groups also support girls in a variety of ways and provide important counterexamples to sexualization.

Recommendations

I. Research

A solid research base has explored the effects of having an objectified body image or viewing objectified body images in the media. Much previous work, however, has focused on women. Future studies focusing on girls are needed. In addition, more culturally competent, focused work is required to document the phenomenon of the sexualization of girls; to explore the short- and long-term harm of viewing, listening to, and buying into a sexualized pathway to power; and to test alternative presentations of girlhood, sexuality, and power. We recommend that psychologists conduct research to:

1. Document the frequency of sexualization, specifically of girls, and examine whether sexualization is increasing.

2. Examine and inform our understanding of the circumstances under which the sexualization of girls occurs and identify factors involving the media and products that either contribute to or buffer against the sexualization of girls.

3. Examine the presence or absence of the sexualization of girls and women in all media but especially in movies, music videos, music lyrics, video games, books, blogs, and Internet sites. In particular, research is needed to examine the extent to which girls are portrayed in sexualized and objectified ways and whether this has increased over time. In addition, it is important that these studies focus specifically on sexualization rather than on sexuality more broadly or on other constructs such as gender-role stereotyping.

4. Describe the influence and/or impact of sexualization on girls. This includes both short- and long-term effects of viewing or buying

into a sexualizing objectifying image, how these effects influence girls' development, self-esteem, friendships, and intimate relationships, ideas about femininity, body image, physical, mental, and sexual health, sexual satisfaction, desire for plastic surgery, risk factors for early pregnancy, abortion, and sexually transmitted infections, attitudes toward women, other girls, boys, and men, as well as educational aspirations and future career success.

5. Explore issues of age compression ("adultification" of young girls and "youthification" of adult women), including prevalence, impact on the emotional well-being of girls and women, and influences on behavior.

6. Explore differences in presentation of sexualized images and effects of these images on girls of color; lesbian, bisexual, questioning, and transgendered girls; girls of different cultures and ethnicities; girls of different religions; girls with disabilities; and girls from all socioeconomic groups.

7. Identify media (including advertising) and marketing alternatives to sexualized images of girls, such as positive depictions of sexuality.

8. Identify effective, culturally competent protective factors (e.g., helping adolescent girls develop a nonobjectified model of normal, healthy sexual development and expression through school or other programs).

9. Evaluate the effectiveness of programs and interventions that promote positive alternatives and approaches to the sexualization of girls. Particular attention should be given to programs and interventions at the individual, family, school, and/or community level.

10. Explore the relationship between the sexualization of girls and societal issues such as sexual abuse, child pornography, child prostitution, and the trafficking of girls. Research on the potential associations between the sexualization of girls and the sexual exploitation of girls is virtually nonexistent, and the need for this line of inquiry is pressing.

11. Investigate the relationships between international issues such as immigration and globalization and the sexualization of girls worldwide. Document the global prevalence of the sexualization of girls and the types of sexualization that occur in different countries or regions and any regional differences in the effects of sexualization. Assess the effects of sexualization on immigrant girls and determine whether these effects are moderated by country of origin, age at immigration, and level of acculturation.

12. Conduct controlled studies on the efficacy of working directly with girls and girls' groups that address these issues, as well as other prevention/intervention programs.

13. Researchers who are conducting studies on related topics (e.g., physical attractiveness, body awareness, or acceptance of the thin ideal) should consider the impact of sexualization as they develop their findings.

II. Practice

As practitioners, psychologists can perform a valuable service by raising awareness of the negative impact of the sexualization of girls—on girls, as well as on boys, women, and men. As individuals and in collaboration with others, practitioners are encouraged to address the sexualization of girls. We recommend:

1. That APA make the Report of the Task Force on the Sexualization of Girls available to practitioners working with children and adolescents in order to familiarize them with information and resources relevant to the sexualization of girls and objectifying behavior on the part of girls.

2. That APA make the Report of the Task Force on the Sexualization of Girls available to practitioners as a source of information on assisting girls in developing the skills necessary to advocate for themselves and counter these adverse messages, taking into account the impact and influence of family and other relationships.

III. Education and Training

Education and training focusing on the prevalence and impact of the sexualization of girls are needed at all levels of psychology to raise awareness within the discipline of psychology and among psychologists about these important issues. We recommend:

1. That APA disseminate information about the Report of the Task Force on the Sexualization of Girls to instructors at the middle-school, high-school, and undergraduate levels and to chairs of graduate departments of psychology.

2. That information from the Report of the Task Force on the Sexualization of Girls be considered for inclusion in future revisions of the *National Standards for High School Psychology Curricula* and *Guidelines on the Undergraduate Psychology Major* by the groups charged with revising these documents.

3. That chairs of graduate departments of psychology and of graduate departments in other areas in which psychologists work be en-

couraged to consider information from the Report of the Task Force on the Sexualization of Girls as curricula are developed within their programs and to aid in the dissemination of the report.

4. That information from the Report of the Task Force on the Sexualization of Girls be considered for development as continuing education and online academy programming, in partnership with APA's Continuing Education in Psychology Office.

5. That the Ethics Committee and APA Ethics Office consider and use this report in developing ethics educational and training materials for psychologists and make this report available to the group responsible for the next revision of the APA "Ethical Principles of Psychologists and Code of Conduct."

IV. Public Policy

APA, in collaboration with other organizations and through its advocacy 25 *efforts, is encouraged to advocate for and better support understanding of the nature and impact of the sexualization of girls, as well as identification and broad implementation of strategies to combat this serious societal problem. We recommend:*

1. That APA advocate for funding to support needed research in the areas outlined above.

2. That APA advocate for funding to support the development and implementation by public agencies and private organizations of media literacy programs, including interactive media, in schools that combat sexualization and objectification.

3. That APA advocate for the inclusion of information about sexualization and objectification in health and other related programs, including comprehensive sex education and other sexuality education programs.

4. That APA encourage federal agencies to support the development of programming that may counteract damaging images of girlhood and test the effects of such programs, for example, Web "zines" (i.e., Web magazines), extracurricular activities (such as athletics), and programs that help girls feel powerful in ways other than through a sexy appearance.

5. That APA work with Congress and relevant federal agencies and industry to reduce the use of sexualized images of girls in all forms of media and products.

V. Public Awareness

The task force offers the following recommendations with the goal of rais-
ing public awareness about this important issue. Achieving this goal will
require a comprehensive, grassroots, communitywide effort. Participants
and stakeholders will include parents and other caregivers, educators, young
people, community-based organizations, religious communities, the media,
advertisers, marketing professionals, and manufacturers. Overarching strate-
gies will be needed to build linkages and partnerships among the community
members. If the goal of raising public awareness is left unmet, the mission of
this work will be significantly curtailed. We recommend:

1. That APA seek outside funding to support the development and implementation of an initiative to address the issues raised in this report and identify outside partners to collaborate on these goals. The long-term goals of this initiative, to be pursued in collaboration with these outside partners, should include the following:

- Develop age-appropriate multimedia education resources representing ethnically and culturally diverse young people (boys and girls) for parents, educators, health care providers, and community-based organizations, available in English and other languages, to help facilitate effective conversations about the sexualization of girls and its impact on girls, as well as on boys, women, and men.
- Convene forums that will bring together members of the media and a panel of leading experts in the field to examine and discuss (a) the sexualization of girls in the United States, (b) the findings of this task force report, and (c) strategies to increase awareness about this issue and reduce negative images of girls in the media.
- Develop media awards for positive portrayals of girls as strong, competent, and nonsexualized (e.g., the best television portrayal of girls or the best toy).
- Convene forums with industry partners, including the media, advertisers, marketing professionals, and manufacturers, to discuss the presentation of sexualized images and the potential negative impact on girls and to develop relationships with the goal of providing guidance on appropriate material for varying developmental ages and on storylines and programming that reflect the positive portrayals of girls.

2. That school personnel, parents and other caregivers, community-based youth and parenting organizations, and local business and ser-

vice organizations encourage positive extracurricular activities that help youth build nurturing connections with peers and enhance self-esteem based on young people's abilities and character rather than on their appearance.

References

Abramson, E., & Valene, P. (1991). Media use, dietary restraint, bulimia, and attitudes toward obesity: A preliminary study. *British Review of Bulimia and Anorexia Nervosa, 5*, 73–76.

Brotto, L., Heiman, J., & Tolman, D. (in press). Towards conceptualizing women's desires: A mixed methods study. *Journal of Sex Research.*

Brown, L. M., & Gilligan, C. (1992). *Meeting at the crossroads: Women's psychology and girls' development.* Cambridge, MA: Harvard University Press.

Durkin, S. J., & Paxton, S. J. (2002). Predictors of vulnerability to reduced body image satisfaction and psychological well-being in response to exposure to idealized female media images in adolescent girls. *Journal of Psychosomatic Research, 53*, 995–1005.

Eder, D. (with Evans, C. C., & Parker, S). (1995). *School talk: Gender and adolescent culture.* New Brunswick, NJ: Rutgers University Press.

Fredrickson, B. L., & Roberts, T.-A. (1997). Objectification theory: Toward understanding women's lived experience and mental health risks. *Psychology of Women Quarterly, 21*, 173–206.

Fredrickson, B. L., Roberts, T., Noll, S. M., Quinn, D. M., & Twenge, J. M. (1998). That swimsuit becomes you: Sex differences in self-objectification, restrained eating, and math performance. *Journal of Personality and Social Psychology, 75*, 269–284.

Gapinski, K. D., Brownell, K. D., & LaFrance, M. (2003). Body objectification and "fat talk": Effects on emotion, motivation, and cognitive performance. *Sex Roles, 48*, 377–388.

Gow, J. (1996). Reconsidering gender roles on MTV: Depictions in the most popular music videos of the early 1990s. *Communication Reports, 9*, 151–161.

Grauerholz, E., & King, A. (1997). Primetime sexual harassment. *Violence Against Women, 3*, 129–148.

Harrison, K. (2000). The body electric: Thin-ideal media and eating disorders in adolescents. *Journal of Communication, 50*, 119–143.

Hebl, M. R., King, E. G., & Lin, J. (2004). The swimsuit becomes us all: Ethnicity, gender, and vulnerability to self-objectification. *Personality and Social Psychology Bulletin, 30*, 1322–1331.

Hofschire, L. J., & Greenberg, B. S. (2001). Media's impact on adolescents' body dissatisfaction. In J. D. Brown & J. R. Steele (Eds.), *Sexual teens, sexual media* (pp. 125–149). Mahwah, NJ: Erlbaum.

Impett, E. A., Schooler, D., & Tolman, D. L. (2006). To be seen and not heard: Femininity ideology and adolescent girls' sexual health. *Archives of Sexual Behavior, 21*, 628–646.

Krassas, N., Blauwkamp, J. M., & Wesselink, P. (2001). Boxing Helena and corseting Eunice: Sexual rhetoric in *Cosmopolitan* and *Playboy* magazines. *Sex Roles, 44*, 751–771.

Krassas, N. R., Blauwkamp, J. M., & Wesselink, P. (2003). "Master your Johnson": Sexual rhetoric in *Maxim* and *Stuff* magazines. *Sexuality & Culture, 7,* 98–119.

Lin, C. (1997). Beefcake versus cheesecake in the 1990s: Sexist portrayals of both genders in television commercials. *Howard Journal of Communications, 8,* 237–249.

Martin, K. A. (1998). Becoming a gendered body: Practices in preschools. *American Sociological Review, 63,* 494–511.

McConnell, C. (2001). An object to herself: The relationship between girls and their bodies. *Dissertation Abstracts International, 61*(8B), p. 4416.

McKinley, N. M., & Hyde, J. S. (1996). The Objectified Body Consciousness Scale. *Psychology of Women Quarterly, 20,* 181–215.

Mills, J., Polivy, J., Herman, C. P., & Tiggemann, M. (2002). Effects of exposure to thin media images: Evidence of self-enhancement among restrained eaters. *Personality and Social Psychology Bulletin, 28,* 1687–1699.

Nichter, M. (2000). *Fat talk: What girls and their parents say about dieting.* Cambridge, MA: Harvard University Press.

O'Donohue, W., Gold, S. R., & McKay, J. S. (1997). Children as sexual objects: Historical and gender trends in magazines. *Sexual Abuse: Journal of Research & Treatment, 9,* 291–301.

Plous, S., & Neptune, D. (1997). Racial and gender biases in magazine advertising: A content analytic study. *Psychology of Women Quarterly, 21,* 627–644.

Rolón-Dow, R. (2004). Seduced by images: Identity and schooling in the lives of Puerto Rican girls. *Anthropology and Education Quarterly, 35,* 8–29.

Schooler, D., & Ward, L. M. (2006). Average Joes: Men's relationships with media, real bodies, and sexuality. *Psychology of Men and Masculinity, 7,* 27–41.

Slater, A., & Tiggemann, M. (2002). A test of objectification theory in adolescent girls. *Sex Roles, 46,* 343–349.

Stice, E., Schupak-Neuberg, E., Shaw, H., & Stein, R. (1994). Relation of media exposure to eating disorder symptomatology: An examination of mediating mechanisms. *Journal of Abnormal Psychology, 103,* 836–840.

Thomsen, S. R., Weber, M. M., & Brown, L. B. (2002). The relationship between reading beauty and fashion magazines and the use of pathogenic dieting methods among adolescent females. *Adolescence, 37,* 1–18.

Vincent, R. C. (1989). Clio's consciousness raised? Portrayal of women in rock videos, re-examined. *Journalism Quarterly, 66,* 155–160.

Ward, L. M. (1995). Talking about sex: Common themes about sexuality in the prime-time television programs children and adolescents view most. *Journal of Youth & Adolescence, 24,* 595–615.

Ward, L. M. (2002). Does television exposure affect emerging adults' attitudes and assumptions about sexual relationships? Correlational and experimental confirmation. *Journal of Youth and Adolescence, 31,* 1–15.

Ward, L. M. (2004). Wading through the stereotypes: Positive and negative associations between media use and Black adolescents' conceptions of self. *Developmental Psychology, 40,* 284–294.

Ward, L. M., & Rivadeneyra, R. (1999). Contributions of entertainment television to adolescents' sexual attitudes and expectations: The role of viewing amount versus viewer involvement. *Journal of Sex Research, 36,* 237–249.

Zurbriggen, E. L., & Morgan, E. M. (2006). Who wants to marry a millionaire? Reality dating television programs, attitudes toward sex, and sexual behaviors. *Sex Roles, 54,* 1–17.

Understanding the Text

1. Early in the report, the APA defines "sexualization." Define this term in your own words and explain why it is a word that needed explanation in the first few paragraphs.

2. What are some of the immediate consequences to young girls of their "sexualization" in the media?

3. Toward the end of the report, the APA outlines things that it can do as an international organization of psychologists. Name a few of the things in that list that you think might be especially effective or useful.

Reflection and Response

4. The report states that it is easy to find examples in popular culture of the sexualization of girls. What current examples spring to your mind as you read and think about this report?

5. What is driving this trend toward sexualization of girls? Who benefits from sexualized images in the media?

6. This report focuses on girls. Consider whether there is a sexualization of boys about which we should also be concerned. Is there any evidence that boys receive conflicted or dangerous messages about sexuality from the media? If not, why not? If so, cite one or two examples to support your position.

Making Connections

7. One of the strategies the APA recommends is girl empowerment, by which they mean alternative media written by girls and girls' groups to support girls in more healthy and nonmediated activities. Find at least one example of this kind of girl empowerment activity and describe whether or not it might effectively provide a positive alternative to existing media narratives.

8. Several of the readings in *Composing Gender* describe the sexualization of contemporary culture. Choose one of these other readings and consider whether the recommendations of these authors are the same as those of the APA. What differences or similarities exist?

9. The APA suggests that there may be positive alternatives to the sexualization of girls, including increased access to athletic and other extracurricular programs, increased discussion with girls about media and their messages, the development and presentation of comprehensive sexuality education programs, and more efforts to empower girls to create their own media. How well do you think these alternatives could counteract the existing media discourse about girls and sexuality?

10. In the APA's call for research, the first recommendation is to "document the frequency of sexualization" in mass media today (p. 272). Do just this, but limit

the range of media to television, music videos, YouTube or Facebook, teen magazines, or some other area of media. Try to "define the problem" in your selected domain and "provide a sense of the consequences."

11. According to the APA, "research on the potential associations between the sexualization of girls and the sexual exploitation of girls is virtually nonexistent" (p. 273). Write about the potential associations between sexualization and sexual exploitation. What kinds of exploitation might be "caused" by the overall cultural emphasis on children, teenagers, and sexuality? Where can those forms of exploitation be seen (especially in the media)? Is there more exploitation now than in the past?

To Catch a Predator

Amy Adler

Amy Adler is a professor at New York University School of Law. Before arriving at New York University, she clerked for a justice in the U.S. Court of Appeals and was a fellow at the Freedom Forum Media Studies Center at Columbia University. Now, she teaches classes on the First Amendment and cultural expression, and her scholarship focuses on the legal issues surrounding the exploitation of children.

[D]esire is never renounced, but becomes preserved and reasserted in the very structure of renunciation.

—JUDITH BUTLER, *EXCITABLE SPEECH* 117

The Scene of the Crime

To Catch a Predator, a wildly popular network television series, netted would-be child predators in a sting operation and filmed them as they were caught and confronted on camera. The series began in 2004, when *Dateline NBC*, the news magazine show, had fallen into a ratings slump. Searching for a new formula, *Dateline* began broadcasting a series entitled *"To Catch a Predator."* Joining forces with a vigilante group called "Perverted Justice," *Dateline* used "decoys," adults posing as 13–15-year-old teenagers on-line, to engage in explicit sex chats with men. The decoys lured the men to a sting house with the promise of sex, but they were met instead by a camera crew and, ultimately, the police.

The show consists of a series of formulaic scenes once the would-be predator arrives at the sting house. First the decoy, usually a young looking woman named Dell who works for Perverted Justice, answers the door for the predator, invites him in, then quickly excuses herself and disappears.[1] She is replaced by Chris Hansen, the host of *Dateline*. A tall, preppy, white guy, Hansen strolls into the kitchen of the house with the air of a man who has just been called off the golf course and is irritated about the interruption. Hansen has been watching on hidden camera and has been privy to the secret online chats between the predator and the decoy. Skeptical, all seeing, all knowing, he's not just a man, but "The Man." In fact, refusing

---

[1] Dell was 22 years old when the show began. Dell is not only accomplished at pretending to be a teenager, but is also a convincing cross-dresser, performing as "male and female and ages 10 to 15 and every ethnicity in-between," depending on the predator. Chris Hansen, *Dateline: Reflections on "To Catch a Predator,"* MSNBC, http://www.msnbc.msn.com/id/17601568 (last visited Aug. 12, 2009).

to name himself, perhaps Hansen is not just "The Man" but some sort of avenging god, or at least daddy or the police. Almost all of the would-be predators believe that Hansen is either the decoy's father or a police officer. In any event, the predator senses Hansen's authority; it is remarkable how many of them obey instantly.

As Hansen begins peppering him with a series of questions—"What are you doing here? Why are you here?"—the predator typically insists that he had no intention to act out his online fantasies.[2] This prompts Hansen to go on the attack. Increasingly incredulous and contemptuous, Hansen reads back in painstaking, salacious detail the predator's sexual chat log with the decoy.[3] This recitation of the sordid chat log often goes on to the point where the predator literally begs for mercy, sometimes sobbing, reduced to his knees, pleading with Hansen to please, please stop.

At this point comes the final blow. Hansen announces: "I'm Chris Hansen with *Dateline NBC*" and tells the predator that he is being filmed for national TV. And then, to drive home the predator's spectacular ruin, comes what I call the "money shot."[4] We watch as a swarm of cameramen surround the predator, pointing their cameras at him. Susan Sontag told us that the camera was predatory like a gun.[5] If only she had lived to see this show. "You are free to leave now," announces Hansen, and the predator, who has been groveling on the ground, stands up and departs. But of course he is not free.[6] When he exits the house, a swarm of heavily armed policemen tackle him, cuff him, and arrest him. As one journalism critic writes, the police handle the predator "as if he has just shot the president."[7]

---

[2] See April 2006 Ohio sting, http://www.msnbc.msn.com/id/12503802/:
Hansen: You ask her if she's horny?
Stacey: What's wrong with that?
Hansen: You ask if she does anal.
Stacey: It's a question. . . . It's just talking. The Internet and real life are two different things.

[3] For example, in one episode, Hansen says, "The problem is that I have the transcript of your online chat. Want to try again?" Hansen then produces some particularly salacious details. "What position do you like? You know how to ride? Do u like doggy?" says Hansen, reciting from the chat transcript. The voiceover then announces, "he gets up and begins to pace." The predator groans, "oh God, stop okay?" September 2006 Georgia sting: http://www.msnbc.msn.com/id/14824427/.

[4] I borrow the term of course from the vernacular of pornography.

[5] Susan Sontag, "In Plato's Cave," in *On Photography* 3, 14 (Macmillan 2001) (1977).

[6] Example from September 2006 Georgia sting, http://www.msnbc.msn.com/id/14824427/: [voiceover] "He's free to leave, but he won't get very far. . . . He's arrested and taken away."

[7] Douglas McCollam, "The Shame Game," *Colum. Journalism Rev.* 28–33, Jan./Feb. 2007.

A major force in public policy, *To Catch a Predator* was also "ratings 5 gold."[8] Indeed, it became a cultural phenomenon, the subject of everything from *Saturday Night Live* skits to college drinking games. *Predator* proved such a ratings bonanza for *Dateline* that it became a staple of sweeps week.[9] NBC built it into a network franchise. The show regularly outdrew anything else in the network's primetime fare.[10]

While *To Catch a Predator* has been repeatedly praised as performing a public service,[11] it also gave rise to two high-profile lawsuits against the show[12] and to a cottage industry of vociferous criticism.[13] Ultimately the controversy was significant enough that NBC halted its investigations in 2008. Although *Dateline* no longer enacts stings, the previous episodes of *Predator* live on: old episodes, with additional, previously unaired, footage have become a new series called *Predator Raw: The Unseen Tapes*, on MSNBC, NBC's sister channel. It is the most popular show on MSNBC. . . .

If you have ever seen it, the show is almost unbearable to watch—so deeply uncomfortable and disturbing, that even I, a seasoned scholar of child pornography law, find it painful to view. What, then, could explain the show's spectacular popular appeal? I want to take the show seriously not as law enforcement or public service but instead as a realm of entertainment, spectacle, pleasure and fantasy. . . .

I have previously written about child pornography law as a realm of discourse that inadvertently replicates and spreads the sexualization of children that it fights.[14] I believe that *To Catch a Predator* repeats but also complicates that problem. The show offers yet another venue in which we are enthralled—anguished, enticed, bombarded—by the spectacle of the sexual child. It purports to be a public service, a crime fighting program that gets predators off the streets and stamps out the horror of child predation. Yet the show continually stages the

---

8 James Poniewozik, "Mark Foley's Real Sin Was . . . : Breaking America's Favorite Taboo," *Time*, Sunday, Oct. 08, 2006.

9 Indeed, it became so popular that it was satirized on *Saturday Night Live*, inspired a *South Park* episode, and became the subject of a drinking game.

10 Douglas McCollam, "The Shame Game," *Colum. Journalism Rev.* 28–33, Jan./Feb. 2007.

11 *To Catch a Predator* has led to numerous convictions. An independent calculation made using the numbers provided on the organization's own website, however, indicates that the per-sting conviction rate for the show ranges from 4% to 92%, and that in total, only 47% of the "busts" on the show have led to convictions in a court of law.

12 See *Conradt v. NBC Universal, Inc.*, 536 F. Supp. 2d 380 (S.D.N.Y. 2008) (plaintiff alleging NBC caused her brother's suicide by humiliating him on show); *Bartel v. NBC Universal, Inc.*, 543 F.3d 901 (7th Cir. 2008) (plaintiff, producer at NBC, alleging wrongful termination for questioning show's ethics).

13 Critics attack the show for a range of issues, including among other things, its apparent violation of journalistic ethics.

14 Amy Adler, "The Perverse Law of Child Pornography," 101 *Colum. L. Rev.* 209 (2001); . . .

spectacle of the sexual child that it disavows.[15] As Butler tells us, "Language that is compelled to repeat what it seeks to constrain invariably reproduces and restages the very speech that it seeks to shut down" (*Excitable Speech* 129).

In my view, *To Catch a Predator* functions as a displaced and disavowed form of child pornography. To break down and castigate the predator, Hansen reads back to him his online pornographic chat. For example, when one predator proclaims his innocence, Hansen replies "But you said you couldn't wait to pour chocolate syrup all over her and lick it off with your tongue."[16] Or, to another predator: "But you said, 'I would love to feel your bleep deep inside my bleep,'" says Hansen. "'What position do you like? You know how to ride? Do u like doggy?'" he quotes sternly. Who is this man scornfully repeating the text of this chat and who are we the viewers, riveted, as the ratings tell us, by this retelling?

Consider this scene between Hansen and a predator called Robert. 10 While Robert insists his online chat with an imaginary 13-year-old boy was just rhetoric, the avenging Hansen replies,

[*To Catch a Predator*] offers yet another venue in which we are enthralled—anguished, enticed, bombarded—by the spectacle of the sexual child.

Hansen: Rhetoric? I've got the transcripts of your conversation here. . . . What it sounds like, Robert, is that you wanted to . . . have [sex] with a 13-year-old boy. You said, ". . . I want to see you and taste your beautiful body? make love to you. You are a gorgeous thirteen year old boy."[17]

Safe within his disgust and contempt, Hansen luxuriates in the details of these imaginary sex scenes, conjuring up again and again another "beautiful" sexualized teenage body. And with righteous indignation, Hansen broadcasts these words to a national audience. "Then you said," quotes Hansen: "'We will be making love all the time.'" "'With my tongue up your [blank].'"[18]

---

[15] The repetition of the prohibition on pedophilic desire becomes a new displaced site of pleasure; as Butler has shown in other contexts, "the prohibition pursues the reproduction of prohibited desire"; it "sustains [and] is sustained by the desire that it forces into renunciation." Judith Butler, *Excitable Speech: A Politics of the Performative* (New York and London: Routledge, 1997).

[16] Douglas McCollam . . .

[17] From February 2006 California sting, http://www.msnbc.msn.com/id/11152602/.

[18] From September 2006 Georgia sting, http://www.msnbc.msn.com/id/14960266/:
Hansen: Now does your boss know that you are on line chatting with 13-year-old girls?
Bhaskaran: I am sure they don't.
Voiceover: So what would his bosses think if they read a transcript of his pornographic online chat?

Nothing deters Hansen from doing his duty of conjuring up the gory details, not even a predator who says, you're right, I'm wrong, I confess, please arrest me right now and take me to jail. There is no apparent reason to go on, yet Hansen persists, "And then you wanted to do blank to his 13-year-old body and then you said you wanted to bleep him." Oral sex, group sex,[19] s and m,[20] Hansen soldiers on.

Please stop says the man. But Hansen can't stop. Even when the man says I confess, I'm guilty, there's nothing to dispute, Hansen can't stop. It's the best part of the show.[21]

In this way, *To Catch a Predator* fits within a long tradition in por- 15 nography, the tradition of the exploitation film. As Eric Schaefer describes in his definitive history of the exploitation film genre, risky films would come with an extra reel that offered a prefatory state-

---

Hansen (reading from chat): You ask if she masturbates.
Bhaskaran: Right.
Hansen (reading): You say you want to have oral sex with this girl you say . . .
Hansen (reading): You say "I feel like kissing you now, and suck on your blank and feel the tummy."
[19] From March 2007 Florida sting: http://www.msnbc.msn.com/id/17491919/: *"one guy has his [bleep] in her mouth. . . . the other guy has his [bleep] in her [bleep] or her [bleep]."*
[20] Hansen (reading) *"I want to lay back on my back. I want to lay on my back with a pillow and let you sit on my chest with your knees over my forearms and punch me repeatedly."*
[21] From March 2007 Florida sting: http://www.msnbc.msn.com/id/17491919/.
Hansen (reading chat): "We will be making love all the time I'm there." "Okay, cool."
Wiles: I said that—
Hansen: "With my tongue up your blank."
Wiles: I said. I say that—
Hansen: What does that mean?
Wiles: I know what it's—means. But I say that on all the—all—
Hansen: You say that all the time.
Wiles: Right.

Voiceover: And when the girl asks about group sex, he describes it in graphic detail.
audiovideo: simply put one guy has is d*** in her mouth
anni_anni_bobanni: o geez
*audavideo: the other guy has his d*** in her p*** or her b****
anni_anni_bobanni: o dANG
audavideo: I love teaching you its so fun
Fine: I don't know what you're talking about.
Hansen: "Can I lick your" blank? And how old is the boy that you came to see today?
Fine: I don't know what you're talking about.
Hansen: 14, male.
Fine: It musta been somebody on my—(TAPE GLITCH)
Hansen: was on your computer who made plans to meet right down here, and magically you showed up?
Fine: I'm not gonna say anything.
Hansen: Okay. "I want to lay back on my back. I want to lay on my back with a pillow and let you sit on my chest with your knees over my forearms and punch me repeatedly."

ment about the moral ill the film claimed to combat.[22] Like that pornographic tradition, *To Catch a Predator* packages titillation as if it were a public service.

The repetition of the prohibition on pedophilic desire becomes a new displaced site of pleasure; as Butler has shown in other contexts, "the prohibition pursues the reproduction of prohibited desire"; it "sustains [and] is sustained by the desire that it forces into renunciation" (*Excitable Speech* xx). In this way, the show may be comparable to Foucault's view of the power of eighteenth century sex manuals that warned parents of the dangers of childhood masturbation. As Foucault writes,

One might argue that the purpose of these discourses was precisely to prevent children from having a sexuality. But their effect was to din it into parents' heads that their children's sex constituted a fundamental problem. . . . [T]his had the consequence of sexually exciting the bodies of children while at the same time fixing the parental gaze and vigilance on the peril of infantile sexuality.[23]

Ultimately, *To Catch a Predator*'s restaging of the sexuality it condemns works to preserve, disseminate, and, in my view, even normalize the predator's sexual fantasies. After all, as the show's spectacular ratings attest, it is no longer merely the "predator," but we, the viewers of NBC, who gain some sort of disturbing satisfaction from these fantasy scenarios. Even though our pleasure is experienced through the veil of disgust and condemnation, doesn't our experience of pleasure align us with the predator? His fantasy is no longer the stuff of furtive, clandestine chats. Now the "pervert's" fantasy is mainstream entertainment, packaged for sweeps week, repeated again and again, long after it is useful or accurate, for a seemingly insatiable viewing audience. Transforming the "pervert's" fantasy into mainstream entertainment, then, the show spreads and normalizes the very imaginings it purports to condemn. In this way, the show participates in what I have called mainstream soft core child pornography—the cultural adulation of the teenager as sexual icon and the concomitant disavowal of that adulation.

---

[22] Eric Schaefer, *Bold! Daring! Shocking! True! A History of Exploitation Films, 1919–1959*, at 69–75 (2d Ed. 1999); . . .

[23] Michel Foucault, *Power/Knowledge: Selected Interviews and Other Writings 1972–1977*, at 120 (Colin Gordon, ed.; Colin Gordon et al., trans., New York: Pantheon Books, 1980) (1977).

Understanding the Text

1. Early in the article, Adler mentions that *To Catch a Predator* has been praised as doing a public service. How might someone make the argument that this show is a public service? Explain why Adler disagrees with this argument and support your explanation with examples from the reading.

2. One of Adler's concerns is that *To Catch a Predator* put explicit sexual fantasies about children on mainstream television for entertainment purposes. What reasons does she cite for being concerned about these fantasies being made so public and commercialized?

Reflection and Response

3. Adler implicates us, the viewers, when she says that we identify with and shame the predator when we watch this show. What do you think about being considered complicit or guilty in maintaining a dangerous system simply by tuning in to a television show? Does this seem fair to you, or is Adler going too far? Support your position by using specific examples from the article.

4. One might argue that there are many forms of entertainment that seem to condemn while glorifying dangerous, illegal, or bad behavior. Crime shows, for instance, often spend a lot of time showing the crime scene and discussing gory details. Physical and sexual assaults are commonly dramatized on television. If we agree with Adler's argument, does it follow that these forms of entertainment are problematic in the same way as *To Catch a Predator*? If not, what differences do you see between *To Catch a Predator* and these other forms of entertainment?

5. Adler spends no substantial space talking about race or ethnicity in her article about *To Catch a Predator*, but she identifies Chris Hansen as a "tall, preppy, white guy" and indicates that Dell, a decoy who works for Perverted Justice, is a young person who can masquerade as any ethnicity or gender. Do you think it would make sense to look more deeply into how the TV show portrayed race and ethnicity? If so, what would be some valuable avenues for investigation? If not, why not?

Making Connections

6. The structure of the TV show *To Catch a Predator* was formulaic, meaning that it had the same basic structure in each episode. How does this repetitive structure work like a ritual? Can you see any connections between the readings in Chapter 3 about rituals, rites, and ceremonies and the events repeated on the show that Adler discusses?

7. Adler's article shows how a form of entertainment has an impact on public policy and legal cases. What other articles in *Composing Gender* have a similarly broad application of their theory to the real world? Or, what current examples from the media might someday give rise to a change in public or legal policy?

Acknowledgments (continued from page iv)

Text Credits

Amy M. Adler, "To Catch a Predator" from New York University School of Law, Public Law Research Paper No. 10-60, October 1, 2010. Copyright © 2012 by Amy Adler. Reproduced with permission of the author. All rights reserved.

American Psychological Association, "Report of the APA Task Force on the Sexualization of Girls." Copyright © 2007 by American Psychological Association. Reproduced with permission.

Sandra Lipsitz Bem, "Dismantling Gender Polarization and Compulsory Heterosexuality: Should We Turn the Volume Down or Up?" from the *Journal of Sex Research*, Vol. 32, No. 4, 1995. Copyright © 1995 by Taylor & Francis Ltd., http://www.tandf.co.uk/journals. Reproduced with permission of Taylor & Francis via Copyright Clearance Center.

Amy L. Best, excerpt from *Prom Night: Youth, Schools and Popular Culture*. Copyright © 2000 by Routledge, a division of Taylor & Francis. Reproduced with permission of Routledge via Copyright Clearance Center.

Jia-Rui Chong, "Beauty and the Bleach" from the *Los Angeles Times*, July 26, 2005. Copyright © 2005 by Los Angeles Times. Reproduced with permission of the publisher. All rights reserved.

Patricia Hill Collins, "Hegemonic Masculinity and Black Gender Ideology" from *Black Sexual Politics: African Americans, Gender, and the New Racism*. Copyright © 2004 by Routledge, a division of Taylor & Francis. Reproduced with permission of Routledge via Copyright Clearance Center.

Aaron H. Devor, "Becoming Members of Society: Learning the Social Meanings of Gender" from *Gender Blending: Confronting the Limits of Duality* by Holly Devor. Copyright © 1989 by Holly Devor. Reproduced with permission of the publisher.

Gail Dines, "Visible or Invisible: Growing Up Female in Porn Culture," from *Pornland: How Porn Has Hijacked Our Sexuality*. Copyright © 2010 by Beacon Press. Reproduced with permission of Beacon via Copyright Clearance Center.

Petra L. Doan, "The Tyranny of Gendered Spaces — Reflections from Beyond the Gender Dichotomy" from *Gender Place and Culture A Journal of Feminist Geography*, Vol. 17, No. 5, August 25, 2010. Copyright © 2010 by Taylor & Francis, Ltd. http://www.tandf.co.uk/journals. Reproduced with permission of Taylor & Francis via Copyright Clearance Center.

Jaclyn Geller, "Undercover at the Bloomingdale's Registry" from *Here Comes the Bride: Women, Weddings, and the Marriage Mystique* by Jaclyn Geller, copyright © 2001. Reprinted by permission of Seal Press, a member of the Perseus Books Group.

Jennifer Goodwin, "Even Nine-Month-Olds Choose Gender-Specific Toys" from *HealthDay*, April 15, 2010. Copyright © 2010 by HealthDay. Reproduced with permission. All rights reserved.

Ruth Hubbard, "Rethinking Women's Biology" from *The Politics of Women's Biology*. Copyright © 1990 by Rutgers University Press. Reproduced with permission of the publisher. All rights reserved.

Emily Kane, " 'No Way My Boys Are Going to Be Like That!' Parents' Responses to Children's Gender Nonconformity" from *Gender & Society*, Vol. 2, No. 2, April 2006. Copyright © 2006 by Sociologists for Women in Society. Reproduced with permission of Sage Publications. All rights reserved.

Image Credits

Index of Authors and Titles